WATER
RESOURCES, MANAGEMENT AND ECONOMIC DEVELOPMENT

Dr. Pallavini Vashishtha is working as an Academic Associate (Economics) at the Indian Institute of Management, Ahmedabad. She obtained her M.A. (Economics) and Ph.D., degrees from University of Rajasthan, Jaipur with specialization in Development Economics and Econometrics.

Dr. Vashishtha has participated in several National Seminars and Workshops on water, health, sanitation and economic development. She has also published several research papers on these themes. Along with this, she has worked on a variety of short term research projects of World Bank and others under the auspices of Kumarappa Institute of Gram Swaraj, Jaipur, Centre for Environment Education, Ahmedabad and National Council of Applied Economic Research, New Delhi.

WATER
Resources, Management and Economic Development

Pallavini Vashishtha

Pointer Publishers
Jaipur 302 003 (Raj.) India

Distributed by
Prem C. Bakliwal for
Aavishkar Publishers, Distributors
807, Vyas Building, Chaura Rasta
Jaipur 302 003 (Raj.) India
Phone : 0141-2578159
e-mail : aavishkarbooks@hotmail.com

2019

ISBN 978-81-7132-626-6

Published by
Mrs. Shashi Jain for
Pointer Publishers
807, Vyas Building, Chaura Rasta
Jaipur 302 003 (Raj.) India
Phones : 0141-2578159, 2708286
e-mail : pointerpub@hotmail.com
Visit us at : www.pointerpublishers.com

Price : ₹ 1350.00

Printed at
Sheetal Printers
Jaipur (Raj.) India

Foreword

Water is a finite but renewable natural resource and, like other natural resources, it is an integral part of our environment. It is essential for survival of all living beings on this planet and so also for socio-economic development of households, communities and nations all over the world. It is also necessary to maintain and enhance biodiversity and quality of environment. Water resources of India are under great biotic and abiotic pressure. Most of the rivers, lakes, tanks and ponds are polluted and the groundwater aquifers are being over-exploited in most of the arid and semi-arid regions and are on the verge of complete exhaustion. Besides, in many areas the groundwater aquifers have been polluted and contaminated.

India, as a whole, is reasonably well-endowed with fresh water resources. It receives nearly 3800 billion cubic metres (BCM) of fresh water annually through rainfall and snowfall. Most of the rainfall is concentrated in 100 to 120 days during the period, from June to September. Besides, there are also wide variations in the annual rainfall from region to region – 100 mm in parts of western Rajasthan to as high as 11, 000 mm in Cherrapunji in eastern part of Meghalaya. Thus, the distribution and availability of water is not uniform over space. Similarly, there are wide year -to -year fluctuations in the rainfall in the country. All these factors together have adversely affected the pace and level of agricultural and industrial development in India and hence the quality of life of people. In view of this, there is an urgent need for improving the management of country's water resources. The book addresses this important dimension of water-related problems, and therefore, is highly salient and relevant in the current context of India as well as Rajasthan, which is one of the most water-scare states of India.

The Jaipur district, which is focal point of the study, is one of the 32 districts of Rajasthan State. The district suffers from water scarcity as it is situated in the semi-arid zone with annual average rainfall as low as 55 cm. Further, it has no perennial rivers to provide water to it through out the year. This study of the water resources and economic development of Jaipur district becomes significant as the water availability in the district has been continually declining for last so many years to the extent that it is on the brink of turning into a water scarcity region. The author argues that this dismal situation could be improved by adopting an integrated water policy, conservation of water resources, effective management and community participation of rural and urban people.

The book comprises six chapters, which together adequately address various issues pertaining to availability, uses and management of water resources in Rajasthan. The first chapter deals with the nature of water problem, objectives of the study, hypotheses, research methodology, scope and coverage and review of relevant studies related to the study. It also describes the ecological and administrative profile of Rajasthan state and Jaipur district. The second chapter presents an assessment of water resources, its uses and related issues in the Rajasthan state with special reference to Jaipur district. It identifies a number of issues such as the lack of surface water resources, depletion, over-extraction and encroachment of groundwater and privatization of common pool water resources.

In the third chapter, the author examines the relationship between water resources and economic development. Additionally, various indices such as Hydrological Water Stress Indicator (HWSI), Social Water Scarcity Index (SWSI), and Water Poverty Index (WPI) are computed and used to assess the water scarcity status of Jaipur district and the regression technique is used to identify the determinants of water poverty. This chapter constitutes the most significant contribution of the author as no other researcher has done this kind of work before. The fourth chapter is devoted to an in-depth study of the institutional framework within which water is managed in India and Rajasthan state, especially in its Jaipur district. It highlights various lacunae in the water management system and explores the strategies for efficient, equitable and sustainable use and management of water so as to accelerate the pace of overall development of the state.

The fifth chapter examines the status of implementation of Rajasthan State Water Policy and water legislations which have gained importance owing to the rapid growth of population, industrialisation and decreasing per capita availability of water. The last, sixth chapter, presents a summary of the major findings, conclusions and policy implications of the author's research work.

The book is an attempt to analyse the status of water availability, its uses and management in the state of Rajasthan with special focus on Jaipur district. I have an opportunity to go through the book under publication. I must commend Dr. Pallavini Vashishtha for having done a very good and pioneering piece of research work.

The book is written in a simple and lucid language. It would be a valuable addition to the scanty literature available on water resources use and management in water- scarce states of Western India. Researchers, teachers, students, policy makers, planners and managers engaged or interested in water resources management would find this book very useful and handy. I highly recommend the book for acquisition by university and college libraries.

Katar Singh

Ph.D. (University of Illinois, USA)

Formerly RBI Chair and Director

Institute of Rural Management, Anand

&

Currently Honorary Chairman

India Natural Resource Economics and Management

(INREM) Foundation, Anand

Preface

Water is a symbol of life. It is crucial for maintaining environment and ecosystem conducive to sustaining all forms of life. It plays a vital role in fulfilling basic human needs for the existence of life and also contributes to socio-economic development. The demand for water for drinking, domestic consumption, livestock, agriculture, industries, power generation and other uses is ever increasing in proportion to the accelerated growth of population, urbanization and industrial development. Hence, water also caters to the enhanced per capita requirements due to rise in living standards.

The availability of water depends on geographical factors, such as, different climatic zones, forest cover, arid and semi-arid areas, hilly tracts and desert plains. It varies in different regions in quantity as well as quality. The benefactions of water have so far been studied with a view to establish relationship of water with various sectors in consumption-production framework. The regional perspective of water – economic development nexus has lately acquired a significant position. This helps in the intensive understanding of the problems and issues related to water which could be tackled at grassroots level to enhance development in a particular region. Such studies will prove to be exemplary models for similar climatic regions at other places. It is in this context that this study on water resources, management and economic development in Jaipur district has been undertaken.

There is always a positive relationship between water and

economic development; but it becomes complex with the process of development in developing countries. The varied contributions of water in poverty alleviation are inevitable. There is a need to shift the use of water from extensive to intensive pattern necessitated by water scarcity and use of technology. The positive trend supports that water remains a major constraint for economic development especially among the lower income range.

This study makes an attempt to develop Jaipur district as a model for water resources, their management and economic development. With the highest rate of population growth and density in comparison to other districts of Rajasthan, Jaipur is obviously growing at a faster pace. The pace of urbanization and industrialization along with accelerated growth of population and expanding economic activities have created serious pressures on water resources and its accessibility, sanitation, health services and environmental balance. Thus, there is a need for improved infrastructure and basic services of water supply, sewerage and sanitation along with other infrastructure facilities like housing, electricity and transportation. On the other hand, rapid expansion in agriculture, population and industries has resulted in dramatic increase in demand for water. The ground water withdrawal has exceeded beyond limits while the surface water resources are inapt to fulfill the demand. The predictions by economists and hydrologists regarding limits of fresh water have been among the motivations behind the present study. In view of various facets of water issues and the pace of economic development of the region, an effort has been made to analyse water resources, causes of scarcity of water, its unequal distribution and its relationship with economic development along with management strategies for the arid and semi-arid regions in general and for the Jaipur district in particular.

The present study is divided into six chapters. The first chapter deals with nature of water problem, the objectives of the study and hypotheses, scope and review of relevant studies related to the subject. It gives the description of physiography, river basins, desert area, natural drainage, and river run-off of Jaipur district along with its rainfall and climatic features, focusing on the effects of all these factors on the availability of water resources. The second chapter presents an assessment of water resources, its uses and related issues in Rajasthan state with special reference to Jaipur district. The assessment of water resources reveals that surface water is exhausted and the level of ground water has also reached the overexploited stage because of environmental changes and erroneous human activities. The changes in land use of river basins, encroachment on catchment areas, afforestation and deforestation, field management, urbanization, drainage and disposal of waste create adverse effects on the availability of water resources. The demand for water has been assessed by including all its uses i.e., municipal (households and others), industrial and agricultural.

The third chapter investigates the relationship between water resources and economic development. It explains the economic, health and other benefits generated through the inter-linkages between water and economic development. Along with this, various indices and regression techniques are used to examine the water scarcity status of Jaipur district and determinants of water poverty, such as, Hydrological Water Stress Indicator (HWSI), Social Water Scarcity Index (SWSI), and Water Poverty Index (WPI). These indices give the water scarcity conditions in the region. The fourth chapter studies the institutional framework and water management of Rajasthan state. The institutional framework of water management includes government departments, non-government organizations, community participation, corporate house and participation of media. This chapter also highlights the existing lapses of water management system and elaborates the strategies of water management for efficient, equitable and sustainable water distribution so as to accelerate development of the region. The fifth chapter examines the Rajasthan state water policy and water legislations which have gained importance owing to growth of population, industrialization and decreasing per capita availability of water. The chapter also discusses the National water policy of India and its adaptation in Rajasthan state along with the possibilities of its implementation in Jaipur district in view of regional variations, physical peculiarities and emerging issues. The last, sixth chapter offers the conclusion and policy implications.

I take this opportunity to record my deep sense of gratitude to Prof. Ranjana, Department of Economics, University of Rajasthan, Jaipur for guidance and continuous encouragement to complete this work. I am specially thankful to the Director, Institute of Development Studies, Jaipur for cooperation. Further, I also express my thanks to the officers and staff of the Census of India, Central Ground Water Board, Jaipur, and also State Ground Water Department, Public

Health Engineering Department, Irrigation Department of Government of Rajasthan for sparing time for discussion and providing facilities for relevant data collection.

I also thank the Librarians and the staff of Central Library, University of Rajasthan, Jaipur; Institute of Development Studies, Jaipur, HCM RIPA, Jaipur; Centre for Arid Zone Research Institute, Jodhpur; Centre for Science and Environment, New Delhi and Indian Institute of Advanced Study, Shimla for extending facilities to consult source-material for my work.

Pallavini Vashishtha

Contents

1

Introduction

1.1 NATURE OF THE PROBLEM

Water is the most vital natural resource. It is essential for the survival and growth of all forms of life – human, animal and vegetable. It is a finite resource, which cannot be produced or added instantaneously by any technological means. Along with existence of life, it is also needed for social, economic and ecological well-being of a man. Water is required for drinking, health, sanitation and other domestic and social purposes. It is indispensable for agriculture, industry, power generation, mining, tourism, navigation, etc. Thus, the uses of water could be largely classified as domestic, agricultural, industrial and recreational.

Water is available through a process of hydrological cycle under the impact of solar energy and gravitation in the forms of rain and snow, surface water in reservoirs, rivers, tanks, etc., and groundwater in wells, tubewells, etc. The problems of water occur due to geophysical features as well as demographic factors. There are complex problems in water distribution with regard to equity and social justice. Lack of access to water for meeting basic needs, such as health, hygiene and food security, undermines development and inflicts enormous hardship on human beings. In view of the coverage of the present study on water resources and economic development, it is essential to analyse the nature of problems related to the distribution of water in Jaipur district.

The district of Jaipur, being situated in the arid and semi-arid zones with meagre forest cover, is characterized by meagre rainfall, no perennial rivers and natural lakes, recurring droughts and dry climate. As a result, the groundwater has been used to the maximum to fulfill the demands of irrigation, industry and domestic water supply. Therefore, water scarcity and its degraded quality have become a natural phenomenon at some places in Jaipur and other districts of Rajasthan State. The main causes of shortage of water are population explosion, destruction of forest, scanty rains, increasing dependence on groundwater, overexploitation of existing water resources, negligence of traditional water conservation systems and techniques, unplanned urbanization and industrialization. All these factors cumulatively make water a scarce commodity.

The study of the water resources of Jaipur district in the spheres of individual households, agriculture and industries is also important because it covers both urban and rural areas of the district. This district is formed from the erstwhile state of Jaipur and possessed some infrastructure of a modern society but substantial work in the direction of water resources and its management could only start after independence with the formation of Rajasthan State under the Indian Republic. In the post-Independence period, Rajasthan State has developed a regular water supply system in the urban areas of Jaipur district for domestic and commercial use. In the rural areas also, water supply is provided for domestic, industrial and agriculture purposes by wells, tubewells, check dams (anicuts), hand pumps, etc. These water supply arrangements have become insufficient because of the pressure of population and industries in the region. The supply of water is not concomitant with the increasing demand of the different sectors. This is mainly due to poor management of water resources in the region.

As a result of faster growth of population, along with sectoral development, there has been growth of suburbs around Jaipur city and towns in the Jaipur district. This process of urbanization has created water scarcity and has given rise to problems related to water availability and accessibility. Thus, increase in irrigation, industrial and domestic needs of water have resulted in more withdrawal of water. On account of the shortage in surface water, pressure increases on groundwater withdrawal leading to salinity in water. The use of land for houses and road networks prevents natural recharge of rainwater to replenish the groundwater. These have led to serious pressures on water resources and have adversely affected its quality and quantity. So also, the farm chemicals and toxic effluents from industries have affected the quality of water. The problems of deepening scarcity of water can be resolved by improving management, by fixing up the priorities of water use and by providing efficient infrastructure and institutional framework for its distribution. The present infrastructure and institutional framework is outdated as it was formulated when water was not scarce, having lesser number of users.

The present study has focused on the water related issues in general and Jaipur district in particular. It is a regional study where global and national perspectives are put to test. Along with this, it also provides an understanding of the national perspective and could be compared to parallel issues of other regions with similar regional circumstances. It would be interesting to note the regional variations and traditional patterns of conservation of water, uses of water for irrigation and domestic purposes, its accessibility in urban and rural areas and the institutional framework of its management. In fact, the regional study provides an opportunity for in-depth study of the problem, so that solutions could be found and implemented at the grassroots level. It could also provide an example for the regions with similar climatic and demographic conditions.

1.2 OBJECTIVES

The main objectives of the study are as follows:

- To examine emerging problems and issues related to surface and groundwater resources, their availability and uses including domestic, agricultural and industrial in rural as well as urban areas of Jaipur district.
- To study the geophysical and ecological factors contributing to the availability of fresh water and groundwater for Jaipur district.
- To study the various aspects of water management, such as, its coverage, accessibility, quality of water supplies, sanitation and health and their linkages with economic development.
- To examine the infrastructure of water management like institutional framework, causes of water crisis and their solutions and the role of Government and NGOs in water management in the rural and urban areas of Jaipur District.

- To examine relation between water and economic development by tracing various economic, health and miscellaneous effects in general with emphasis of Jaipur district.
- To evaluate the water policy, law and emerging problems prevalent in the State of Rajasthan with special reference to Jaipur District.

1.3 HYPOTHESES

Following hypotheses will be tested :

- Water management is effective in controlling water scarcity.
- There is a positive relationship between water resources accessibility and economic development.
- There is positive relationship between water management and availability of drinking water.

1.4 REVIEW OF LITERATURE

There have been several studies in the past to examine the issues related to water resources, its management in rural and urban areas and its uses in agriculture, industry and domestic sectors. These studies have focused mainly on international, national or state level issues. Very few studies have concentrated on the issues related to water resources with emphasis on water management and economic development of Rajasthan and especially of Jaipur district. However, review of some of the relevant studies illustrating the general trends of the studies on water is as follows:

Shuval (1980) in his book, *Water Quality Management under conditions of Scarcity*, has examined the problems of water management in the areas of severe water scarcity with special reference to Israel covering a period of thirty years from 1950 to 1980. The author has identified the reasons of groundwater pollution as overuse and overexploitation of water resources for municipal and agricultural purposes. He has concluded that most of the problems allied to water quality are universal. Organizational, economic, legal and political measures would resolve and control the water quality issues. Therefore, the institutional set-up needs to be revamped, and economic and legal measures should be implemented for the improvement of water quality management, which is an integral part of water management.

Vangani, Sharma and Chatterji (1988) in their article on "Tanka – A Reliable System of Rainwater Harvesting in Indian Desert", have given a comprehensive framework of the construction and maintenance of *tanka* (underground reservoir) in arid zones of Rajasthan. They emphasized rainwater harvesting to combat water scarcity. The authors have concluded that rejuvenation of traditional system of water conservation is one of the measures to compensate the scarcity of water.

The World Bank Water Demand Research Team (1993) in their article, "The Demand for Water in Rural Areas: Determinants and Policy Implications", have investigated the determinants of water demand in the selected rural areas of Latin America, Africa and South Asia covering India and Pakistan. The team conducted the survey during 1987-1990 and used both direct (contingent valuation) and indirect (revealed preference) methods to estimate households' willingness to pay for improved water supply. The determinants of demand for water supply have been identified as size, socio-economic and demographic features of the household, and characteristics of existing water supply versus improved supply in terms of cost, distance, quality, reliability, and attitudes of households towards government policy in water sector. They have concluded that the households are willing to pay for improvement of water supply in contrast to the prevalent view that people do not wish to pay.

Misra (1995) in his work, *Rajasthan ki Rajat Bunden*, has examined the causes for scarcity of water resources in Rajasthan state. He has ascribed it to the climatic and geographical conditions of the region. Further, he has elaborated the traditional measures of rainwater conservation especially in the arid zones of Rajasthan covering Barmer, Jaisalmer, Jodhpur, Bikaner and Churu districts. The author has concluded that the revival of traditional system of storage and conservation of water resources would resolve the water scarcity problem in the region, provided the resources are fitted with latest equipments for using water for domestic and agricultural purposes. The management of these traditional systems should be entrusted to the community after training them to operate these resources.

Murty (1995) in his book, *Watershed Management in India,* has studied the methods of conservation of rain water and its management in the context of India. He has attempted to put together essential details of the multidisciplinary approach in watershed management in relation to land, agriculture, energy, technology and several systems of water conservation, such as, water harvesting, dams, etc. The author has concluded that revival of watershed is an important measure of water resource management in agriculture sector.

Carruthers and Morrison (1996) in their article on "Institutions in Water Resources Management: Insights from New Institutional Economics", have focused on the importance of institutional factors in the successful implementation of the policies in water sector. The authors have analysed the interaction between water policy and the complex institutional arrangements and have classified the institutions for the allocation of water as market, government and community. They have studied several aspects related to water sector, such as, privatization versus cultural values, traditional institutions and external pressures caused by urbanization, tourism and industrial demands of water. The authors have suggested unification of these aspects in formulation of water policy and stressed the need for coordination of market, government and community.

Purohit and Siddiqui (1996) in their article on "Urban Water Supply in Rajasthan: A Case Study of Jaipur City", have studied the water supply system of Jaipur city in 1995. The study is based on secondary data from Public Health Engineering Department (PHED) covering major water production zones - Ramgarh lake and Amanishah. The authors have estimated the demand and production of water in the city for 1995 and have concluded that there is a deficit in water supply of 8 million litres of water per day. There have been economic and technical problems in management and distribution of water in the city, besides low rainfall causing low availability of water in Ramgarh lake led to increased groundwater dependence with low recharge, high production losses, leakages in the distribution system and low cost recovery. These problems can be resolved by investments in water sector to improve and augment water supply, and increasing the capabilities of PHED, by establishing a research and development wing, and organizing formal management training programmes.

Gleick (1998) in his article on "Water and Human Health" has emphasized the provision of basic water services for drinking and sanitation which are the key elements for human health. He has reviewed the water scenario of the continents of the world during 1980 and 1990 and has highlighted Africa and South Asia as those parts of the world which lack access to safe drinking water and adequate sanitation facilities for their population. He has ascribed the reasons of failure in providing these services as rapid growth of population, growing urbanization, under investment, lacunae in government planning and laxity in the implementation of its programmes. He concluded that in order to eliminate water-related diseases there is a need for the improvement and maintenance of water infrastructure to provide clean water, to inculcate adequate hygienic habits and to retain proper food habits. The minimum basic water requirement of a person for drinking, sanitation, bathing and cooking is 50 litres per person per day. Failure to meet the basic water needs, results in high social and economic costs, such as, high morbidity and mortality.

Vaidyanathan (1999) in his book, *Water Resource Management: Institutions and Irrigation Development in India,* has made a comparative study of water institutions in different agro-climatic regions of China, Japan and India for a better understanding of the problems of water management across countries. The author has approached the issues in holistic manner taking technology, structural systems, awareness and regional pattern of availability of water resources together and highlighted the contribution of NGOs for the first time. He has discussed the salient features of irrigation development in India during 1990-1995 and concluded that emphasis on the utilization of water for irrigation has resulted in overexploitation of groundwater. This increased the problems of salinity and saturation of groundwater. Hence, restructuring of different institutions is required for irrigation through planning and operation of large surface system, rehabilitation and expansion of local irrigation works based on rain water through integrated watershed development, and regulation of groundwater.

Rao (2000) in his article on, "Watershed Development in India: Recent Experience and Emerging Issues", has studied the watershed projects launched in India under the Drought Prone Area Programme (DPAP) in 1994. He has concluded that the overall impact of the programme was positive and impressive. The expenditure on drought relief can be spent more productively by allocating it for watershed development bearing very little extra cost. Effective participation of people on a sustained basis can be ensured by effective institutional framework and strong leadership.

Singh, Waris, Chauhan and Rathore (2000) in their article entitled, "Tanka - A Boon for Arid Zone Farmers", have focused on the growing scarcity of water in arid zone of Rajasthan and on measures to conserve rain water. The authors have presented a cost-benefit analysis of the construction of *tanka* and plantations of agroforest products. They have designed a low cost structure of *tanka* for small farmers of arid and semi-arid zones of Rajasthan. Plantation of trees which require little water and could be grown in the field along with foodgrains using water supply from *tanka* would be highly remunerative for farmers. Therefore, this traditional system of water harvesting should be revived to solve the problem of water scarcity in summer as well as add to their income.

Zerah (2000) in her book, *Water: Unreliable Supply in Delhi,* has studied the water supply situation of Delhi. The author has combined the global and theoretical approach with the field observations from a survey of 600 households of Delhi conducted in 1995. It has covered the issues regarding infrastructure, problems and constraints of public water supply system, along with price, subsidy, cost, cost recovery, losses and poor maintenance. The author has studied the household behaviour on water tariff, pilferage and leakages in water supply and also examined the reliability of water supply in the city. She has concluded that there is a necessity of a vigourous drive for generating mass awareness for the judicious use of water and for roof top water harvesting to combat water scarcity. The inequalities in water distribution are due to the individual strategies of water access, such as, individual tubewells and storage tanks. This has accelerated the pace of environmental degradation. Though the municipal authorities emphasise the lack of water resources as the main constraint, yet inadequate supply is most often caused by poor management of the distribution network. Tariff augmentation is also justified as there is both households' ability and willingness to pay if improved supply of water is ascertained.

Mayor and Binde (2001) in their book, *The World Ahead: Our Future in the Making,* have concentrated on the specific objectives of the futuristic development in the 21st century on the issues of water, environment, food, education, women and science. The authors have dealt with various issues of water resources, such as, growing demand of water, the threat of water scarcity, prospects of water in 2025, control on irrigation, water quality and environment. They have concluded that reliable supplies of water would require saving the resources through judicious management and renewal of water resources to augment water supply. This could be achieved by the "political will" and also by rational use of water by the users. Further, realistic pricing of water should be implemented according to its use in view of the capacity of users to pay for it. There is need of equitable distribution of water resources for striking a balance of power on international level for preventing a war for water in the 21st century. The solution of this problem is visualized in the adoption of a genuine international legislation.

Vaidyanathan (2001) in his article on, "Policy Dimensions: Reviving Decaying Systems : A Case for Rainwater Harvesting", has advocated for the resuscitation of traditional measures and the efforts of the government in the field of water conservation. He has stated the causes of decline of the traditional water conservation system as physical degradation, siltation of tank beds, damage of sluices and surplus weirs and, above all, deterioration of local institutions. These traditional systems should be renovated and fitted with modern equipment according to the local needs and circumstances. He has recommended expansion of the tanks by linking them to other big tanks of the region as a measure for augmenting the capacity of water storage during heavy rains. The existing schemes affecting land, water and forests should also be merged into a single unified programme of watershed development.

Lawrence, Meigh and Sullivan (2002) in their paper entitled, "The Poverty Index: An International Comparison", have elaborated on the preparation of an International Water Poverty Index. The authors have obtained the index for 140 countries for the year 2001. This index is an interdisciplinary measure which links household welfare with water availability and indicates the degree of impact of water scarcity on human population. The Water Poverty Index facilitates management and monitoring of existing water resources, and socio-economic factors affecting the access to water resources and their use.

Ballabh (2003) in his article on, "Politics of Water Management and Sustainable Water Use", has analysed the major causes of failure of water policy in India. He has highlighted that failure to achieve sustainable reforms in this sector is due to politics of water management between the different water sectors and interest groups. These interest groups obstruct the implementation of reform for maintaining the *status-quo* so that they remain 'dominant and resilient' in water sector. The real reform in water sector could only be initiated by restructuring the government departments related to water resources and by providing space to local bodies for meaningful participation in deliberations for reforms in the water resource sector. He has suggested restructuring of irrigation bureaucracy for making them more accountable and transparent, and restoring balance of power between them and farmers' organization.

Iyer (2003) in his book entitled, *Water Perspectives, Issues and Concerns*, has adopted analytical approach in dealing with management of water during drought, water scarcity, pollution and wasteful utilisation of water. He has examined critically the varied water provisions of Indian Constitution, Inter-State Water Dispute Act 1956, the Cauvery dispute and National Water Policy of 1987 and its revised version of 2002. He has concluded that an integrated holistic river basin planning along with water harvesting and other major water projects is the need of the time.

Marothia (2003) in his article on, "Enhancing Sustainable Management of Water Resources in Agriculture Sector: The Role of Institutions", has discussed the policy, problems of institutional choices and hierarchy for enhancing sustainable development of water resources in agricultural sector. He has stated that the major issue in management of water resources in India is the dominance of agriculture sector and neglect of demand of water in other sectors. He has analyzed the problems of canal, tank and groundwater irrigation. The author has concluded that restructuring of institutional set-up is required for governing demand and supply of water and for reallocating inter-sectoral water use. He has suggested for extensive research on integrated river basin management. The policy makers should give more emphasis on the change in cropping pattern, technical use of appliances for irrigation and adoption of water saving technologies.

Sivaraman and Govindarajan (2003) in their work entitled, *Manual on Rainwater Harvesting*, have elaborated on the techniques of rainwater harvesting. The authors have evaluated the impacts of rainwater harvesting in Chennai metropolis as a case study. They have concluded that harvesting of rain water is the primary step for the increase in groundwater table, and for the augmentation of water supply. Hence, water harvesting in individual houses and buildings and method of rainwater harvesting in rural and urban areas must be introduced. Besides, different ways of recharging of rainwater, such as, percolation pits, recharge trenches and wells, open wells and tube-wells or through abandoned wells must be implemented. Along with this, various methods of rainwater harvesting for agriculture, such as, contour bunding, check dams, gully control structures, farm ponds and percolation ponds should also be encouraged. There should be proper guidelines to arrest the flow of subsurface dams and the advantage of these structures must be publicized in the region.

Janakrajan (2004) in his article on, "Conflict over the Use of Groundwater: Some Evidence from Tamil Nadu", has explored the nature and extent of the problem of exploitation of groundwater and the response of users to conflicts generated by it. He has elaborated the reasons and results of the conflicts and concluded that conflicts arise mainly due to ambiguous property rights. The author has conducted the study to assess the fragmentation of wells in the villages in the river basins of Tamil Nadu during 1992. He has suggested the review of the relationship between water and land rights and the need to clarify the legal rights on groundwater. It has been emphasized that the state should be responsible for its execution and for nominating farmers to participate in decision-making bodies.

Natarajan and Kallolikar (2004) in their book entitled, *Rainwater Harvesting–New Approaches for Sustainable Water Resources Development*, have paid attention to conditions of water scarcity and the trends of groundwater extraction in the districts of Tamil Nadu over three time periods - 1989, 1992 and 1997 with its use in domestic and agriculture sectors. They have also reviewed the rainwater harvesting methods practised in Maharastra and Rajasthan. The authors have discussed different strategies to improve water scenario in all the river basins in districts of Tamil Nadu and suggested rainwater harvesting and construction of new water storage structures to overcome water scarcity. They have suggested both negative and positive measures for saving water and preventing its misuse, such as, restrictions on farmers to the access of free supply of power, popularization of small-scale irrigation techniques, recycling of waste water, etc.

Saleth (2004) in his research report on "Strategic Analysis of Water Institutions in India: Application of a New Research Paradigm", has studied the evolution of water related institutional set-up, and their performance in India focusing on macro institutional arrangements and their micro counterparts. He has developed a new research paradigm which is useful for analyzing the structure and performance of water institutions. The author has concluded that the present structure of water institutions in India is still far from meeting the basic water challenges at present and in future also. The functioning of the existing institutions is substandard in terms of the overall physical, financial, and economic performance of the water sector. Further, there is need to bring about 'real reforms' in water sector, by reviewing centre-state relations in the water sector, by declaration of an exclusive water law, by creation of a system of water rights at various levels, and by introducing administrative reforms for sub-sectoral coordination in all water sectors and balanced functional specialization.

Shah (2004) in his paper on "The Deepening Divide: Diverse Responses to the Challenge of Ground Water Depletion in Gujarat", has analysed the strengths and weaknesses of the policy for augmenting the supply of water in Gujarat state. He has dwelt on the need for integrated management of water resources and evaluated the role of NGOs, government and other socio-religious groups in water resource management. According to the author, water resource management and water conservation are equally important to meet the challenge of water scarcity. Regulatory and promotional framework, taxes and subsidies, action plan and recharge technologies can address the groundwater depletion issues.

Black and Talbot (2005) in their book entitled, *Water – A Matter of Life and Health*, have reviewed the role of UNICEF in rural water supply and sanitation in India since its inception in 1969. The authors have evaluated UNICEF's programmes of rural water supply projects and have pointed out its failures and deficiencies in resolving the causes of the scarcity of water, groundwater overexploitation and rapid depletion of the aquifer. They have concluded that community participation in rainwater harvesting and micro-watershed development programmes have the potential prospect to overcome water scarcity.

Narain, Khan and Singh (2005) in their article on "Potential for Water Conservation and Harvesting against Drought in Rajasthan, India", have examined the potential of water harvesting, conservation of rainwater and floods to mitigate scarcity of water during summers and droughts in Rajasthan. The area of their study concentrated on the arid zone of Marwar, Bikaner, Jaisalmer and Barmer. The authors have enumerated the groundwater recharge potential of all the districts of Rajasthan in case of normal rainfall. They have suggested several means of integrated water resource management, proper policies and latest technologies. The total roof top areas and non-agricultural land can be utilized for water harvesting and recharge of groundwater. So also, the water stored from rooftop harvesting can be utilized during severe drought and would be sufficient to meet nearly 69 per cent of the drinking water requirements of villages under study. The traditional water harvesting system of Rajasthan should be implemented to achieve the objectives of conservation of water.

Briscoe and Malik (2006) in association with World Bank published a book entitled, *India's Water Economy Bracing for a Turbulent Future*. They have examined the evolution of water management in India, its achievements in the past and the challenges ahead and also suggested ways of evolving a sustainable water management system. The authors have emphasized the concepts of water management and economic development by referring to some instances of efficient private management and public systems. They have concluded that the uncertainty of water in future could be resolved by the adoption of comprehensive policies, management, active participation of public water institutions and increased investments in water sector in India.

Holland (2006) in her book, *The Water Business Corporations Vs. People*, has dealt with the controversial issue of privatization of water supply for domestic use. She has pointed out the inability of the public water systems to improve efficiency and failure to mobilize the resources for expansion and modernization. This has led to privatization. But, on the other side, there is a widespread dissatisfaction among users over the poor quality of service of private companies and their arbitrary increase in water rates. The private companies also fail to fulfill their commitments to serve the poor. Hence, the author has suggested to improve the water supply system rather than to give it to private companies.

Pangare, Pangare and Das (2006) in their book, *Springs of Life–India's Water Resources*, have evaluated the water resource programmes in India with a focus on the need of sustainable development and water resource management for drinking, domestic, irrigation and industrial uses. They have emphasized on the micro-level reality of availability, access, quality of water and its equitable supply. The authors have concluded that the policies of the state have encouraged the use of surface and groundwater for irrigation purposes to increase the foodgrain output, which has resulted in overexploitation and privatization of water resources. This resulted in the conflicts over sharing of water by different users and widening inequalities between the rich and the poor. The authors have propagated development of a legal framework for defining water rights or for regulating the loss of water. The state should intervene and prevent privatisation of community water resources.

Mohile (2007) in his article on "Government Policies and Programmes" has traced the evolution of water policies in India since 1866. He has critically examined the National Water Policy 2002, with a view to identify the difficulties in the implementation of the policy. He has concluded that there are two difficulties, one is lack of clear guidelines for water allocation and the other is non-establishment of river basin authorities. The major issues are related to water supply and sanitation, water auditing systems, and inter-basin transfers of water to non-basin states. There is a need for legal and institutional changes and revision of water allocation according to uses. The author has suggested drawing clear guidelines on the role of private sector and the maintenance of proper water accounts at basin and sub-basin levels. The strategy for water use should be designed according to water zones.

Shaban and Sharma (2007) in their article on, "Water Consumption Patterns in Domestic Households in Major Cities", have studied the water supply and consumption patterns in the households of the seven major cities of India covering Delhi, Kanpur, Kolkata, Ahmedabad, Mumbai, Hyderabad and Madurai in the year 2005. They have selected two factors for their study - water use activity and socio-economic groups. The sample was representative of five different categories of socio-economic groups viz., high income, middle income and low income groups residing in planned buildings, and slums and mixed areas having non-planned buildings. The information was collected on different water activities, sources of water supply and perception of households on the subjects, such as, quality, duration of municipal water supply and awareness for water conservation. The authors have concluded that domestic consumption per household per capita per day of the different socio-economic groups in all the seven cities was inadequate and unreliable. The dismal picture of water supply indicated that 65 per cent of the households, specially belonging to low income and slums remain water deficient. The duration of water supply was for limited hours and that too erratic and unreliable. Their study reveals that even high literacy does not lead to relatively a high level of awareness of rain water harvesting. The norms of water supply were much lower than the standard laid down by Indian Bureau of Standards.

Vyas (2007) in his article on "Economic Reforms through Principled Pragmatism" has stated that the principle of all reforms must aim at a viable mix of equity and efficiency. The main focus was on the reforms in water sector in India. The author has suggested the need of an integrated and holistic approach to water related problems and involvement of users in conservation and management of water. There should be a consensus in favour of reforms and the reforms must focus on the benefits of larger sections. The strategies should be adopted in consonance with social values and political institutions. The author has concluded that to achieve successful implementation of the reforms there are some prerequisites like water literacy, awareness, cost recovery, participation of stakeholders and setting up priority in implementation of the projects.

Kumar, Patel, Ravindranath and Singh (2008) in their article, "Chasing a Mirage: Water Harvesting and Artificial Recharge in Naturally Water Scarce Regions", have studied economic viability of water harvesting and recharge programmes in arid and semi-arid zones of India with hard rock formations, and closed and open basins. Their analysis is based on macro level hydrological and geo-hydrological data of India for the last fifty years (1969-2007). The authors have taken the data of annual rainfall, number of rainy days and evapotranspiration from selected river basins of Narmada, Cauvery, Pennar, Krishna and Sabarmati and the data of impact of rain water harvesting on river Ghelo in Saurashtra, Gujarat State. The objective of the study is to assess the effectiveness of the efforts of runoff water harvesting in water scarce regions. The authors have concluded that water harvesting and artificial recharge in water scarce areas is not economically viable because (i) water harvesting in closed basins have negative hydrological impact, (ii) water harvesting has become unreliable due to variability in annual rainfall in the basin, and (iii) water harvesting would be deficient due to poor storage capacity of aquifer in these regions. Hence, the paradigms of water supply, the equity in access to water, social justice, water security for the poor and realization of greater economic value from the use of water can be hardly achieved in water scarce region. Therefore, the authors have suggested that assessment be made of variability of physical features, pattern of rainfall, and quantum of runoff, rate of evapotranspiration and situation of river basin to avoid construction of inefficient and expensive structures. In their opinion a better understanding of the catchment and basin hydrology should be acquired with the help of new technical inputs, such as, rainfall intensity, analysis of properties of soil topography and geo-hydrological parameters before introducing designs of water harvesting schemes and recharge structures in a region.

The above review of literature reveals that the recent studies related to water have laid emphasis on the different dimensions of water availability, management and guiding principles for its supply. The present study is an attempt to highlight the vitally significant relationship between water and economic development with emphasis on the management of water resources. The study adopts a holistic approach. It also identifies the effects of water resources on health, education and productivity of the people. It examines the accessibility to drinking water and sanitation facilities in rural and urban areas with surface and groundwater availability.

Cullet's book (2009), *Water Law, Poverty, and Development: Water Sector Reforms in India,* discusses water legislation, water sector reforms related to rights of landowners, groundwater, water pollution and environmental impacts of water uses. It also examines the water law reforms in different states in India. It stresses on the formulation of an appropriate water law in India in the context of different water uses. Further, it proposes a series of alternative ideas for broad-based reforms starting from a human rights equity and sustainability perspective. Water should not be treated as an economic good in relation to drinking water uses. The author clarifies that water law has a prime role in poverty eradication and must be conceived as a strategy of development. The book is based on primary documents and sources of ancillary subjects.

1.5 SCOPE OF STUDY

The coverage of the study is Rajasthan state and Jaipur district during the post-Independence period. Rajasthan has the distinction of being the largest state of India in terms of its area. It is situated in the north-western region of India and has the neighbouring country of Pakistan as its north-western boundary, states of Uttar Pradesh, Punjab and Haryana as its north-eastern and northern frontiers; Madhya Pradesh and Uttar Pradesh on its east and south-eastern rims and Gujarat on its south-western borders. The state has an area of 3.42 lakh sq. kms, which is 10.41 per cent of India's geographical area, but shares only 1.2 per cent of water resources for 5.5 per cent of India's population.

Jaipur district is situated in north-eastern part of Rajasthan state. It is located between 26° 25′ and 27° 51′ North latitude and 74° 55′ and 76° 10′ East longitude. Its neighbouring districts are Sikar in the north-west, Alwar in north-east, Dausa in east, Tonk in south, Ajmer in south-west and Nagaur in west. Jaipur district has an area of 10,878 sq. km, which is 3.18 per cent area of the state. The city of Jaipur is located in the centre of Jaipur district and extends over 5 per cent of the district's total area. The total area of Jaipur city in 1961 was 64.75 sq. kms, which increased to 200.40 sq. kms in 1991 and within a decade it has doubled to 484.64 sq. kms in 2001.

Population

The total population of Rajasthan state was 564.73 lakhs as per 2001 Census. The State is predominantly rural as 76.62 per cent of the total population resides in rural area with agriculture and animal husbandry as its major occupations. Agriculture in Rajasthan is mostly dependent on the monsoon, which is erratic and uncertain and has a short span. The population growth rate of Rajasthan is higher as compared to that of India. It is 28.33 per cent in Rajasthan while the growth rate of India is 21.34 per cent for the period 1991-2001 as given in table 1.1. Besides, there has been an increase in density of population of Rajasthan from 129 in 1991 to 165 in 2001.

TABLE 1.1

Area and Population of India, Rajasthan and Jaipur District, 2001

S.No.		India	Rajasthan	Jaipur
1.	Area (lakhs sq.km)	32.87	3.42	0.10
2.	Total Population (lakhs)	10,270.15	564.73	52.52
3.	Growth rate 1991-2001, (per cent)	21.34	28.33	35.10
4.	Urban Population (lakhs)	2,853.54	132.05	25.92
5.	Urban Population (Per cent of total population)	27.78	23.38	49.36
6.	Rural Population (lakhs)	7,416.60	432.67	26.59
	Rural Population (Per cent of total population)	72.22	76.62	50.64

Source : Census of India, Rajasthan, Jaipur District, 2001.

Jaipur district had a total population of 52.52 lakhs as per 2001 Census, which was 9.3 per cent population of the state. Among the districts of Rajasthan, Jaipur has the largest population but holds tenth position in terms of area. The degree of urbanization in the region is indicated by the composition of its population. About 50 per cent of the population of the district resides in rural area. It is observed from table 1.2 that the pace of urbanization is fast in Jaipur district as the urban population has increased from 26.26 per cent to 49.36 per cent of the total population of the district during the period 1961-2001.

TABLE 1.2

Area and Population of Jaipur District, 1951-2001

(lakhs)

S. No.	Year	Area (sq.km.)	Total Population	% Decadal Variation	Rural Population	% of Total Population	Urban Population	% of Total Population
1.	1951	N.A.	15.24	28.14	10.89	71.43	4.35	28.56
2.	1961	14,000	19.02	24.75	14.02	73.74	4.99	26.26
3.	1971	14,000	24.82	30.53	17.37	69.95	7.46	30.05
4.	1981	14,068	34.21	38.42	21.70	63.44	12.51	36.56
5.	1991	14,068	47.23	37.44	28.56	60.47	18.67	39.53
6.	2001	10,878	52.52	11.20	26.59	50.64	25.92	49.36

Source: Census of India, Rajasthan, Jaipur District for relevant years.

There has been rapid growth in population of urban agglomerations and cities of Rajasthan. The population of Jaipur urban agglomeration is highest in the state and has registered the highest population growth rate of 59.4 per cent for the period 1991-2001 followed by Hanumangarh (56.7 per cent) and Gangapur City (52.9 per cent). Jaipur urban agglomeration ranks eleventh in terms of population amongst the urban agglomerations of India. Table 1.3 gives the growth of population in Jaipur urban agglomeration from 1951 to 2001. The population increased from 3.04 lakh in 1951 to 23.24 lakhs in 2001, which is around eight times upsurge. This population outburst has outstripped the supply of the basic amenities of life like drinking water, electricity, sanitation, sewerage, drainage, etc.

Rapid urbanization in the region is also evident from the growth of population and expansion of area of Jaipur city. The population of the city has increased from 4.03 lakhs in 1961 to 14.58 lakhs in 1991 and then to 23.24 lakhs in 2001 as given in table 1.4. The city has over 44 per cent of the population of the district. The density of population of the city in 2001 is 4796 persons per sq. km. Along with the increase in the area and population of Jaipur city, its Municipality was raised to the status of Municipal Council in 1991 and finally to Municipal Corporation in 2001 covering Amber and Sanganer municipalities as well as 93 villages. This growth of Jaipur city ordains appropriate planning for its water resources for the sustenance of its population.

TABLE 1.3

Area and Population of Jaipur Urban Agglomeration, 1951-2001

S.No.	Year	Area (sq.km.)	Persons	Decadal Variation	% Decadal Variation
1.	1951		3,04,380	+12344	+68.22
2.	1961	104.40	4,10,376	+105996	+34.82
3.	1971	258.57	6,36,768	+226392	+55.17
4.	1981	210.09	1,015,160	+378392	+59.42
5.	1991	218.26	1,518,235	+503075	+49.56
6.	2001	484.64	2,324,319	+806084	+59.37

Source : Census of India, Rajasthan, Jaipur District for relevant years.

TABLE 1.4

Area and Population, Jaipur City, 1951-2001

S.No.	Year	Status of Town	Area (sq.km.)	Persons	Decadal Variation	% Decadal Variation
1.	1951			291130	+115320	+65.59
2.	1961	Municipality	64.75	403444	+112314	+38.58
3.	1971	Municipality	206.06	615258	+211814	+52.50
4.	1981	Municipality	181.23	977165	+361907	+58.82
5.	1991	Municipal Council	200.40	1458483	+481318	+49.26
6.	2001	Municipal Corporation	484.64	2324319	+865836	+59.36

Source : Census of India, Rajasthan, Jaipur District for relevant years.

Physiography

Rajasthan stretches in the shape of an irregular rhombus. It is considered as a desert state of India, as 61 per cent of its area is either desert or semi-desert. The Aravalli hill ranges, running from north-east to south-west, divides the state like a mid-rib into two major parts – western arid and eastern semi-arid regions. The present land form and drainage systems have been greatly influenced and determined by the geological formation and structure of the mountain ranges of the Aravalli. The area, to its east, is well-drained by several integrated drainage systems of non-perennial rivers, such as, Banas, Kothari, Khari, Chambal, Kalisindh, Parvati, etc., while the area to the west has only one integrated drainage system–the Luni drainage system. The state is divided into four major physiographical regions, which are as follows :

(i) Western Sandy Plains
(ii) The Aravalli Range and Hilly Region
(iii) The Eastern Plains
(iv) South eastern Rajasthan Plateau (Hadoti)

The Jaipur district extends partly in Aravalli hill region and partly in the eastern plain. Its area is characterized by flat and undulating topography and isolated hills in the central-northern, north-eastern and south-western parts. The shape of the district is elliptical; it is broader at the centre and tapering towards the north-east. The eastern and northern parts of the Jaipur district are occupied by the hill range of Aravalli hills, with its forests which have suffered erosion and deforestation due to large scale quarrying of the mountain ranges. The main peaks of the Aravalli hills in the district are Jaigarh, Nahargarh, Barwara, Manoharpura and Bichun. The Eastern plain region of Jaipur district is divided into two zones: (a) the Banas plain and (b) the Chhappan plain. These plains have rich alluvial soil and are drained by non-perennial rivers. The integrated drainage of Banas plain constitutes several tributaries, namely, Kothari, Dain, Sohadra, Manshi, Bandi, Dhundh, Morel, Kareli, Berach, Wagan and Gambhiri. Banas is the major tributary of Chambal which ultimately joins Yamuna. Another non-perennial river, Banganga has been impounded near Jamwa Ramgarh which provides drinking water to Jaipur city. The western part of the district comprises the Sambhar salt lake basin and an extensive sand dune field.

Jaipur city is located more or less centrally in a valley on a sandy triangular plain "conjectured to be on a bed of dried up lake"

(Imperial Gazetteer). The city is enclosed on three sides by the Aravalli ranges; in the north by Nahargarh, Jaigarh and Amber hills, with a fort on each hill, in the north-east by Purana Ghat known as Galta hills in the form of a gorge and on the east by the Jhalana and the Amagarh hills. The area has a number of rain-fed streamlets and nallahs which collect rain water flowing down from the hills around the city, such as, (i) Amanishah nallah from Nahargarh hills flowing parallel to the city in the west and turning south-east of the city; (ii) Jawahar Nagar nallah from Jhalana and Amagarh hills in the east joins Amanishah nallah in the south. (iii) Another streamlet from the north-eastern hills of Galta flows along the southern wall of the city and joins Amanishah nallah.

Climate and Rainfall

The climate of Rajasthan varies from arid to sub-humid. The annual rainfall in the state differs significantly. The western part of the state (60-75 per cent area) is arid as well as semi-arid with low and erratic rainfall, high summer temperatures, low humidity and high velocity of wind causing an average potential evapotranspiration of 2000 mm, negative water balance and acute water deficit. The average annual rainfall in this part ranges from less than 10 cm to 40 cm. The climate differs between semi-arid and sub-humid in the east of Aravalli range, characterized by more or less the same extremes of temperatures but relatively having lower wind velocity and high humidity with better rainfall. The average annual rainfall in this part ranges from 55 cm to 100 cm. The south-west monsoon starts in the end of June and lasts till mid September. The number of rainy days during this period varies widely in different places ranging from 10 to 48 days. Rainfall during the rest of the year ranges from 2 cm to 7 cm. Though monsoon winds from Arabian Sea and Bay of Bengal pass over Rajasthan, but it does not receive the amount of rainfall as other parts of India. The monsoon clouds from Bay of Bengal, coming from a distant sea are drained off all its water and humidity before reaching Rajasthan. So also, the monsoon from Arabian Sea only gives a part of rain to this arid region. The Aravalli ranges are not able to obstruct the monsoon winds to cause rainfall as the direction of the range is parallel to the monsoon winds.

Climatic changes have been observed in Rajasthan, as could be gauged from variations in rainfall and temperature. The analysis of the temperature data of the last 100 years indicates a rise of 0.60° C in temperature. The changes in rainfall and temperature are largely caused by human negligence and by emission of greenhouse gases, such as, carbon-dioxide, which prevents heat from dissipating into space.

The climate of Jaipur district is dry and salubrious, ranging between extremes, with hot winds blowing during May and June and cold waves during winters. The temperature in summer reaches around 45° C and generally in winters the minimum temperature falls to 3° C. The mean temperature is 24° C. The annual rainfall varies from 50 to 60 cm. and the normal annual rainfall is 54.82 cm.

Land Use Pattern

The state presents a variety of land use pattern which exhibits the availability of soil and water resources and the human efforts to harness them. The land utilization includes agricultural, non-agricultural, forest and other uses of land. There is significant change in this pattern over the years. In the areas having greater concentration of population, the significance of agricultural cropping of the land increases as is evident from the relatively high net sown area in the district. Table 1.5 shows the changes in the land utilization pattern of Rajasthan state and Jaipur district. The net sown area of the state was 38.75 per cent in 1960-61, which increased to 46.3 per cent in 2000-01 and that of Jaipur district was 47.21 per cent in 1960-61 which increased to 58.95 per cent in 1991. This increase is due to the expansion of the irrigation facilities in the state during these plan periods, as irrigation and agriculture were on priority. The irrigated area of the Jaipur district was 12.78 per cent in 1960-61 which increased to 32.70 per cent in 2001. Similar is the case with the forest cover of the state which is an important factor affecting water resources. The forest cover of Jaipur district has also increased from 2.02 per cent in 1960-61 to 7.29 per cent in 2001. Table 1.6 shows that the state has a forest cover area of 9.32 per cent and only 1.05 per cent is dense forest and most of it is confined to the hilly areas in the eastern and southern regions. The per capita forest of the state is only 0.07 hectares. The role of forest becomes important in rain water conservation. It works in two ways. It is effective in saving rain water and silt of rivers during over flow by making anicuts, small ponds, contour trenches along the river in forest area. Moreover, the roots of trees stop the flowing of the silt, increase the level of groundwater and keep the forest green, control the temperature and help in the process to have more rainfall. The Forest Department plans for the conservation of water in the forest around Banganga river i.e., in Shahpura, Bilwadi and Viratnagar area which would also help in soil conservation.

TABLE 1.5
Land Utilisation of Rajasthan and Jaipur District

(000' hectares)

S.No.		Rajasthan 1960-61	Rajasthan 2000-01	Jaipur District 1960-61	Jaipur District 1991
1.	Forest	814 (2.41)	2606 (7.61)	28.33 (2.02)	70.7 (5.05)
2.	Land put to non-agricultural use	1095 (3.24)	1740 (5.08)	62.32 (4.45)	85.04 (6.08)
3.	Barren and uncultivable land	5153 (15.23)	2566 (7.49)	133.95 (9.57)	97.36 (6.96)
4.	Uncultivated land	1700 (5.02)	1721 (5.02)	101.98 (7.29)	108.33 (7.74)
5.	Cultivable waste	6841 (20.22)	4908 (14.32)	208.01 (14.86)	64.21 (4.59)
6.	Fallow land	5126 (15.15)	4859 (14.18)	204.37 (14.60)	148.67 (10.63)
7.	Net area sown	13112 (38.75)	15865 (46.30)	660.87 (47.21)	824.75 (58.95)
8.	Total geographical area	33841 (100.00)	34265 (100.00)	1399.83 (100.00)	1399.06 (100.00)

Note : Figures in parentheses are percentage share of land utilization.

Source : Trends in Land Use Statistics, Department of Agriculture, Government of Rajasthan, for Rajasthan; Census of India, Rajasthan, Jaipur District for Jaipur District.

TABLE 1.6
Forest Cover in Rajasthan, 2001

S.No.	Rajasthan	Area (hectares)	Share (%)
1.	Total forest area	31.9 lakh	9.32
2.	Dense forest	3.6 lakh	1.05
3.	Open forest	9.5 lakh	2.78
4.	Barren forest	18.8 lakh	5.49
5.	Total geographical area	3.422 crore	
6.	Per capita forest	0.07	

Source : Rajasthan Development Report, 2006

1.5.1 Administrative Profile

The state of Rajasthan is divided into 32 districts (Pratapgarh district has been formed in 2007), 30 Zila Parishads, 241 Tehsils, 237 Panchayat Samitis (development blocks) and 222 cities and towns. The district of Jaipur is divided into four sub-divisions (Amber, Kotputli, Sambhar and Jaipur), 13 tehsils, 13 Panchayat Samitis, 16 towns and 2131 villages. The sub-divisions have been evolved to facilitate better administration. Initially, Jaipur district included Dausa sub-division, which later on became a separate district of Dausa in 1996. The tehsils of Dausa, Lalsot, Baswa and Sikrai were transferred to district of Dausa.

Tehsils

A tehsil is a small administrative unit for collecting land revenue and is administered by a Tehsildar. At present, the state has 241 tehsils spread over its 32 districts. The number of tehsils in a district is largely determined on the basis of its population. The tehsils of Jaipur district are Kotputli, Bairat (Viratnagar), Amber, Jaipur, Sanganer, Jamwa Ramgarh, Bassi, Chaksu, Phagi, Phulera, Dudu and Chomu. The tehsils also include towns and villages; hence the population of a tehsil is divided into rural and urban population. Table 1.7 gives rural and urban population of the tehsils of Jaipur district. The tehsils of Dudu, Phagi, Jamwa Ramgarh and Bassi are completely rural. Jaipur tehsil has the highest population of 19.60 lakhs of which 95.46 per cent is urban.

Panchayat Samitis

Panchayat Samiti is a cluster of Gram Panchayats, which is headed by a Pradhan. The Panchayat Samiti is also termed as Development Block. A Gram Panchayat is an elected body representing a group of villages coming in around an area of 8 sq. km. and with population ranging from 2000 to 5000. There are 13 Panchayat Samitis in Jaipur district viz., Kotputli, Viratnagar, Shahpura, Govindgarh, Amber, Jamwa Ramgarh, Sambhar, Dudu, Sanganer, Jhotwara, Phagi, Bassi and Chaksu.

1.5.2 City of Jaipur

The city of Jaipur was founded on 18 November 1727 by Maharaja Sawai Jai Singh II and was completed in 1750. It was the capital of erstwhile Princely State of Jaipur which was also known

TABLE 1.7

Population of the Tehsils, Jaipur District, Rajasthan, 2001

(lakhs)

S.No.	Name of Tehsil	Name of the Town	Total Population	Rural Population	Col. 5 as per cent of Col. 4	Urban Population	Col. 7 as per cent of Col. 4
1	2	3	4	5	6	7	8
1	Kotputli	Kotputli	3.40	3.00	88.19	0.40	11.81
2	Viratnagar	Viratnagar	1.36	1.18	87.29	0.17	12.71
3	Shahpura	Shahpura	2.26	1.98	87.54	0.28	12.46
4	Chomu	Chomu	3.26	2.76	84.47	0.51	15.53
5	Phulera		3.89	3.07	78.94	0.82	21.06
(i)		Phulera				0.22	5.56
(ii)		Sambhar				0.22	5.73
(iii)		Jobner				0.10	2.70
(iv)		Kishangarh Renwal				0.28	7.08
6	Dudu		1.75	1.75	100.00	0.00	0.00
7	Phagi		1.62	1.62	100.00	0.00	0.00
8	Jaipur	Jaipur	19.60	0.89	4.54	18.71	95.46

Contd.

Contd..

1	2	3	4	5	6	7	8
9	Sanganer		5.73	1.31	22.91	4.42	77.09
(i)		Sanganer				4.20	73.24
(ii)		Bagru				0.22	3.85
10	Amber	Amber	2.94	2.62	89.11	0.32	10.89
11	Jamwa Ramgarh		2.50	2.50	100.00	0.00	0.00
12	Bassi	Bassi	2.30	2.30	100.00	0.00	0.00
13	Chaksu	Chaksu	1.90	1.61	84.70	0.29	15.30

Note : Percentages are from respective population total.

Source : Census of India, Rajasthan, Jaipur District, 2001.

as State of Amber. The city is famous for its scientific town planning which was modern in its approach and was designed in view of the future growth of population and economic development. It had the potential to support the population of 1.50 lakh persons and to provide them with adequate drinking water, good drainage system, and transport and communication facilities. These facilities were developed and modernised specially during the reigns of Maharaja Sawai Ram Singh II (1835-1880) and Maharaja Man Singh II (1921-1949). The area of the city in the beginning was 6 sq. kms which increased to 64 sq. kms within a period of 100 years. In the year 1961 the population of Jaipur city was 4.03 residing in an area of 64.75 sq. km and presently it is 484.64 sq. km. with a total population of 23.24 lakhs. The accelerated pace of urbanization has resulted in the conversion of the agricultural land in several residential colonies on the fringes of the city. The emergence of new colonies has obstructed the natural drainage system resulting in the decline of water table. In view of accommodating the increased population, new residential areas have been identified on the outskirts of the city under Master Plan 2011 towards the north-west of Jhotwara, west of Vaishali Nagar, south of Sanganer between Diggi-Malpura Road and Tonk Road, south of Sanganer Airport up to Sitapura and east of Tonk Road and areas west of Mansarovar along the western bypass. In Jaipur city the growth of slum is also very high. A total of 164 slums have been reported in Census 2001 with a population of 3.5 lakhs which is around 15 per cent of the total population of the city. This reveals the rapid urbanization of the Jaipur city in all directions having organized system of railways and air service connecting Jaipur with all metropolises of the country.

❑❑❑

2

Water Resources, Uses and Emerging Issues

Water is the most essential need of life. It is the natural resource, which is abundantly available on earth, but limited for the use of man. It is renewed through the hydrological process which depends on the ecological factors and controls the availability of water. The fresh water provides a link between the physical and social environment of man. It touches every aspect of life, from the health of aquatic ecosystems to human health, from the need to grow food to generate energy for the growing population of the world. The human demand for water has also multiplied owing to the increase in population and economic development.

The source of all fresh water on earth is precipitation in the form of a drizzle or rain or from hail, snow, dew and even frost. The total global supply of water can neither be increased nor be diminished like other natural resources. Hence, it has a fixed total stock but it is potentially inexhaustible as it is continuously being renewed through nature's hydrological cycle. The implications of water cycle differ from region to region owing to climatic changes. In dry climatic regions with rapid population growth, the water cycle may affect self-sufficiency in food and availability of fresh water. It has its bearing on all functions of nature and mankind, namely, climate and vegetation, health and habitat, psychological, religious, and socio-economic functions. In this context, this chapter gives an overview of water resources, their availability and uses in Rajasthan state with special reference to the district of Jaipur. It also highlights the emerging issues related to water resources in Jaipur district.

2.1 STATE WATER RESOURCES

Rajasthan is among the most water scarce states. It has 1.2 per cent of the nation's water resources. Its water availability suffers mainly due to erratic rainfall and high evapotranspiration in arid and semi-arid zones of the state. In Jaipur district rainfall is 55 cm and evapotranspiration is 174.52 cm. If rainfall is higher than the potential evapotranspiration, then it provides water surplus in the region. This feature is visible only in few southern and south-eastern parts of Rajasthan where water surplus ranges from 10 to 30 cm per year, whereas the entire north and west of the Aravalli range extending over Jaipur district has been characterized as moisture deficient. The physical features of Rajasthan state exhibit signs of land degradation, desertification, constant droughts, deforestation, and depletion of water resources due to high degree of water use and population growth. This is evident by per capita per annum availability of water in Rajasthan, which was 840 cubic metre in 2001, and is estimated to decrease to 561 cubic metre by 2025 and 439 cubic metre by 2050, against the national average of 1140 cubic metre in 2050.

According to the State Water Resources Plan, 1993, the total surface water in Rajasthan was 39.59 BCM, out of which 21.71 BCM was internal flow and 17.88 BCM was external flow (Ravi, Beas, Satluj, Chambal, Mahi and Yamuna) (table 2.1). However, the economically utilizable surface water at 50 per cent dependability is estimated as 16.05 BCM. There are 203 major and medium tanks and reservoirs in the state, which store about 13.72 BCM of water at their full capacity and a reduced volume of 11.51 BCM during low rainfall years. Besides, there are a large number of minor rainwater harvesting structures with storage capacity of 2.28 BCM, which increase the total storage at full capacity level to 16 BCM. However, during droughts, the estimated total surface water availability is reduced to 12.88 BCM creating a shortfall of 3.12 BCM. It has been assessed that mean annual natural replenishable groundwater in the state is 7.413 BCM, while the total available groundwater in the state is 10.09 BCM including return flows from irrigated areas, urban and other water utilization sectors.

Groundwater is regarded as the major source for both irrigation as well as domestic consumption. An assessment of available groundwater resources in Rajasthan state was made in 1995, 1998 and 2005 as given in table 2.2. The total draft from groundwater aquifer in 1995 was 7746.94 MCM which increased to 9260 MCM in 2005. Thus, the development of groundwater resources increased from 59 per cent in 1995 to 73 per cent in 2005. This is significantly high in the eastern part of Rajasthan as compared to its western part because of geological features of rock formations. The groundwater level has declined by 12-15 metres, the shallow wells have dried up, the deep wells have further been deepened, and the quality of water in the deep wells has deteriorated due to overexploitation of groundwater resources. Figure 2.1 describes the groundwater potential zone and aquifer of Rajasthan state. It shows the spread of the water bearing rock formations in the state. The western region is non-potential or has saline groundwater. The 'good to moderate' water potential zone of alluvium lies in the north-east region of Rajasthan state comprising the districts of Jaipur, Jhunjhunun, Sikar, Bharatpur, Karauli and in some parts of Dholpur.

TABLE 2.1

Water Availability in Rajasthan, 1993

(billion cubic metre)

	Rajasthan
Average Annual Rainfall	57 cm
Total Surface Water	39.59 BCM
Internal Flow	21.71 BCM
External Flow	17.88 BCM
Annual Utilizable Water Resources	23.46 BCM
(a) Surface Water	16.05 BCM
(b) Groundwater	7.413 BCM

Note : BCM = billion cubic metre

Source : Vision 2045, Department of Water Resources, Government of Rajasthan, Jaipur.

In order to facilitate the assessment of groundwater resources, the Rajasthan state has been divided into 594 groundwater zones. Out of these, 322 zones (54 per cent) fall in the 'White' or 'Safe' category

Fig. 2.1 : Groundwater Potential Zone & Aquifer in Rajasthan

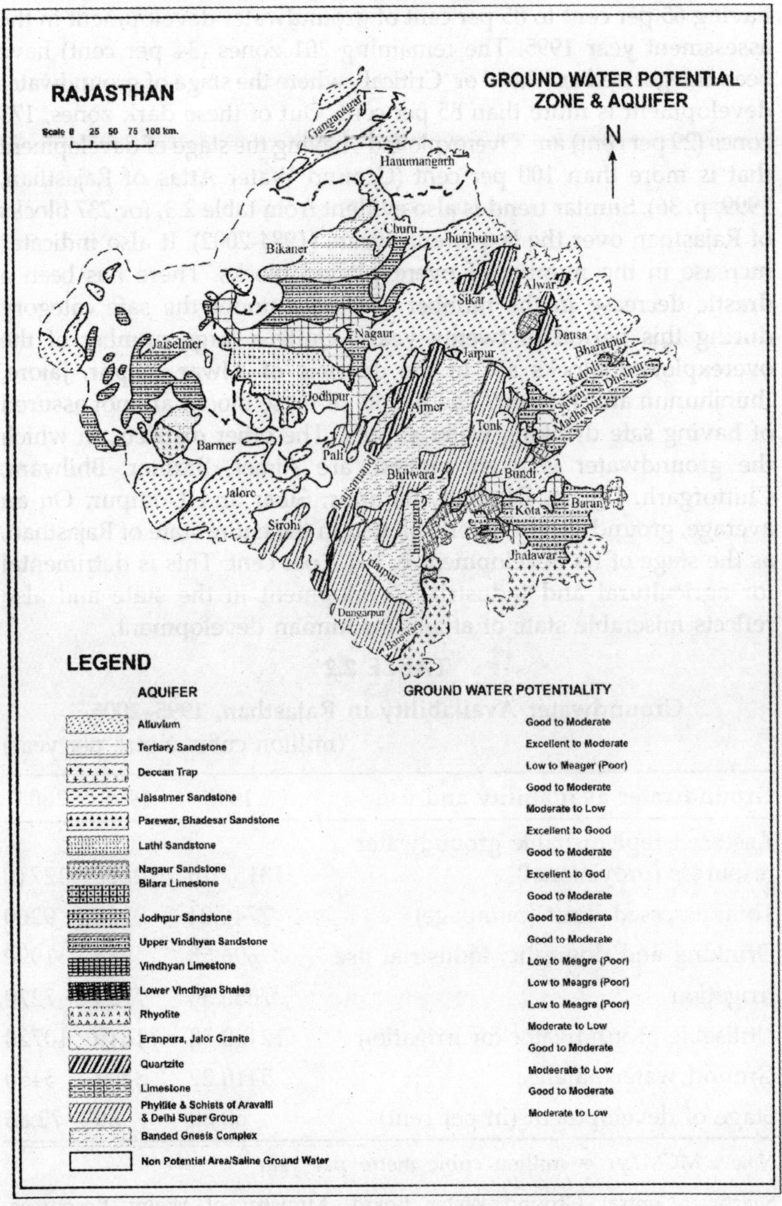

Source : Groundwater Atlas of Rajasthan, Department of Groundwater, Government of Rajasthan, Jodhpur, 1999.

where groundwater development is less than 65 per cent; 71 zones (12 per cent) fall in the 'Grey' category also known as 'Semi-critical', having 65 per cent to 85 per cent of groundwater development in the assessment year 1995. The remaining 201 zones (34 per cent) have been categorized as 'Dark' or 'Critical', where the stage of groundwater development is more than 85 per cent. Out of these dark zones, 173 zones (29 per cent) are 'Overexploited', having the stage of development that is more than 100 per cent (Ground Water Atlas of Rajasthan, 1999, p. 36). Similar trend is also evident from table 2.3, for 237 blocks of Rajasthan over the last twenty years (1984-2002). It also indicates increase in the number of overexploited blocks. There has been a drastic decrease in the number of blocks under the safe category during this period of twenty years. Quite a large number of the overexploited blocks are in the districts of Alwar, Jaipur, Jalore, Jhunjhunun and Nagaur. The people of these blocks are not assured of having safe drinking water supply. The other districts, in which the groundwater is overexploited, are Ajmer, Barmer, Bhilwara, Chittorgarh, Dausa, Dholpur, Jodhpur, Sikar and Udaipur. On an average, groundwater is overexploited in the entire state of Rajasthan, as the stage of its development is 104.3 per cent. This is detrimental for agricultural and industrial development in the state and also reflects miserable state of affairs for human development.

TABLE 2.2

Groundwater Availability in Rajasthan, 1995-2005

(million cubic metre per year)

Groundwater availability and use	1995	1998	2005
Assessed replenishable groundwater resources (provisional)	13157.16	12602	12710
Total assessed draft (pumpage)	7746.94	8708	9260
Drinking and domestic, industrial use	696.58	983	1990
Irrigation	7050.36	7725	7270
Utilisable groundwater for irrigation	12460.58	11619	10720
Ground water balance	5410.22	3894	3450
Stage of development (in per cent)	58.88	69	72.86

Note : MCM/yr = million cubic metre per year

Source : Central Ground Water Board, Ministry of Water Resources, Government of India, Jaipur, for relevant years.

TABLE 2.3

Status of Ground Water in Rajasthan, 1984–2002

Category	Percentage of development of Ground water	Number of Blocks 1984	1998	2001	2002
Safe	< 70	203	135	54	49
Semi-critical	70-90	10	34	32	21
Critical	> 90	11	26	65	80
Over-exploited	> 100 (Areas with declining trends in groundwater levels)	12	41	85	86
Fully saline water (Taranagar block, Churu)		1	1	1	1

Source : Report of the Group on the estimation of Groundwater Resources of Rajasthan, Department of Ground Water, Government of Rajasthan, Jaipur, for relevant years.

The **State Water Plan,** 1995 estimated that the surface water utilization would increase from 8.20 BCM in the year to 12.97 BCM in 2015 and 16.87 BCM in 2045 which is almost an increase of 105.73 per cent in fifty years period from 1995 to 2045. Similarly, the groundwater utilization would increase by 14.71 per cent during the same period (table 2.4). The State has 136 lakh hectares (ha) of total irrigable land and if all of it is irrigated, the agricultural water demand will be about 100 BCM, which obviously is not available. The State had the irrigation potential of only 4 lakh ha at the time of India's independence, which increased to 28.12 lakh ha in fifty years. This is 5.64 per cent of the country's total irrigation potential as against 2.46 per cent at the time of independence. The analysis of this data clearly shows that the surface water utilization has to be increased by 60 per cent from present position of utilization of about 10 BCM. So also, the efficiency of distribution system has to be increased to 74 per cent from present estimated efficiency of 54 per cent. Along with this, average on-farm irrigation efficiency has to be increased significantly to about 70 per cent from present estimated efficiency which is below 27 per cent. It is envisaged in the plan that with all the development and increase in efficiency and after meeting the non-agricultural demands, water would be available in the year 2045, to irrigate only about 46 lakh ha which is only 30 per cent of total irrigable area of 136 lakh ha.

TABLE 2.4

Projections on Water Utilisation as per State Water Plan for 2015 & 2045

Particulars	1995	2015	2045
Surface water availability (BCM)	21.17	22.17	23.38
Surface water utilization (BCM)	8.20	12.97	16.87
Groundwater utilization (BCM)	9.45	10.37	10.84
Non-agricultural demand (BCM)	3.29	5.05	8.07
Agriculture area irrigated (lakh ha)	27.07	50.59	57
On-farm irrigation efficiency (percentage)	27	44.20	70
Off-farm irrigation efficiency (percentage)	54	61.20	72

Note : BCM = billion cubic meters

Source : Vision 2045, Department of Irrigation, Government of Rajasthan, Jaipur, 2004.

The State Water Plan has projected an increase of non-agricultural demand of water from 3.29 BCM in 1995 to 5.05 BCM in 2015 and to 8.07 BCM in 2045, which is around one and a half times increase from 1995 to 2045 (table 2.4). The non-agricultural demand primarily includes domestic and industrial demands. The projections for the water demand in non-agricultural sectors in Rajasthan for the year 2015 is given in table 2.5. There is an estimated increase of 58.64 per cent in the water consumption by domestic sector and about 51 per cent increase in the industrial sector during 1995 to 2015.

TABLE 2.5

Water Demand for Non-agricultural Uses in Rajasthan

(million cubic metre per year)

Year	Domestic	Industrial	Livestock	Others	Total
1995	2002	47.2	1069	167	3285.2
2005	2584	57.2	910	645	4196.2
2015	3176	71.4	1089	715	5051.4

Note : MCM/year = million cubic metre per year.

Source : Water Resources Planning for the State of Rajasthan, Tahal & WAPCOS, 1998.

In Rajasthan, as per Census 2001, 70 per cent of the population is dependent upon groundwater for both drinking and irrigation uses.

About 90 per cent of the drinking water and 60 per cent of the irrigation water is drawn from groundwater resources. About 70 per cent towns have no access to surface water for drinking purposes and these mainly depend on groundwater resources. About 69 per cent towns draw water through deep wells and 30.62 per cent towns use hand pumps along with deep wells. Among urban households, 88.2 per cent have access to drinking water but supply of water is insufficient to them. Only 80 per cent of urban households of the state have tap facility and 10 per cent draw water from hand pumps. About 50 per cent of the rural households have access to safe drinking water, out of which only 21.6 per cent are connected through taps, 31.3 per cent depend on hand pumps and 30 per cent depend on wells. About 20 per cent of the total households of the state have proper sanitation facilities, but still more than 70 per cent do not have any sanitation facility as per Census 2001. In the state 63.5 per cent of the total households do not have access to any sort of drainage system. Moreover, 56 per cent urban households still rely on open drainage. The net water demand is estimated to increase by 69.75 per cent in cities and 159 per cent in towns of Rajasthan between 1991 and 2015.

TABLE 2.6

Total Capacity of Various Tanks in Jaipur District, Rajasthan, 2007

Name of Tank	Capacity (Mcft)
Ramgarh	2650
Chhaparwara	1236.3
Kalakhsagar	581.4
Chitoli	861.12
Buchara	588
Kanota	499
Khard	417
Hingonia	265
Ramsagar Newata	236.72
Patan	183.5
Baneri	176.45
Total Capacity	7694.49

Note : Capacity at Full Tank Level (FTL). Mcft = million cubic feet

Source : Department of Irrigation, Government of Rajasthan, Jaipur.

2.2 WATER RESOURCES : AVAILABILITY IN JAIPUR DISTRICT

The availability of water depends on the groundwater as well as surface water resources. These resources are interdependent in the sense that river run-off and its basin also add to storage of groundwater. Therefore, the availability of water resources in a region is determined by the river run-off and the groundwater aquifer. For instance, the rivers during summer and winter survive on the groundwater, while in rainy season their basins become the main source of recharge of the groundwater aquifer. Thus, the surface water and groundwater are the two faces of the same coin. In summer, the level of groundwater is low, the river beds also dry up and the surface water evaporates. The level of groundwater rises only after precipitation. In view of this, the water resources in Jaipur district can be studied under two categories: (a) river basins and reservoirs, and (b) groundwater resources. The district is drained by non-perennial rivers and their basins serve as sources of surface water and also as a prime source of groundwater recharge. The reservoirs include dams, natural and artificial lakes and tanks. There are other water resources which include watershed structures and traditional water sources including reservoirs, stepwells (*baodis*), ponds and tanks (*tanka*) known by various names according to their size and use.

2.2.1 Surface Water Resources

River Basins

There are two major non-perennial rivers - the **Banas** and the **Banganga** and their tributaries together drain the Jaipur district. The **Banas** is the principal river, which originates in Udaipur, but flows near the borders of Jaipur district for about 110 miles (164 km) and finally merges into the Chambal river. Its basin covers eastern and central Rajasthan extending over some parts of Jaipur district. The total catchment area of the basin is 45,833 sq. km. The main tributaries of Banas like Berach, Kothari, Khari, Dai, Mashi, Dhundh and Morel also drain Jaipur district. There are seven major surface water projects on the Banas, out of which Chhaparwara, Kalakh Sagar and Bisalpur irrigation projects are in Jaipur district and operated by the Panchayat Samitis. The other major river is the **Banganga** which flows for about 90 miles (144 km), in the north-eastern part of Rajasthan and extends over Jaipur district having the total catchment area of 8878 sq. km. It originates from the hills of Bairat (Viratnagar) in Jaipur district. The

Ramgarh dam is constructed on this river in Jamwa Ramgarh tehsil which lies about 20 kms from Jaipur city. Other non-perennial tributaries flow through different Panchayat Samitis of Jaipur district.

The **Bandi** river flows through Amber and Phagi; the Dhundh river passes through Bassi, Chaksu and Jhotwara; the Mendha river proceeds through Govindgarh and Sambhar; the Banganga and Tala move to Jamwa Ramgarh; Amanishah (Dravyavati) inundates Jhotwara and Sanganer; the Sabi and the Sotanala rivers rush through Kotputli; and the Sabi spills on Shahpura. These rivers serve as sources of surface water, provide recharge to the groundwater aquifer through their basins and also provide opportunity for the development of watershed projects in the Panchayat Samitis of Jaipur district. The groundwater in the district is mainly dependent on the basins of Sabi, Bandi and Banganga rivers as their greater part is underlain by gravel and pebbles.

Reservoirs

The district of Jaipur has only one natural lake at **Sambhar** (Phulera tehsil), which is the largest salt lake in India. It has an area of 145 sq. kms. Moreover, the district has 116 tanks both big and small in size and many reservoirs and artificial lakes. The water of small tanks only serves as a source of irrigation but that of the bigger tanks is used both for drinking and irrigation purposes. The State Irrigation Department maintains some of the bigger and important tanks, such as, Ramgarh, Chhaparwara, Kalakh Sagar, Chhitoli, Hingonia, Buchara, Baneri, Kharad, Ramsagar Nevata, Patan, Kanota, Sainthal Kalakh, Madho Sagar, Marali Gudu Bandh and Kheri (table 2.6). The total capacity for the storage of water of the major and medium tanks of the district is 7694.49 MCFt. Besides, some of the minor irrigation projects which are below the capacity of 150 MCFt have been handed over to the Panchayat Samitis for their operation and maintenance. At present there are four medium irrigation projects and about 96 minor irrigation projects in the district, and these provide water for irrigation, drinking and other purposes. Table 2.7 gives the medium and minor irrigation projects in each tehsil of Jaipur district. The medium irrigation projects are concentrated in Dudu, Jamwa Ramgarh and Kotputli tehsils only. The minor irrigation projects are spread over all tehsils. Dudu and Phagi have the highest number of such projects (23 and 22 respectively).

Table 2.7
Medium and Minor Irrigation Projects in Jaipur District, Rajasthan, 2007

Name of Tehsil	Medium Irrigation Projects with Capacity	Minor Irrigation Projects (number)
Amber		5
Phulera		3
Dudu	Chhaparwara (10770 CCA)	23
Dudu	Kalakh Sagar (7920 CCA)	
Bassi		7
Jamwa Ramgarh	Ramgarh Dam (12160 CCA)	8
Sanganer		4
Phagi		22
Chaksu		10
Viratnagar		11
Shahpura		2
Kotputli	Buchara (2840 CCA)	1

Note : CCA = Canal Command Area in hectares.

Source : Department of Irrigation, Government of Rajasthan, Jaipur.

There are a large number of traditional water resources in Jaipur district, such as, *baodis* (stepwells), *tanka, nadi, johad,* etc. These traditional systems of water storage are, in general, in the state of dilapidation. The traditional sources served as watershed structures and fulfilled the water requirements of the district. These traditional water sources have still the potential to cater the demands, especially in the domestic and agriculture sectors. These could be revived by state level efforts.

2.2.2 Status of Groundwater

The groundwater and its recharge are also important in supplementing water resources in Jaipur district. Groundwater is collected from precipitation and seepage of water from other water bodies down the soil. Therefore, the availability of groundwater in the region depends upon the nature of rocks and their water bearing character. The water yield of Alluvium in Jaipur district is the highest, ranging from 50 to 280 cubic metres per day, while that of Quartzite is between 30 to 120 cubic metres per day and that of Granite and Gneiss are below 60 cubic metres per day. These formations are responsible for bearing groundwater and its recharge at different levels in the district. The occurrence of groundwater in the district mainly depends upon the hard rock formations and Alluvium in the region. Younger Alluvium and Older Alluvium are the main water bearing formations, which consist of sand, *bajri*, silt and gravel and retain more water as compared to hard rocks. They cover almost 72 per cent of the potential zone area of the district extending over 11 Panchayat Samitis as illustrated in figure 2.2. The hard rocks in the district mainly consist of Quartzite (Q), Schist (S), Gneiss (Gn) and Granite (G), which cover about 27 per cent of the potential zone area of the district and lie in the Panchayat Samitis of Dudu, Phagi and parts of Jamwa Ramgarh. Table 2.8 shows that the percentage of Alluvium in the groundwater potential zone area is higher in most of the Panchayat Samitis of Jaipur district except in Dudu and Phagi. In fact, Dudu has the lowest percentage (18 per cent), whereas, Panchayat Samitis of Govindgarh, Jhotwara, Sambhar, Sanganer and Shahpura have 100 per cent of Alluvium. According to the 2005 survey of the State Ground Water Department of Government of Rajasthan, Jaipur, the depth of groundwater level varies from 10m to 69m in the district as given in table 2.8. In 1984, the pre-monsoon water level varied between 10 to 20 metres in the district except in Jhotwara, Govindgarh, Shahpura and Viratnagar, where it was below 20 metres. During 1984 and 1997, the water level decreased by 3 to 15 metres in the district. In fact during this period, it is only in parts of Phagi and Dudu Panchayat Samitis where the change in water level is 0 to 3 metres, whereas in Amber, Jamwa Ramgarh and parts of Dudu and Phagi Panchayat Samitis it is 0 to (-) 3 metres. In most parts of Jaipur district the change in water level is from (-) 3 to (-) 7 metres. In the Panchayat Samitis of Sambhar, Shahpura, Bassi and Amber the change is upto (-) 15 metres between 1984 and 1997 as illustrated in the figure 2.3. In the areas of Alluvium, the depth of groundwater varies from 8.80 m to 65.00 m below ground level whereas in the hard rock areas (Quartzite, Granite and Schist), it varies from 9.80 m to 36.00 m below ground level as investigated by the Groundwater Department during the pre-monsoon period in 2003.

Fig. 2.2 : Groundwater Potential Zones in Jaipur District, Rajasthan

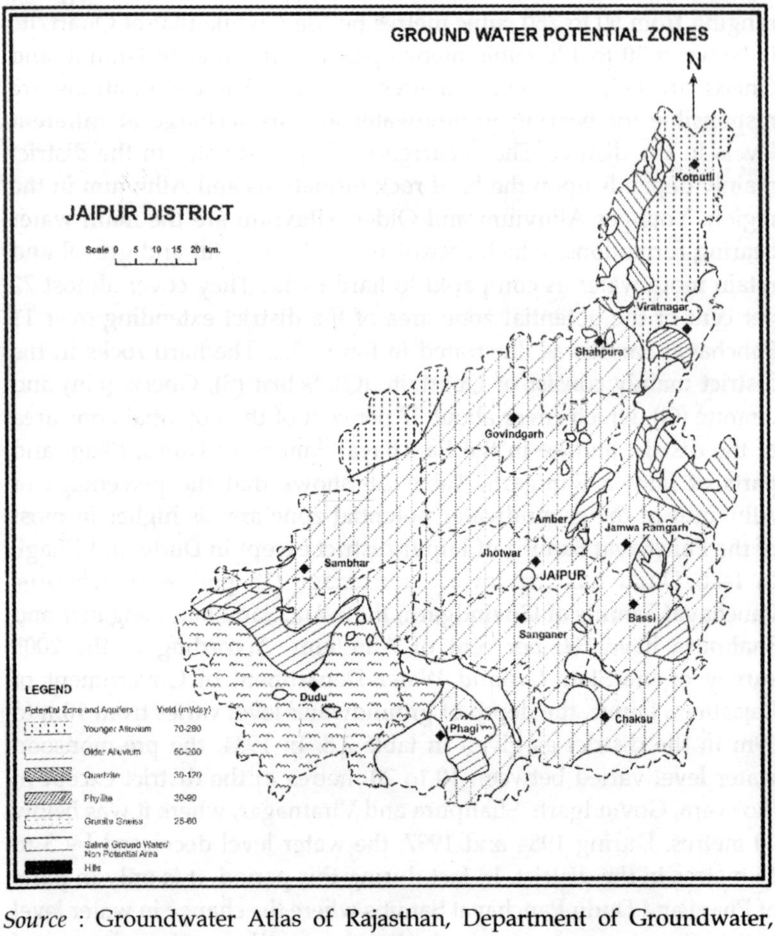

Source : Groundwater Atlas of Rajasthan, Department of Groundwater, Government of Rajasthan, Jodhpur, 1999.

Thus, the situation of groundwater in all the Panchayat Samitis of Jaipur district is **overexploited** except in Dudu and Phagi, where it is **critical**. There is a continuous decrease in the groundwater level since 1984, because of the arid and semi-arid climate, shortage in rainfall, less recharge and excessive extraction and the ignorance of the people about the scarcity of water resources. The survey conducted by the Ground Water Department for the period 1984-2001 reveals that the level of groundwater has decreased by 6.68 m i.e., about 40 cm a

TABLE 2.8

Ground Water Level and Potential Zone Area in Jaipur District, Rajasthan, 2004

Panchayat Samiti	Name of the river	Area (sq km)	Potential zone area (sq. km)	Alluvium Percentage	Hardrock (S,G,Q,Gn) Percentage	Rainfall (mm)	Ground water level (metre)				
							North	South	East	West	Middle
Amber	Bandi	898.64	850.48	87	13	629.67	32	39	23	40	25
Bairat		706.1	663.98	89	11	594.62	34	12	25	17	20
Bassi	Dhundh	654.69	631.23	91	9	545.34	27	16	31	31	24
Chaksu	Dhundh	811.92	729.36	76	24	572.42	22	22	32	18	10
Dudu		1870.64	1790.87	18	82	493.19	17	11	22	18	19
Govindgarh	Mandha	685.12	638.08	100		531.14	24	69	25	31	17
Jamwa Ramgarh	Banganga & Tala	1033.7	961.88	60	40	566.73	10	24	12	34	10
Jhotwara	Dhundh & Amanishah	568.79	553.04	100		575.38	24	34	13	34	55
Kotputli	Sabi & Sotanala	691.71	572.75	77	23	535.08	30	19	15	21	24
Phagi	Bandi	1114.34	773.51	51	49	504.82	17	12	12	14	19
Sambhar	Mandha	938.4	831.48	100		494.09	14	26	49	23	24
Sanganer	Amanishah	657.54	613.87	100		566.78	50	35	23	22	32
Shahpura	Sabi	429.85	384.14	100		542.61	24	26	12	21	43
Jaipur District		11061.4	9994.67	72.31	27.69	544	25	26	23	25	25

Note : Alluvium includes both Young and Old Alluvium. S for Schist, G for Granite, Q for Quartzite, Gn for Gneiss.

Source : Department of Groundwater, Government of Rajasthan, Jaipur.

Fig. 2.3 : Groundwater Level Trends in Jaipur District, Rajasthan

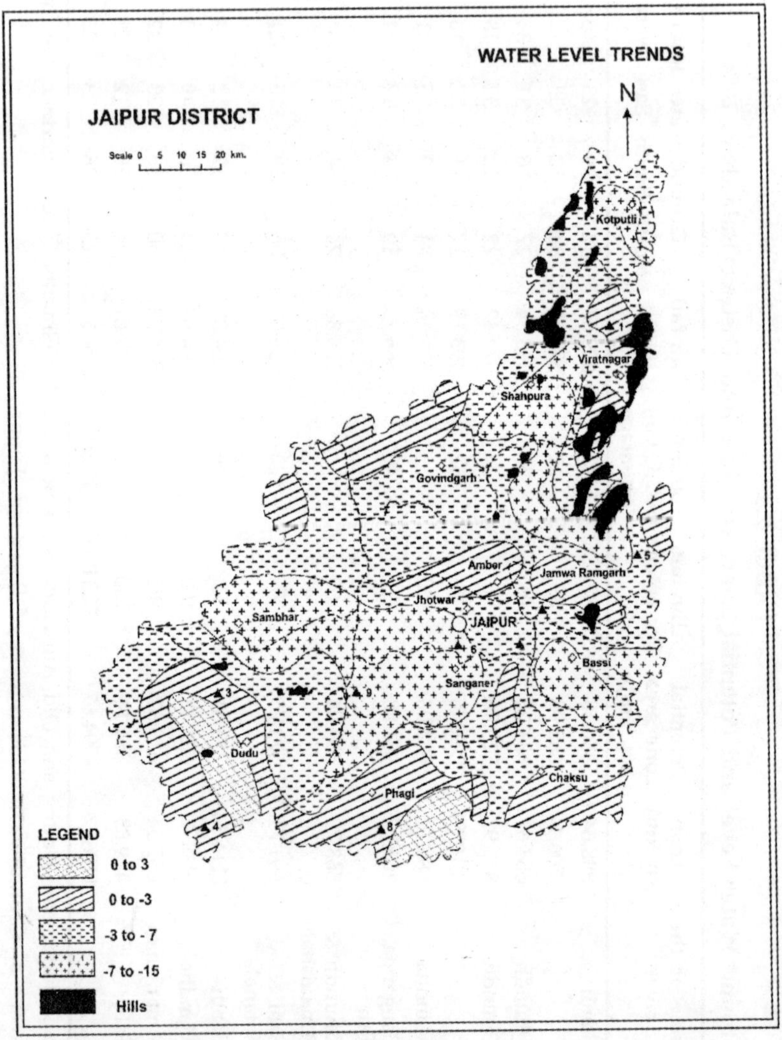

Source : Groundwater Atlas of Rajasthan, Department of Groundwater, Government of Rajasthan, Jodhpur, 1999.

year. This excessive extraction of groundwater is indicated by the increase in the number of dark zones. For instance, the number of dark zones in 1984 was 11 which increased to 80 in 2001. It is revealed from table 2.9 that the net annual recharge of groundwater in Jaipur district is 609.25 MCM, which is less than the annual extraction of 1136.86 MCM of water for irrigation, domestic and industrial use, thus creating a deficit of 527.60 MCM in groundwater aquifer. This revealed a significant overexploitation of groundwater resources and depletion of water level in Jaipur district. The stage of groundwater development in Jaipur district is 186 per cent, therefore, the district is categorized as **overexploited** as could be observed from table 2.9. In Jhotwara block it is more than 300 per cent (highest) and Phagi has the lowest (80 per cent). In Govindgarh, Sanganer, Shahpura and Sambhar it is over 200 per cent; and in Amber, Bassi, Chaksu, Bairath, Kotputli and Jamwa Ramgarh the stage of groundwater development is over 100 per cent. It is only in the potential zones of Dudu and Phagi and some parts of Bairath and Jamwa Ramgarh blocks, that stage of development is between 80-100 per cent. Therefore, the blocks of Dudu and Phagi are categorized as 'critical'. Future groundwater development has been recommended for potable use only in an area of 407.93 sq. km of Dudu block of the Jaipur district.

In general, the groundwater in the Jaipur district is considered suitable for drinking and irrigation purposes and characterized as 'bicarbonate' type water. Figure 2.4 marks the areas of potable and unpotable groundwater in Jaipur district. It also reveals that groundwater in some parts of Dudu, Sambhar, Phagi, Sanganer, Chaksu, Jhotwara, Jamwa Ramgarh, Govindgarh and Kotputli is not suitable for drinking due to salinity, fluoride and nitrate concentration. The Phagi block has an area of 340.06 sq. km, which has chemically unsuitable water for drinking purposes and the stage of groundwater development of this block has been calculated as 80.50 per cent. In Jaipur district the level of salinity vacillates between low (0-2000 μS/cm) to high (more than 4000 μS/cm) as shown in figure 2.4. The maximum salinity is found in village Untirampura (12000 μS/cm) in Sanganer block and the minimum in village Mozamabad (390 μS/cm) in Dudu block. The permissible limit of nitrate is 100 mg per litre and that of fluoride is 1.5 mg per litre. There is high concentration of nitrate i.e., more than 100 mg/L in the northern part of the Jaipur district including Kotpuli and parts of Govindgarh block (table 2.10).

TABLE 2.9
Ground Water Recharge, Draft and Stage of Ground Water Development in Jaipur District, Rajasthan, 2004

Block	Area of Block (sq.km.)	Potential zone area (sq. km.)	Total annual ground water recharge (MCM)	Natural discharge during non-monsoon season (MCM)	Net annual ground water availability (MCM)	Existing ground water draft for all uses (MCM)	Ground Water Balance	Stage of ground water development (%)	Category
1	2	3	4	5	4 - 5 = 6	7	6 - 7 = 8	9	10
Amber	898.64	850.48	69.92	6.99	62.93	120.28	-57.35	191.14	Overexploited
Bairath	706.1	663.98	51.28	5.13	46.16	48.22	-2.07	104.48	Overexploited
Bassi	654.69	631.23	43.92	3.07	40.85	78.50	-37.65	192.16	Overexploited
Chaksu	811.92	729.36	43.64	2.51	41.13	68.40	-27.26	166.28	Overexploited
Dudu	1870.64	1790.87	70.02	7.00	63.02	59.05	3.96	93.71	Critical
Govindgarh	685.12	638.08	56.58	5.66	50.93	125.89	-74.96	247.2	Overexploited
Jamwa Ramgarh	1033.7	961.88	51.71	5.17	46.54	66.28	-19.74	142.42	Overexploited
Jhotwara	568.79	553.04	55.50	5.55	49.95	165.38	-115.43	331.07	Overexploited
Kotputli	691.71	572.75	57.99	5.80	52.19	90.56	-38.37	173.51	Overexploited
Phagi	1114.34	773.51	45.18	2.82	42.36	38.70	3.67	91.34	Critical
Sambhar	938.4	831.48	47.85	3.47	44.38	119.05	-74.67	268.23	Overexploited
Sanganer	657.54	613.87	45.69	4.57	41.12	99.94	-58.82	243.04	Overexploited
Shahpura	429.85	384.14	30.77	3.08	27.69	56.60	-28.91	204.42	Overexploited
Saline zone Phagi		340.06	20.47	1.02	19.44	15.65	3.79	80.5	
Jaipur District	11061.4	9994.67	670.06	60.81	609.25	1136.86	-527.60	186.6	Overexploited

Note: MCM = million cubic metre
Source: Department of Ground Water, Government of Rajasthan, Jaipur.

Fig. 2.4 : Groundwater Potability and Salinity in Jaipur District, Rajasthan

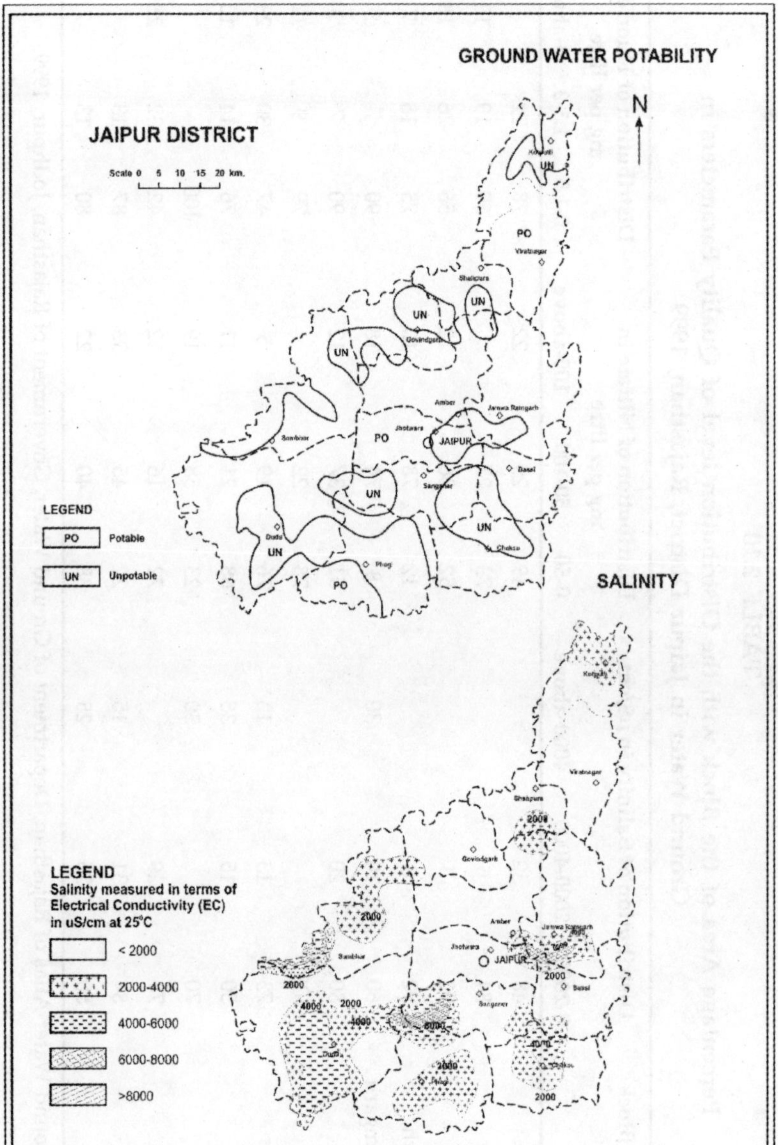

Source : Groundwater Atlas of Rajasthan, Department of Ground Water, Government of Rajasthan, Jodhpur, 1999.

TABLE 2.10

Percentage Area of the Block with the Distribution level of Quality Parameters in Ground Water in Jaipur District, Rajasthan, 1999

Name of Block	Distribution of Salinity in µS/cm			Distribution of Nitrate in mg per litre			Distribution of Fluoride in mg per litre		
	0-2000	2000-4000	4000-above	0-50	50-100	100-above	0-1.5	1.5-3	3-above
Kotputli	48	52		49	29	22	78	22	
Viratnagar	84	6		73	27		69	19	12
Shahpura	92	8		52	36	12	56	26	18
Govindgarh	92	8		12	78	10	75	18	7
Jamwa Ramgarh	60	10	30	8	74	18	90	7	3
Amber	80	20		51	37	12	90	7	3
Bassi	100			78	22		79	9	12
Chaksu	73	13	13	76	19	5	47	30	23
Dudu	50	15	35	68	21	11	76	14	10
Jhotwara	70		30	23	58	19	100		
Phagi	71	29		72	16	12	42	32	26
Sambhar	84	31	15	22	45	33	87	13	
Sanganer	50	25	25	38	40	22	80	13	7

Source : Ground Water Atlas of Rajasthan, Department of Ground Water, Government of Rajasthan, Jodhpur, 1999.

The fluoride concentration is between 1.5 mg/L to 3.0 mg/L in Kotpuli, Amber, Shahpura, Govindgarh, Dudu, Phagi and Chaksu. The groundwater also shows characteristics of hardness ranging between 0 to 300 mg/L in the blocks of Viratnagar, Kotputli, Bassi, Govindgarh, Phagi and Shahpura and the higher range (301- 600 mg/L) in parts of Dudu, Chaksu and Kotputli blocks.

The above analysis shows that the major water resource in Jaipur district is groundwater. It is accessed through dug wells, pumps and tube wells. The surface water is very limited and is available only through non-perennial rivers, lakes and reservoirs. It meets the needs of a small portion of water demand and that too for three to four months in a year, in case of normal rainfall. In the areas of **Alluvium**, the average yield of the wells fitted with pump sets varies from 57,000 to 96,500 litres per day, whereas the average discharge from the tube wells varies from 8 to 15 cubic m per hour. In the **hard rocks**, the average yield of the wells with pumps varies from 38,000 to 55,000 litres per day, whereas the average discharge of the tube wells varies from 2.5 to 9 cubic m per hour. This difference is because of the existence of younger and older Alluvium and hard rocks.

This trend of growing water scarcity in Jaipur district is not only because of environmental changes but also due to erroneous pattern of human activities. The changes in land use of river basins, such as, afforestation and deforestation, field management, urbanization and drainage, transform the river catchment areas and also control the water resources availability. The human activities administer the demand for water. The water supplied from reservoirs, tanks, and groundwater aquifer fulfills the direct demand for irrigation, industrial and domestic purposes. Besides, there are also indirect demands of water related to forest, drainage, and waste disposal and to maintain the balance of ecosystem. All these factors affect differently the total volume of water resources, river run-off regime and water quality.

2.3 WATER USES IN JAIPUR DISTRICT

Water is used as a consumption good, production good and as an environment good. As consumption good, water is used for drinking and sanitation purposes and as production good, it is an intermediate good which acts as a means to obtain the final good, such as, in agriculture and industry. Besides, water is also an environmental good as it is an essential component for maintaining the environmental balance and providing sustainable life. In this way, freshwater plays a central role in human health and development. Therefore, the demand of water is for drinking, removing, or diluting wastes, producing manufactured goods, growing food, generating and using energy, and so on. The water required for each of these activities varies with climatic conditions, lifestyle, culture, tradition, food habits, technology and wealth. Even the type of access to water is an important determinant in total use. The uses of water can be broadly classified into (i) municipal, (ii) industrial and (iii) agricultural sectors. The water utilized in each sector is assumed as the water withdrawn from the source.

Municipal uses of water sector are connected with the quantity of water primarily withdrawn and consumed for drinking and sanitation, gardening, washing, and other domestic uses in cities, towns, housing, estates, domestic, private and public service enterprises. Besides, water is also required for waste disposal. The use of the quantity of public water is determined by the size of urban and rural population, services and utilities. So also, the demand for water by urban and rural community is based on number of inhabitants, their income level, the climate, population density and other planning parameters and on the purchase price. It has been recommended by the World Health Organisation (WHO) that a standard of 50 litres per person per day (l/p/d) of water is the basic water requirement for human needs and survival. **Industrial uses** of water are mainly for cooling and washing, as a solvent, and also as a component of some finished goods. It is also an energy resource, used to produce hydropower. Thus, the industrial sector also consumes potable quality water from the water supply system. **Agricultural uses** of water are mainly for irrigation purposes. In this category the demand for water is derived from the final good i.e., the importance of water depends on the price of the final good along with the other inputs, such as, seeds, fertilizers, etc. Land irrigation has been practiced to maximize food supply for the humanity and there has been dramatic expansion in irrigated land since Independence.

2.3.1 Municipal and Industrial Uses

The main source of water withdrawal for municipal and industrial uses in Jaipur district is groundwater. According to the State Ground Water Department, about 19 per cent (216.90 MCM) of the total groundwater withdrawal for the year 2004 in Jaipur district is for domestic and industrial uses. It is observed from table 2.11 that the

TABLE 2.11

Groundwater Use in Jaipur District, Rajasthan, 2004

Panchayat Samiti	Net Annual Ground-water Availability (MCM)	Existing Groundwater Draft for All Uses (MCM)	Existing Gross Groundwater Draft for Irrigation (MCM)	Percentage Draft for Irrigation (%)	Existing Gross Groundwater Draft for Industry & Domestic Use (MCM)	Percentage Draft for Industry and Domestic Use (%)
Amber	62.93	120.28	105.96	88.10	14.32	11.90
Bairat	46.16	48.22	37.81	78.40	10.42	21.60
Bassi	40.85	78.50	68.00	86.62	10.50	13.38
Chaksu	41.13	68.39	64.04	93.63	4.36	6.37
Dudu	63.02	59.05	44.49	75.34	14.56	24.66
Govindgarh	50.93	125.89	114.95	91.31	10.93	8.69
Jamwa Ramgarh	46.54	66.28	61.07	92.13	5.22	7.87
Jhotwara	49.95	165.38	71.00	42.93	94.38	57.07
Kotputli	52.19	90.56	81.42	89.91	9.14	10.09
Phagi	42.36	38.70	35.52	91.79	3.18	8.21
Sambhar	44.38	119.05	108.71	91.31	10.34	8.69
Sanganer	41.12	99.94	78.75	78.80	21.19	21.20
Shahpura	27.69	56.60	48.24	85.23	8.36	14.77
Total	609.25	1136.86	919.96	80.92	216.89	19.08
Percentage		186.60		80.92		19.08

Source : Department of Ground Water, Government of Rajasthan, Jaipur.

highest withdrawal for domestic and industrial uses is in Jhotwara Panchayat Samiti, which is 43.51 per cent (94.38 MCM) of the total withdrawal (216.89 MCM) for this sector. This is because the area of Jhotwara Panchayat Samiti includes Jaipur city. Moreover, 57 per cent of the total extraction of groundwater in Jhotwara is for domestic and industrial uses. Among the other blocks of Jaipur district, the groundwater withdrawal in this sector is below 10 per cent of the total extraction. The per capita withdrawal for domestic and industrial use in Jaipur district is around 42 cubic metre. The total withdrawal of groundwater for domestic and industrial purpose is estimated to increase by 51.33 per cent from 2004 to 2015 and then by 75 per cent in 2045 as given in table 2.12.

TABLE 2.12

Projected Groundwater Demand for Drinking and Industrial Use in Jaipur District, Rajasthan, 2015–2045

Block	Projected demand (MCM)		
	2015	2025	2045
Amber	22.433	28.0413	39.2578
Bairath	10.4808	13.1011	18.3415
Bassi	18.2258	22.7823	31.8952
Chaksu	8.3368	10.421	14.5894
Dudu	16.989	21.2362	29.7307
Govindgarh	15.328	19.16	26.824
Jamwa Ramgarh	5.872	7.34	10.276
Jhotwara	153.272	191.59	268.226
Kotputli	12.08	15.1	21.14
Phagi	3.776	4.72	6.608
Sambhar	16.4666	20.5833	28.8166
Sanganer	29.0652	36.3315	50.8641
Shahpura	15.9066	19.8833	27.8366
Jaipur District	328.232	410.29	574.406

Note : MCM = million cubic metre.

Source : TAHAL consultants, Reappraisal of Groundwater Resources of Jaipur District, Department of Ground Water, Government of Rajasthan, Jaipur, 2004.

The rural population of the Jaipur district has access to drinking water through taps, handpumps, wells, tubewells, tanks, etc. According to Census 2001, 17.38 per cent of rural households of Jaipur district draw water through taps, 35.09 per cent depend on handpumps, 37.96 per cent rely on wells, and 7.85 per cent get water from tubewells and the remaining 1.72 per cent have access to other sources like tank, lake, canal, spring, etc. Among the villages of Jaipur district, 54 villages do not have access to any source of drinking water within a range of 5 kms., which belong to the Panchayat Samitis of Viratnagar, Amber, Jamwa Ramgarh, Bassi, Dudu, Phagi, Sanganer and Chaksu.

The urban population in Jaipur district primarily depends on groundwater supplied through pipelines. According to Census 2001 almost 81 per cent of urban households residing in 17 towns of the district draw water from taps connected to the pipeline network of the government department. The remaining urban households depend on handpumps (6.86 per cent), tubewells (6.24 per cent), wells (4.53 per cent), etc. This includes Jaipur Urban Agglomeration (Jaipur, Sanganer and Amber) where 81.96 per cent households have taps, 6.19 per cent use handpumps, 6.55 per cent have tubewells and 3.5 per cent depend on wells and 1.5 per cent on other sources. The drinking water scheme covers 22.15 lakh population of Jaipur city out of the total population of 23.24 lakhs. The per capita per day water supplied in Jaipur city is 149 litres per day, while in other towns of the district it is only 92 litres per day. The water supplied in the city from different sources is 3275 lakh litres from tubewells, 10 lakh litres from the seepage of Ramgarh dam, 75 litres from hand pumps and 24 lakh litres from tankers, which comes to a total of 3290 lakh litres.

2.3.2 Agricultural Use

In the rural areas of Jaipur district water utilisation is mainly for fulfilling the agriculture and domestic needs. The Jaipur district has total irrigated area of 338044.84 ha which is about 33 per cent of its total area (1033748 ha). In semi-arid and arid zones of the district, 80.92 per cent of the total annual groundwater withdrawal is for irrigation purposes, and in almost all the blocks it is above 80 per cent as observed in table 2.11. Except in Dudu, Viratnagar and Sanganer, the canal irrigation system is around 75 per cent, in Jhotwara block it is 42.93 per cent due to dominance of urban population of Jaipur city. The major sources of irrigation are wells in the district, which irrigate about 95 per cent of its total irrigated area, 4 per cent is irrigated by canals and only 1 per cent by ponds and tanks (table 2.13). Irrigation through canal is practised in very small percentage in some parts of the tehsils of Jaipur district, such as, Dudu, Phagi, Jamwa Ramgarh and Chaksu, while in others irrigation is completely dependent on groundwater resources drawn through wells as illustrated in the figure 2.5. It is also observed from table 2.13 that the total irrigated area has increased about 89 per cent from 1960-61 to 2001. The irrigation potential created through groundwater resources in the district is 306653 ha, but in view of the increasing domestic demand and its projected requirement by the year 2025, the irrigation potential would be reduced and will remain only 66323 ha, as observed from table 2.14. There are two cropping seasons in the district – *rabi* and *kharif*. The crop of *rabi* completely depends on irrigation from groundwater and *kharif* depends on monsoon rains. The total irrigated area of *rabi* is 2903.75 sq. km and that of *kharif* is 251.04 sq. km. Therefore, the gross irrigated area of the district is 3154.79 sq. km for which the water requirement is 889.9530 MCM, out of this the *rabi* crop requires 871.125 MCM and *kharif* 18.828 MCM.

TABLE 2.13

Irrigation by Different Sources in Jaipur District, 1961–2001

(hectares)

Sources of Irrigation	1961	1971	1991	2001
Canals	10098.34 (5.64)	5553.62 (2.21)	4168.58 (1.22)	7801.47 (2.31)
Tanks	4331.85 (2.42)	8487.66 (3.38)	385.13 (0.11)	575.15 (0.17)
Wells	164462.16 (91.87)	236169.16 (94.02)	316596.4 (92.8)	299516.4 (88.60)
Other Sources	122.22 (0.068)	966.82 (0.39)	757.68 (0.22)	3694.38 (1.09)
River				208.3 (0.06)
Tubewell			19246.16 (5.64)	26482.34 (7.83)
Total Irrigated Area	179014.57	251177.26	341153.9	338278.1

Note : Figures in parentheses are percentage of total irrigated area in respective year.

Source : Census of India, Rajasthan, Jaipur District, for relevant years.

TABLE 2.14

Irrigation Potential of Jaipur District by 2025

Name of Block	Net available ground water recharge (ha.m/y)	Net irrigation requirement (m)	Groundwater draft for irrigation (ha. m/y)	Irrigation potential created (ha) (col. 4/3)	Allocation of domestic and industrial need for the year 2025 (ha. m/y)	Groundwater balance (ha.m) (col. 2-4-6)	Balance irrigation potential from ground water (ha.) (col. 7/3)	Ultimate irrigation potential from ground water (ha.) (col. 5+8)
1	2	3	4	5	6	7	8	9
Amber	6293	0.3	10596	35320.00	2804.00	-7107.00	-23690.00	11630.00
Bairath	4616	0.3	3781	12603.33	1310.00	-475.00	-1583.33	11020.00
Bassi	4085	0.3	6800	22666.67	2278.00	-4993.00	-16643.33	6023.33
Chaksu	4113	0.3	6404	21346.67	1042.00	-3333.00	-11110.00	10236.67
Dudu	6302	0.3	4449	14830.00	2124.00	-271.00	-903.33	13926.67
Govindgarh	5093	0.3	11495	38316.67	1916.00	-8318.00	-27726.67	10590.00
Jamwa Ramgarh	4654	0.3	6107	20356.67	734.00	-2187.00	-7290.00	13066.67
Jhotwara	4995	0.3	7100	23666.67	19159.00	-21264.00	-70880.00	-47213.33
Kotputli	5219	0.3	8142	27140.00	1510.00	-4433.00	-14776.67	12363.33
Phagi	4236	0.3	3552	11840.00	472.00	212.00	706.67	12546.67
Sambhar	4438	0.3	10871	36236.67	2058.00	-8491.00	-28303.33	7933.33
Sanganer	4112	0.3	7875	26250.00	3633.00	-7396.00	-24653.33	1596.67
Shahpura	2769	0.3	4824	16080.00	1988.00	-4043.00	-13476.67	2603.33
Total	60925		91996	306653.33	41028.00	-72099.00	-240330.00	66323.33

Note: ha.m / y = hectare metre per year, m = metre, ha = hectare.

Source: Department of Ground Water, Government of Rajasthan, Jaipur.

Fig. 2.5 : Irrigation by Different Sources in Jaipur District, Rajasthan

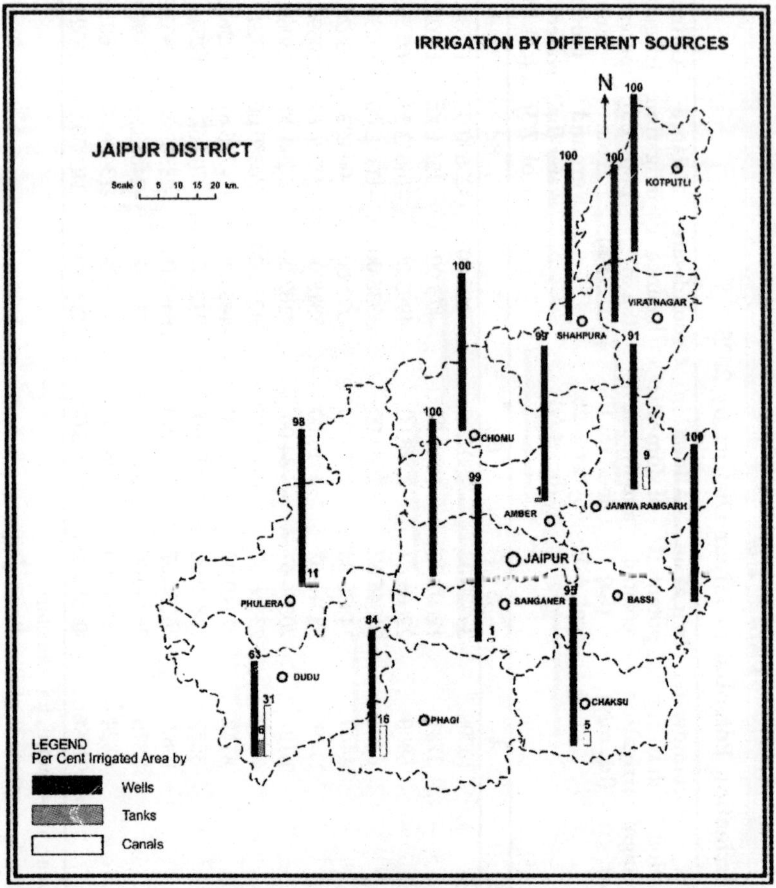

Source : Groundwater Atlas of Rajasthan, Department of Groundwater, Government of Rajasthan, Jodhpur, 1999.

2.4 EMERGING ISSUES

The assessment of total water availability and its use in the Jaipur district has given rise to several issues, such as, lack of surface water resources, encroachment in catchment areas, groundwater depletion, natural resources property rights, water quality, etc. These issues are complex and interrelated. The understanding of these issues would facilitate the formulation of management strategies and water policy for the state of Rajasthan.

2.4.1 Lack of Surface Water Resources

The existing surface water resources are unable to fulfill the requirements of the people. These resources are very few and do not serve the needs of the people throughout the year due to high evapotranspiration, deforestation, soil erosion and lack of water infrastructure. In spite of normal rainfall these surface water reservoirs do not get ample water to serve the irrigation and drinking water requirements. The traditional water sources, such as, stepwells, tanks, etc., have been abandoned and do not serve the purpose at all. There has been no expansion of the water infrastructure in the recent years to fulfill the requirements of water.

2.4.2 Encroachment in Catchment Areas

The constructions and encroachments in the catchment areas of the water resources in Jaipur district obstruct the inflow of water. The catchment areas of the water resources of Jaipur city have been used in the post-independence period for developing new colonies and roads by land mafia owing to the negligence of government authorities. For instance, the land of the Amanishah Nalla in Jaipur city was acquired by the land mafia and plots were sold for residential colony resulting in the building of 25 thousand houses in its catchment area during the past 20 years. The residential colony of Amanishah Nalla is illegal according to the Law and Convention for the protection of land property of surface water resources of Rajasthan state and the Rule 1955, Clause 16 of Rajasthan Agriculture Law.

The cultivation and construction of unplanned and illegal anicuts in the catchment areas of water resources in Jaipur city by the local people and the government for the diversion of rainwater for irrigation purposes has resulted in the decrease of the surface water run-off. It is also evident from such constructions in the catchment areas of Talkatora and Man Sagar in Jaipur city. So also, the lopsided constructions in the catchment areas of Tala and Banganga streams have obstructed the inflow of water to Ramgarh lake due to the negligence of the authorities. The construction of about 25 big anicuts over the past decades in the catchment area of Ramgarh lake under the drought relief works have resulted in decreasing the inflow of water in the dam. It cannot be denied that these anicuts are of great help to people as they result in recharge of groundwater and wells in the down stream, facilitate agriculture, promote livelihood, and provide drinking water to cattle, but the government should have planned the construction of anicuts in the catchment of Ramgarh lake in such a way as to have avoided any obstruction to the inflow of water in it. As a preventive measure, the farmers should be prohibited from using the catchment area for cultivation and from extracting the water from the lake by pump sets as it reduces the water level.

The construction of colonies in the catchment area of a river is also dangerous for the residents. According to the Rajasthan State Water Resource Department, the colonies in the catchment areas of Ring Bandha (Sambhar), Gangasagar (Dudu), Morija (Chomu), Amanishah Nallah (Jaipur), Gunavata (Amber), Jawanpura, Manoharpura and Devan Road (Shahpura) and Baneri Bandh (Kotputli) in Jaipur district would submerge in case of excessive rainfall (more than 431mm) or flood while the dams would not receive sufficient water due to obstructions in the inflow of water.

2.4.3 Groundwater Depletion

The groundwater depletion has created shortage of water in Jaipur district. The replenishment of groundwater is very little in the district due to low rainfall, aridity and excessive withdrawals. Besides, the urban areas of the district are mostly covered with road networks and cemented constructions, which affect the natural groundwater recharge leading to decline in groundwater level. Similarly, excessive pumping or closely spaced pumps and natural obstacles also cause slow movement of water in the wells from the groundwater aquifer. In such cases wells become dry and pumps start squeezing the water from greater depth from the neighbouring wells. This results in high cost of pumping, deficiency of water and further exhaustion of potential of water. It can be summarized that groundwater is exhausted when the total replenishment is less than the draft as in case of Jaipur district where groundwater is 'overexploited' and its stage of development is over 186 per cent.

The shortage of surface water resources and increase in groundwater withdrawals in Jaipur and other districts of Rajasthan state are due to increase in population, urbanization, industrial and agricultural development. It is also caused due to misuse of water, scanty and erratic precipitation and ignorance of consumers which do not permit recharge of extracted groundwater. As a result, the groundwater resource indicates 'critical' and 'overexploited' stages and signs of increasing depletion. The report of State Ground Water Department reveals that during 1984 and 1999 there has been an average depletion between 0.13m to 6.86m in 27 out of the 32 districts of Rajasthan and for Jaipur district the average decline in the water level for the period 1984 to 2001 was 6.68 m, about 40 cm a year. There has been further decline in the water level of Rajasthan state till 2003 ranging between 0.18 m to 10.3 m in 29 districts out of the 32 districts. This has created a receptive space for groundwater recharge in the state. The area of potential groundwater aquifer recharge in the state is 63.7 per cent (217,947 sq. km) of the total area of the state. The average groundwater depletion for the period 1984-2003 and specific yield of the aquifer varies from 1.5 to 8 per cent, depending on the hard rock formations of the aquifer. Therefore, the total net space available in Rajasthan for recharging the aquifer is 55,748 MCM which could be higher if the period prior to 1984 is considered. The total net space available in the groundwater aquifer for recharging in Jaipur district is 5654.07 MCM and the estimated net storable water in 10 years is 1111.57 MCM. This situation of groundwater is alarming as it has resulted in depletion of water level, drying of wells, tubewells and handpumps and emergence of salinity in water especially during summer (Narain, 2005: 6-8).

Jaipur district has 13 blocks out of which 10 blocks have been declared in dark zone of groundwater level. The Jhotwara block has been declared as notified area where groundwater exploitation through tubewells has been prohibited as the water level has decreased more than 700 ft. In the other nine blocks, the groundwater level has depleted to the extent that it may provide water only for a few years. Phagi and Dudu blocks are in the 'critical' category as the water contains high amount of fluoride. During the last two decades there is a continuous decline in the level of groundwater and the rate of depletion has accelerated in Jaipur city from 4 m to 16 m between 1995 and 2003. It is observed from table 2.15 that the groundwater level has declined by almost 20 m in various areas of Jaipur city between 1995 and 2005-06. It is estimated by the Central Ground Water Board that by 2010 the groundwater level in Jaipur city would decline by 50 metres. According to the hydrologists the extraction should not be more than 100 per cent of the recharge whereas presently it is 300 to 541 per cent in Jhotwara, Sanganer and Murlipura areas of Jaipur city. The roof top harvesting has been made mandatory but the residents of Jaipur city have not taken it seriously. Hence, it could only be implemented in the government buildings but it could be enforced effectively by law in residential buildings.

TABLE 2.15

Groundwater Level in Jaipur City, Rajasthan, 1995–2006

Localities of Jaipur City	Groundwater Level (metres)					
	1995	2001	2002	2003	2004	2005-06
Banipark		39.10	40.35	42.00	35.80	43.82
Durgapura	19.50	21.10	26.40	29.70	31.70	38.80
Mansarovar		26.65	29.54	31.40	32.10	35.30
Ajmer Road Hirapura						49.50
Galta		7.00	12.15	12.15	6.35	9.45
Jhotwara	36.83	45.57	47.28	48.37	45.70	54.50
Kaladera		14.21	16.10	17.65	23.30	21.85
Surya Nagar, Jagatpura	15.40	16.37	17.95	18.10	19.25	21.50
Sirsi Road	38.25	43.20	47.25	48.78		54.70
Kalwad Road		17.00	23.52	21.30	23.50	24.80
Jawaharlal Nehru Marg	31.45			47.25		48.60
Vatika	17.50			30.66		

Source : Department of Ground Water, Government of Rajasthan, for relevant years.

2.4.4 Natural Resource as Common Property

The issue of common property resources has not received proper attention of the government for its maintenance. Common property resources are understood as those natural resources which cannot be claimed exclusively by an individual. These comprise pasture land, forest produce, and wasteland, common threshing grounds, dumping places, watershed drainage, ponds, tanks, rivers, streams and riverbeds. When the number of users was small the natural resources were sufficient but the increase in the number of users has resulted in their overexploitation and conflicts which could only be resolved by legal regulations. The issue of government control on water resources is important in the formation of water policy (Jodha, 1994: 150-151).

The property rights regarding water are not clearly defined in India, as groundwater is accessible to those who own the overlying land. The absence of well-defined property rights on water has made it an open access resource, a resource that is everybody's property and hence not managed properly. Besides, there are two other important characteristics of groundwater that make its management difficult, one, indivisibility of the groundwater aquifer, and second, technical difficulties in the assessment and monitoring of the stock and withdrawal of water. An aquifer cannot be divided on the basis of ownership of overlying land and its water cannot be confined to the extent of individual's land. This leads to overexploitation of stock, degradation of quality and misappropriation of water as is also evident from the situation of groundwater in arid and semi-arid areas of Jaipur district (Singh, 2005: 1-13).

Similarly, there are no explicit Ordinances or Acts which clearly recognize rights of people even on the surface water. The public ownership of surface water is implied in the government appropriation and regulation of surface water through irrigation projects.

2.4.5 Water Quality

Water pollution has become a serious threat to surface and ground water. Pollution originates from land based activities. This includes municipal, industrial and agricultural waste, and atmospheric deposition. The major cause of water pollution is the discharge of waste water. In urban areas it occurs from sewers and industrial effluents and in rural areas from seepage of fertilizers and pesticides in agricultural fields. The analytical survey of groundwater for fluoride and nitrate has revealed that all villages of Phagi and Chaksu tehsils in Jaipur district have excess quantity of these pollutants. This survey was conducted in 1986 villages, which revealed that 1519 villages had excessive quantity of fluoride and nitrate. Besides, large quantity of pollutants have been discovered in 8 tehsils out of 13 viz., Sanganer, Kotputli, Phulera, Shahpura, Viratnagar, Amber, Bassi and Govindgarh. This is a clear indicator of overexploitation of groundwater and seepage of pollutants. Among them Sanganer, Kotputli and Phulera have the highest number of villages with excessive quantity of pollutants in groundwater. This could be compared to the blocks in Jaipur district where development of groundwater has reached the stage of overexploitation and there is fast depletion in the water level.

The analysis of water supplied from PHED in the Jaipur city also indicates presence of high level of fluoride and nitrate, characteristics of hardness and total diluted solvents (TDS) in different parts of the walled city of Jaipur and in its circumscribing areas as clarified in table 2.16. The quantity of pollutants in water is greater than standard level of the contents permissible in drinking water. The TDS is higher than 500 mg/l in all the areas of the city. Fluoride is on the borderline, nitrate is higher due to the mixing of sewer line with the groundwater aquifer at various places.

TABLE 2.16
Level of Water Quality Parameters in Groundwater in Jaipur City, Rajasthan, 2003

Localities of Jaipur City	Total Dilution of Solvents (TDS) (mg/l)	Fluoride (mg/l)	Nitrate (mg/l)	Hardness (mg/l)
Adarsh Nagar	5040	0.95	98	280
SMS	910	0.96	298	590
Civil Lines	980	0.72	326	640
Chomu House	1120	0.82	350	710
Shanti Nagar	1050	1.3	350	660
Banipark	5950	0.95	188	360
C-Scheme	1960	0.92	1000	1430
Badi Chaupad	1470	1.2	750	1070
Subhash Chowk	1680	0.85	770	1130
Zorawar Singh Gate	1680	0.88	610	1220
Ramganj	1610	1.3	370	920
Ramganj Chaupad	910	0.95	40	380
Chandpole	980	1.2	200	580

Note : All quantities are in mg per litre. Permissible Quantity of TDS is 500 mg/l; Fluoride is 1.5 mg/l; Nitrate is 100 mg/l; Hardness is 300 mg/l.

Source : Central Groundwater Board, Jaipur, 2003.

The poor maintenance of water supply pipelines, leakage in the sewer lines, interception of water supply and sewer lines, and deep dug waste disposal pits have aggravated the water pollution in Jaipur city. In some colonies there are individual sewage disposal pits which are dug so deep that the sewage waste mixes with the groundwater aquifer. The project of covering open drainage by installing sewer lines in Jaipur city has not yet been completed. Moreover, the manholes of the sewer line have been made on the points from where water supply pipelines also pass. Due to corrosion of water pipelines, sewer water often gets mixed with the drinking water. This has led to an increase in the pollutants of water. Thus, the water quality has declined though there has been increase in quantity of chlorine from 1.75 to 2 ppm in the chlorination plants of water treatment and purification. However, the RUIDP has started changing the old pipelines in the city as a permanent cure for this malady.

The seepage of water from agriculture also pollutes the groundwater as it includes pesticides. For instance, the remains of pesticides in water are transmitted to animals, birds consuming that water and vegetables irrigated with that water. The accidental spillages of oil and chemical from industries, disposal of sludge, and solid and semi-solid wastes in water bodies are the major causes of pollution. These sources of pollution give rise to chemical pollution, i.e., man-made additions of chemical contaminants to water. This type of water pollution is continuing within the areas of Sanganer and Amanishah Nalla in Jaipur city, and it has proved harmful to animal and human life. In Sanganer and Bagru, 400 small, medium and large-scale textile units, and domestic sewage are identified as responsible for water pollution. In Sanganer, the chemical discharge of the textile industries and other waste in the local river and also in Gullar dam is a permanent source of bad odours and health hazard in Sanganer. The consumption of polluted water and vegetables grown in that water have become a cause for enteric and other water borne diseases. Gullar dam was initially constructed as a storage dam to provide water to Chandlai and Nevata dams but due to technical fault, it could not achieve its objective. The height of the slip lane of this dam is so low that excess water during rain overflows and is wasted. The sewer water from Amanishah Nalla and pollutants from the industrial area of Vishvakarma and Bais-Godown are drained into this dam. Besides, there are about 125 units of textiles in colonies of Khatri Nagar, Jaipur Gate and Namdev Colony in Sanganer, which also drain their waste water into this dam. This dam was destroyed during the flood of 1981, and was renovated in the year 2000 by the orders of High Court for the benefit of farmers who used its water for growing vegetables. Further, the judiciary imposed a pollution tax on 8 March, 2003 to check water pollution and ordained to install a cooperative water purifier plant with the financial assistance of RIICO and other agencies. Ultimately, the Court closed 486 textile units to control pollution in the Amanishah Nalla and in Gular dam and ordered to shift them from Sanganer.

2.4.6 Wastage of Water

The drinking water is wasted due to technical faults and uncivil habits of people and their negligence in their daily routine life. According to a survey report of a French Company (Sureca) on the water supply system of Jaipur city, 37.8 per cent water is wasted due to leakage, 4.4 per cent due to faulty meters, 0.2 per cent through public taps, 0.5 per cent through illegal connections, and 1.3 per cent is unaccounted water. Thus, the Government department does not get returns on 44 per cent of total water supply.

The Ground Water Department of Rajasthan Government had also taken cognizance of the wastage of water in the Jaipur city in 2004. It had been calculated that in Jaipur city 3.75 crore litre water is wasted per day, which is more than the water required per day by its population. The habit of keeping the tap open during daily toilet practices including bathing, shaving, brushing, washing hands, etc., dripping of water from taps; leakage at joints of supply lines and washing of vehicles and clothes, etc., cause wastage of considerable quantity of water per day. It has been calculated by Ground Water Department, Government of Rajasthan, that the population of Jaipur requires 2.5 crore litres drinking water per day and the water supplied is 37 crore litres. Approximately, 25 per cent of population wastes about 60 litres of water per day per person. Thus, 3.75 crore litres of water is wasted per day. This wastage of drinking water is sufficient for next 15 years for the population, if it is conserved. The Ground Water Department has also suggested the ways in which the people can save water and reduce their daily consumption in routine chores as elaborated in table 2.17. These ways are easy to adopt but the urban population does not follow them due to their leisurely lifestyle and laxity.

2.4.7 Privatization of Water Supply

The issue of privatization of water has come to the fore as the total available water for use in different sectors is becoming lesser than its rising demands. The concept of privatization upholds water as commodity but not as natural resource. Privatization in water sector

TABLE 2.17

Water Requirement for Domestic Daily Chores

Daily chores	Present habits	Usage of water (litre)	Suggested change	Water requirement (litres)	Water saved (litres)
Brushing of Teeth	Keeping the tap open for 5 mins	20	Use of mugs	0.5	19.5
Washing of hands	Keeping the tap open for 2 mins	10	Use of mugs	2	8
Shaving	Keeping the tap open for 8 mins	15	Use of mugs	1	14
Shower bath	Keeping the shower open all the time	70	Use of mug and bucket	20	50
Flush toilets	Use of cistern	13.5 or more	Dual flush system for solid and liquid waste	9 and 4.6 respectively	4.5 and more
Watering of plants	5 mins with pipe	80	Watering sprought	5	75
Washing floors	5 mins with pipe	80	Use of mug and bucket	18	62
Washing of cars	10 mins with pipe	160	Use of mug and bucket	25	135
Dripping of Tap		20 in 24 hours	Use of washers	0	20

Source : Department of Ground Water, Government of Rajasthan, Jaipur.

means outsourcing, regulation and monitoring of supply, billing, maintenance, repair and disconnection for non-payment of dues. It has already started in the states like Delhi, Maharastra and Bangalore. However, the issues relating to it are complex as the groundwater supplied by the suppliers is not potable, and the purified water is expensive for common man, whereas the treated water is not evenly distributed to all by the Government.

On the issue of privatization of water there are two lines of thought; **one** believes water as a commodity, and therefore, it should not be free even for people who live near a river or for the poor and the rural communities. Hence, it should be charged. **Second,** believes that water is a common natural resource to support life for which the poor cannot afford to pay. It should not be treated as commodity or private property. It should be managed by the government.

The policy of privatization will deprive the poor from an essential resource, as the poor and slum dewellers even do not have a tap for water at their residence and do not have the money to pay for it. Privatization will lead to exorbitant increase in price of water. This has been experienced by Delhi Jal Board which has now decided to abandon the policy of privatization. This decision tallies with the spirit of Constitution of India which provides that water especially the drinking water is a fundamental right of the people.

2.5 REMEDIAL MEASURES

Some corrective measures have already been introduced to resolve the above mentioned issues by striking a balance between demand and supply of water in domestic, industrial and agricultural sectors. These measures comprise recycling of waste water and treatment of chemical waste, reduction in pumping from wells, prohibition on further borings in the overexploited zones, etc. Along with these, other remedial measures could be taken to augment water supply and provide access to safe drinking water. These measures are concerned with recharge of groundwater, rejuvenation of water resources, restoration and renovation of the supply line, rainwater harvesting, watershed structures and common property rights. These are interrelated and result in overall augmentation of water resources.

2.5.1 Recharge Measures for Groundwater

There is good scope to recharge the depleted aquifers during rainfall through artificial recharge. The selection of recharge area is of considerable importance for the artificial replenishment of groundwater aquifer of a particular region, which must be made according to hydrological and geophysical features of the region, such as, drainage, rock formations, open surface area, etc. This information could be gathered through remote sensing system and extensive use of hydrological and geological maps. In urban areas also artificial recharge points can be selected according to the slope of land, near flyovers and at the points where water accumulates. Recharge wells can also be made in residential houses to utilize the rainwater. The wells and the handpumps which have been abandoned in the Jaipur city should be revived and recharged from rain water harvesting. The water structures, such as, dams, anicuts, reservoirs, etc., also act as a source of recharge of groundwater through seepage and deep percolation. It is estimated that the recharge from a *talab* in arid region, covering 2.25 ha and having a storage capacity of 15,000 cubic m in an alluvial area may have a recharge capacity of 10,000 cubic m in one rainy season (Khan, 1989: 20-23, 1996: 147-150).

2.5.2 Rejuvenation of Surface Water Resources

The traditional water resources have been neglected after the introduction of piped water supply system by the government. In order to increase the capacity of water in reservoirs and dams, the catchment areas are to be properly maintained, cleaned annually and should be notified as 'no construction zone.' The sale of land in these catchment areas of water resources should be banned, all encroachments should be removed from this land, and dumping of waste and garbage in these areas must be prohibited. Legal action should be taken by the government for removing encroachments from the catchment areas of water resources. Along with these reformatory measures, there should be an integrated action plan for cleaning the catchments and rehabilitation of displaced persons of these areas. The traditional water sources have the capacity to fulfill the demand of safe drinking water. Therefore, these should be revived, repaired and fitted with modern equipment for pumping and filtering for the supply of water.

The survey of all sources of water and measures for their revival should be undertaken with the assistance of government, NGOs, and other social groups. Proper monitoring of distribution of water should be undertaken in coordination with the concerned departments, Water Users' Associations and Committees. Regular cleaning of the tanks, such as, removing its silt, foliage and using filter can augment the regular and safe water supply from groundwater. Moreover, prevention of disposal of untreated chemical waste, sewage outfalls and other contaminated wastes in water bodies would help in environmental hygiene. Water pollution causes bad smells, fly swarms and mosquito breeding which in turn cause malaria, enteric and other diseases borne by flies, mosquitoes and bacteria. It also indirectly affects aquatic environment that subsequently becomes harmful to human life.

2.5.3 Restoration and Renovation of the Supply Network

The habitations of new colonies have clogged the old pipelines and natural drainage of rainwater in Jaipur city. For instance, the Talkatora tank had lost its underground pipelines which were used for collecting rainwater from Brahmapuri, Chaugan Stadium and other places around it. Due to new construction and habitation of Raj Hans colony this inflow of rainwater has stopped and it has gone dry. Now, it has been altered by installing other pipelines. The consumers of the new colonies should contribute for the change of pipelines and new connections must be fitted with reflectors. The reflectors are installed on service lines to resolve the problem of water pollution. The use of boosters should be stopped as its use terminates the proper supply to 20 other consumers. In order to check the use of booster pumps, power supply should be suspended to the area during the water supply hours.

2.5.4 Rainwater Harvesting

The natural storage of rainwater in tanks, *talabs* or dugout ponds (*nadi*) is the oldest form of rainwater harvesting, and this water is used for drinking purposes by man and livestock in Jaipur district as well as parts of rural Rajasthan. Due to lack of maintenance, such *talabs* suffer from high evaporation, seepage and biotic factors which cause siltation and pollution. These must be fully revived to cover the growing water scarcity due to climatic changes and population growth. In Rajasthan, the houses were built with stone and lime and the rainwater from rooftop and ground was drained through pipes to underground tanks (Misra, 1995). This tradition for the conservation of rain water has been abandoned with the implementation of piped water supply by the government in towns, cities and even in rural areas. Hence, the measures to revive rooftop water harvesting and other measures of rainwater harvesting would certainly alleviate the present state of scarcity of drinking water and reduce the rapid depletion of groundwater. The estimated water yield from a 1,500 sq. m roof top with an effective rainfall of 250 mm and a 0.8 runoff coefficient is 300 cubic m, which is enough to provide drinking water for the consumption of 30,000 person days at 10 litres per capita per day (lpcd). Roof water harvesting for the recharging of groundwater can also be recommended for areas having suitable aquifers. This approach requires harvesting and channellizing roof water to existing wells, tube wells, borewells or specially designed wells. It is most suitable for urban housing complexes or institutional buildings located in drought-prone, arid and semi-arid regions. The scientists of Central Arid Zone Research Institute (CAZRI) have also calculated the run-off efficiency of different roof materials. The rooftop harvesting in a planned way would be beneficial for the state of Rajasthan, as its 216 cities and big towns have the capacity to generate nearly 522 MCM of roof runoff annually, of which nearly 12 per cent is stored in surface water resources and groundwater aquifers. Excluding losses, a potential 265 MCM of roof runoff is available to meet domestic water requirements on a sustainable basis and to mitigate drought for an urban population of 8.8 million.

The undergroundwater reservoirs (*tanka*) generally exist in villages and can be introduced in every house, public building and residential complex in cities and towns for conservation of rainwater from surface and rooftop. Electric pumps can be used for withdrawal of water. In villages, these can be constructed in circular or rectangular shape on ground where surface run-off can be diverted to underground tank by creating a clean catchment around it. The CAZRI had improved upon the design of traditional underground tanks with a capacity ranging from 10,000 to 6 lakh litres. There is a provision for three inlets with a wire mesh and silt trap to prevent polluting material and silt. There is one outlet for overflow. The water is withdrawn both manually and through electric pumps. This system is highly economical and easily accessible as compared to bringing water from distant surface water sources in villages.

The depleted high-capacity aquifer can be replenished by adopting integrated artificial recharge techniques, such as, dams, tanks, anicuts, percolation tanks, etc. These integrated techniques would improve water availability and create a water buffer to sustain

8-10 droughts in Rajasthan. Analysis of long-term rainfall data and water balance studies have shown that during a high magnitude flash flood, 22.6 to 54.8 BCM of excess water is available in the state. The harvesting and conservation of this excess water will not only minimize the colossal damage to life and property but also serve as an undergroundwater bank for drought mitigation for a long time. A survey of groundwater covering the period 1984-2003 pointed out that there is empty space of 55.7 BCM in the groundwater aquifer in Rajasthan state. Hence, the maximum available flood water of 54.8 BCM could be easily accommodated in the aquifer through the integrated recharge techniques. Practically, it is not possible to harvest 100 per cent of the flash flood water to groundwater. But even the utilization of 10-20 per cent of flood water will result in an equal proportion of aquifer replenishment (Narain, 2005: 9-17).

2.5.5 Watershed Structures

The check dams, anicuts, percolation tanks and underground reservoirs are some of the watershed structures which can be developed for conservation of excess overflow and rainwater. The check dams with drop inlet spillways can be constructed in ravines or heavily gullied land. These check dams have a small pondage and help retention of the silt load. Further, these can supplement irrigation and contribute to recharge of groundwater and can also enhance the overall biomass production. So also, dams have been constructed across ephemeral streams at several locations in Jaipur district under watershed management programmes to impound 40,000 to 800,000 cubic metres of water behind each structure.

Similarly, the anicuts are small water harvesting masonry dams which are constructed across a stream to hold sufficient water and submerge the upstream area during the rainy season. The stored water is used for lift irrigation and for recharging groundwater in adjacent wells used for drinking. A study has been conducted by CAZRI, which shows the significant rise of water level in wells in the vicinity of anicuts and dams. It revealed an annual increase in water level of 1.8-2.2 m in the zone of influence of anicuts as against a 0.5 m rise in outside wells (Khan, 1996: 147-150). By constructing anicuts at all identified locations, it is possible to harvest and conserve nearly 25.8 MCM of additional water, from which a population of nearly 470,000 people can benefit by using it both for drinking and limited supplemental irrigation. The structures of percolation tanks can be installed as these are more useful for recharge of rainwater from surface run-off.

There are other **water harvesting and moisture conservation technologies**, which are field based, low-cost and specific to soil. These are highly useful in drought mitigation and in enhancing land productivity. Among these, **contour furrowing** is practised on mild slopes by creating large numbers of mini-storage structures across the slope. So also, **contour bunding** is adopted in the semi-arid region for soil and water conservation for rain-fed farming. The specifications of contour furrowing and contour bunding vary as these depend upon rainfall and soil. These bunds are placed in a series from the ridge to the bottom of a valley, one below another, to form terraced slopes with drainage. It was observed that 25 mm of rainwater could be stored in 130-150 mm of soil depth for growing crops. On average, contour bunds had 27 per cent higher soil moisture and 14 to 181 per cent higher fodder yield than flat surfaces on grasslands (Wasi-Ullah, 1972: 179-182). **Contour vegetative barriers** (CVB) of suitable grass and shrub species are cheap and environment friendly. These varied types of bunds help in soil and water conservation, and also in the improvement of land productivity. These can be implemented in rural areas especially in pasture land to increase the yield of fodder and soil moisture. The CAZRI has developed a system of vertical contour of hedge named as CVB with the objective of checking the flow of water against the slope, soil erosion and conservation of moisture. The study of CAZRI claims that with CVB the runoff volume was reduced by 28 to 97 per cent and that the soil stored about 2.5 times more moisture than in control sites.

There is another technique known as **Box Trench Technique** (BTT), to conserve rain water specially in hilly region. Under this technique the drained rainwater from the hill slopes is protected and conserved by making trenches at the interval of 2.25 metres. This technique was evolved by K.K. Kotia, Chief Forest Conservator, in the forest areas of Udaipur in 1990 and was also implemented by him in 400 hectare hilly area of Daulatpura and Kotra villages of Amber tehsil in Jaipur district. It added about 4 crores litres of water in the groundwater which increased the water level by 20 feet. Within a period of five years (2000-2005), the groundwater level increased by 15 to 20 metres.

2.5.6 Water as Common Property Resource

The loss by overexploitation and low recharge in groundwater can be restored through government intervention and through formation of appropriate property rights. Common property resources (CPR) play important role in the life and economy of rural people. It helps poor farmers in saving their land for cultivation by using common pasture land for their cattle for regulating livestock production. The common dry river beds and tanks could be used for off season cropping and irrigation respectively. The forest is used for procuring fodder, fibre, fuel and timber for buildings and furniture. The catchment area of rivers is used for growing summer vegetables and crops and drawing silt to enrich the soil of their land. The dependence on CPR is greater among poor as compared to rich as it augments their resources.

The grazing land can be used for recharge and conservation of rainwater in reservoirs. It gives support to poor in growing varied types of food stuffs, especially in sparsely populated areas of Rajasthan during the food shortage, non-crop season or drought. The farming of food stuffs like *ker, sangri,* melons and water-melons in dry non-perennial riverbeds give considerable support to human life in summer. The awareness for the use of groundwater as common property resource would lead to prevention of its misuse and exploitation of the poor farmers. The poor farmers can further strengthen themselves by organizing in a Water Users' Association and installing peizometers to regulate the groundwater withdrawals.

In urban areas as well, the overexploitation of groundwater can be checked by enforcing common property rights on groundwater aquifer. This will prohibit the individual households from digging borings in their houses. There is an urgent need of a licensing or permission authority to check the digging of bore wells in urban as well as rural areas.

❑❑❑

3

Water Resources and Economic Development

Water resources contribute to economic, ecological and human welfare and help in sustaining all forms of life. Water is essential for drinking, sanitation, health, agriculture, industry, power generation, etc. Availability of clean and safe water is a basic condition for social and economic development. The provision of clean water for drinking and sanitation has broader links, as it has positive effects on health and hygiene, productivity and efficiency of human beings. Besides, it safeguards natural environment. Thus, over all human progress depends on access to clean water and on the ability of societies to harness the potential of water as a productive resource. Water for life in the households and water for livelihoods through production are the two pillars on which rest the social and economic development. Therefore, water availability and accessibility complement economic development of the region. This relationship between water and economic development can be measured by Water Poverty Index, which is based on the capital entitlements.

The present chapter analyses the inter-linkages between water and economic development with special reference to Jaipur district. Accessibility and availability of water generate economic, health and other benefits which have been examined for Jaipur district as a whole. Additionally, various indices and indicators have been calculated to measure water stress and water poverty condition in the district. The Water Poverty Index has been calculated for all the 32 districts of Rajasthan state with special focus on Jaipur district. Regression technique has also been used to further strengthen the analysis.

3.1 ECONOMIC DEVELOPMENT : CONCEPT

Economic development implies capital formation to enhance human potential and human freedom. It encompasses the acceleration of economic growth, reduction of inequality and eradication of poverty. In broader context, economic development can be visualized as improvement in the quality of life by higher income, better education, better health and nutrition, healthy environment, economic and social equality, elimination of poverty, greater individual freedom and a richer cultural life. This depends on developing capabilities to empower people to make choices and to lead lives of their choice.

Desai (1995) has identified five basic capabilities which enhance human potential, such as, capability to stay alive and enjoy prolonged life; capability to ensure biological reproduction; capability for healthy living; capability for social interaction; and capability to have knowledge and freedom of expression and thought. Access to safe and adequate water supply for domestic and productive use can be linked to most of these capabilities. These incorporate the formation of different capital types and capital entitlements as outlined in the sustainable livelihood framework given by Scoones (1998) and Carney (1998). These are identified as natural capital, physical capital, financial capital, human capital and social capital. The potential of economic development of a region is greatly influenced by its endowment of these capital entitlements. These capital entitlements generate all forms of economic and non-economic benefits. Among these entitlements, human capital plays a key role. The investments in human capital economizes the use of physical capital, optimizes the exploitation of natural resources and, above all, results in spreading greater benefits.

3.2 WATER–ECONOMIC DEVELOPMENT NEXUS

Water provides the basis for the accumulation of human capital that leads to economic development. Access to safe drinking water is the foundation for better health, education, food, livelihood and environment. Availability of water depends on the natural capital endowments and its accessibility depends on the provision of water through infrastructural and institutional set-up and has positive impacts on the accumulation of human capital. Improved, safe and clean water accessibility is ensured only when water is supplied through pipelines with no time constraint. Improved access encompasses three dimensions of water security – quality, proximity and quantity. Therefore, availability and accessibility to water generate a number of benefits which can be classified under three categories as economic benefits, health benefits and other benefits. Economic benefits include increase in productivity and levels of income. Health benefits ensure good health and secure life, free from water-borne diseases. Other benefits include increase in opportunities for education, improvement in standard of living and more leisure time, enhancement of skill and efficiency, and restores ecological balance. These benefits are shown in the flow chart (figure 3.1).

3.2.1 Economic Benefits

Surface and ground water availability generate economic benefits, which are assessed in terms of increase in productivity and levels of income. In agriculture, irrigated cultivation leads to higher net and gross area sown under different types of food and non-food crops. It also enables adoption of high yielding varieties (HYVs) of seeds and improved technology, which increases cropping intensity and crop yields and helps in diversification of cropping pattern. This in turn, transforms living standard of farmers, giving rise to their income, employment, and higher investible resources (figure 3.1). The forward linkages, help in developing secondary and tertiary sectors of the economy and thereby contribute to overall growth of the economy.

In **Jaipur district**, irrigation mainly depends upon groundwater owing to scanty rainfall and lack of surface water resources. The farmers with tubewells have much better control over water for irrigation purposes than with canal irrigation. The performance of irrigated agriculture is evident from the expansion of cultivated and irrigated areas. In the district, there has been an increase in net irrigated area and net sown area as a per cent of total area from 13.76 in 1971 to 18.92 per cent in 1996, and 47.21 in 1961 to 58.95 per cent in 1991 respectively (table 1.5). The gross irrigated area also increased from 17.57 per cent in 1971 to 21.36 per cent in 1996. The net sown area in Jaipur district was 63.2 per cent in 1998-99 and 63 per cent in 2005-06, i.e., net sown area has almost remained stagnant in relative terms during the last eight years. But the gross irrigated area increased from 40.7 per cent to 44.4 per cent and the cropping

Fig. 3.1 : Water–Economic Development Nexus

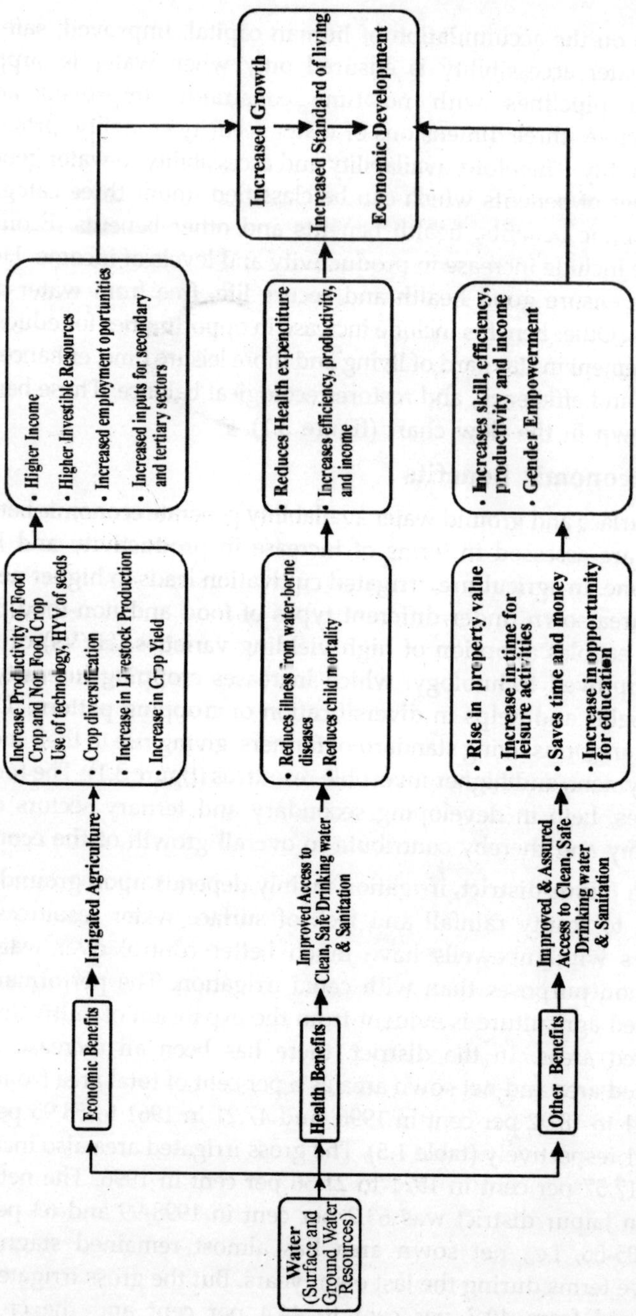

intensity also increased from 142.66 to 159.05 during the same period. This indicates positive improvement in agriculture with increased irrigation facilities.

3.2.2 Health Benefits

Access to clean and safe drinking water is the prime factor for good health and nutrition. It reduces illnesses caused by water-borne diseases, specially among children. This in turn reduces the expenses on health, time and opportunities foregone due to sickness. It increases work efficiency and productivity giving rise to higher level of income, higher standard of living, higher economic welfare and economic development (figure 3.1). Water-borne diseases, such as, typhoid fever, cholera, jaundice, hepatitis-A disorders and a wide array of serious or fatal diarrhoeal illnesses occur at higher rates in low income or poor communities, such as, urban slum settlements and rural areas where safe and clean drinking water accessibility is missing. The water related diseases from intestinal parasites are also impediments to child's mental and physical development.

There has been an increase in the reported cases of water related diseases in **Jaipur district** during the period 1978-93 as given in table 3.1. The total number of patients of diahrroea was around 6600 in 1978-79 which increased to 34607 in 1992-93. Similarly, the number of reported cases of water related diseases from intestinal parasites also increased from 311 to around 5120 during the same period (table 3.1). The number of infected hepatitis patients increased from 1,951 to 4,214 between 1984-85 and 1991-92. The total number of patients having diahrroea, worms and infected hepatitis increased in Jaipur district by 1.4 times during the period of fifteen years from 1978 to 1993.

In rural Rajasthan, there have been reported deaths of children due to water-borne diseases between the age groups of 1-4 years and 5-14 years. There were 20.4 per cent total deaths of children in the age group of 1-4 years due to typhoid fever, 13.9 per cent due to diarrhoea and 6.1 per cent due to gastro-enteritis during 1994-95. These percentages were 11.9, 7.9 and 6.3 respectively for the age group of 5-14 years (table 3.2). More deaths were caused by jaundice in the older age group of children.

There is another aspect related to health benefits. Consumption of contaminated water imposes high risk to the mental and physical development of children. In Jaipur district, above 90 per cent of drinking water is withdrawn from groundwater, which has high levels of salinity, fluoride and nitrate. Around 10-20 per cent area of the blocks of Phagi, Chaksu, Bassi, Viratnagar, Shahpura and Dudu have above 3 mg per litre of fluoride level and most of these blocks of Jaipur district except Viratnagar and Bassi have above 100 mg per litre of nitrate level (table 2.10). Fluorosis is one of the major diseases among the children and adults of Jaipur district. The population of these blocks of the district suffers from problems of untimely decay of tooth and bones, kidney disorders, etc.

TABLE 3.1

Number of Patients of Water-related Diseases reported in Jaipur District, 1978-93

Year	Diahrroea		Worms		Infected Hepatitis	
	Internal Patients	External Patients	Internal Patients	External Patients	Internal Patients	External Patients
1978-79	1441	5157	115	196		
1984-85	3036	18915	241	6028	195	1756
1985-86	4334	10220	325	1481	129	985
1990-91	3647	14987	13	1990	55	727
1991-92	2964	21334	2	1127	47	4167
1992-93	12260	22347	3890	1230	63	871

Source : District Abstract, Directorate of Economics and Statistics, Government of Rajasthan, Jaipur, 1981, 1987 and 1994.

Access to improved and safe drinking water directly impacts health and hygienic conditions and infant mortality. The infant mortality rate (IMR) in Rajasthan has reduced from 114 in 1951 to 68 in 2005 and in Jaipur district it has decreased from 67 in 1991 to 63 in 2002-04, but still it is higher than the national figure of 58 in the year 2005 (table 3.3). This can be further reduced by increasing the access to clean drinking water and proper sanitation. The relationship between improved water and sanitation is clearly revealed from other studies conducted in countries like Uganda, Peru and Egypt. In Uganda, the risk of infant mortality was reduced by 23 per cent after access to improved water and sanitation. As a result of introducing flush toilets, infant mortality has decreased by 57 per cent in Egypt and 59 per cent in Peru (HDR, 2006: 43).

TABLE 3.2

Percentage of Deaths to Reported Total Deaths (excluding senility) in Rural Areas of Rajasthan, 1994-95

Disease	Rajasthan
Children (1-4 Years) 1994-95	
Typhoid	20.4
Dysentery	0.7
Gastro-enteritis	6.1
Jaundice	0.7
Diarrhoea in New Born	13.9
Children (5-14 Years) 1994-95	
Jaundice	2.8
Typhoid	11.9
Gastro-enteritis	6.3
Diarrhoea in New Born	7.9

Source: Registrar General of India, "Survey of Causes of Death (Rural) India Annual Report 1995", New Delhi.

TABLE 3.3

Infant Mortality Rate of Rajasthan and India, 1961-2005

(per 1000 live births)

Year	Rajasthan	India
1961	114	115
1981	87	77
1999	79	70
2000	78	68
2002	78	63
2003	75	60
2005	68	58

Source : Office of the Registrar General of India, Ministry of Home Affairs, for relevant years and Ministry of Health and Family Welfare, Government of India, 2002.

The long term growth in productivity is impeded due to poor health and the foregone opportunities, caused by lack of clean and safe drinking water and their management. Hansen and Bhatia (2004) have stated that widespread water related diseases and illness also determine investments at the macroeconomic level. Where the level of such diseases is chronic, all the sectors of the economy viz., agriculture, mining, manufacturing and tourism suffer. High rates of disease or illness introduce a new source of business risk that deters investment.

Jeffrey Sachs (2001) has empirically demonstrated the adverse impacts of drinking water and sanitation mismanagement on health and education, and more generally, on economic welfare and growth. He argued that countries with access to improved water and sanitation services experience higher economic growth and higher level of health indicators. Clean water and sanitation are among the most powerful preventive factors for reducing child mortality. In addition to saving lives, upstream investments in water and sanitation make economic sense because they would reduce the downstream costs facing health systems. Therefore, universal access to the most basic water facilities would reduce the financial burden on health systems.

3.2.3 Other Benefits

The other benefits exclude economic and health benefits as these are indirectly related to improved access to safe drinking water and sanitation. Improved and assured access to clean and safe water leads to better sanitation conditions and increases school going opportunities (figure 3.1). The availability of drinking water and sanitation facility within household premises with tap, handpump or tubewell saves lot of time of women and girls and also saves substantial amount of money. This time can be utilized in other productive activities, which would increase income, provide opportunities to girls to attend school regularly and result in rise of literacy and education among them. The lack of proper sanitary environment in schools and insufficient water supply for sanitation and hand-washing facilities makes them susceptible to diseases. Even in the case of the availability of these facilities, they are often not adapted to the needs of children, or are dirty, unsafe and in ruinous conditions. In the absence of sanitation facilities in schools, the girl child is quite often deprived of school education or resorts to absenteeism.

The time consumed in collection of water deprives women from other useful activities, such as child care, leisure, or productive work. This sort of restraint also adversely affects women's health due to the physical burden involved in transporting heavy pitchers of water (Wickramsinghe, 2001). People, who have good water access, can use the time saved in water procurement for productive purposes, such as small scale cottage industries, small enterprises, etc. In case of poor water services to communities or households, the labour supply from these households is also reduced owing to the time consumed in the collection of water.

Moreover, it is not only the loss of income but the empowerment of women brought about by their economic independence is also valuable. Education of girls has lifelong impacts which are transmitted over generations. As adults, educated girls are more likely to have smaller and healthier families and their children are less likely to die and likely to receive education more than the children of less educated or uneducated mothers. These gains are cumulative, as are the losses associated with gender inequalities linked to water and sanitation. The absence of sanitation facilities threatens life, destroys opportunity for work and undermines human dignity. Lack of access to toilets forces people to defecate in public or open places which pose severe health hazards and insecurity for women and young girls.

The percentage of girls enrolled in primary school of Jaipur district was only 21 per cent in 1964-65, which increased to 37 per cent in 1992-93, while that of boys was over 70 per cent during this period (table 3.4). Similarly, in Rajasthan the gross enrollment ratio in primary and middle school was low for girls. The gross enrollment ratio in primary school for girls in Jaipur district was 60.9 in 1992-93, which increased to 83 in 2001-02, but in the span of next five years (2001-05) it has increased to around 117 by 2004-05. A similar trend is observed in the gross enrollment ratio of girls in middle school. The combined gross enrollment ratio for girls also increased from 70.25 in 2000-01 to 94 in 2004-05 (table 3.5). The total female literacy rate in Jaipur district in 1951 was 4.11 per cent which increased to 25.37 per cent in 1991 and further improved to 55.52 per cent in 2001. Despite this increase in total female literacy rate in Jaipur district, the literacy rate of the rural female for the district was significantly lower. It was 3.6 per cent in 1971, which rose to 9.59 per cent in 1991, but tremendously rising to 43.86 per cent in 2001 (table 3.6).

TABLE 3.4

Percentage of Students Enrolled in Primary Education, Jaipur District, 1964-93

Year	Number of Boys	Percentage of Boys	Number of Girls	Percentage of Girls	Total Number of Students
1964-65	88115	78.60	23990	21.40	112105
1965-66	96583	78.32	26728	21.68	123311
1966-67	99154	78.10	27811	21.90	126965
1967-68	83374	80.52	20169	19.48	103543
1968-69	152513	79.45	39460	20.55	191973
1975-76	127655	74.26	44239	25.74	171894
1976-77	123361	77.58	35645	22.42	159006
1977-78	123062	77.33	36069	22.67	159131
1978-79	143052	78.87	38317	21.13	181369
1979-80	147222	77.68	42310	22.32	189532
1981-82	163970	78.04	46133	21.96	210103
1982-83	181456	77.15	53736	22.85	235192
1983-84	192590	76.17	60266	23.83	252856
1984-85	189849	72.82	70880	27.18	260729
1985-86	365734	79.81	92524	20.19	458258
1988-89	183415	66.96	90521	33.04	273936
1989-90	125989	62.85	74490	37.15	200479
1990-91	136306	60.01	90838	39.99	227144
1991-92	215953	64.48	118967	35.52	334920
1992-93	184901	62.82	109455	37.18	294356

Source : District Abstract, Directorate of Economics and Statistics, Government of Rajasthan, Jaipur, 1971, 1981, 1987 and 1994. (Later figures not collected by the Department).

The opportunities of education for girls increase with improved access to drinking water and sanitation facilities at school and at home. For instance, in Bangladesh, the UNICEF school sanitation programme between 1990 and 2000 was instrumental in increasing the number of enrollment of girls by 11 per cent (HDR, 2006: 47).

TABLE 3.5

Gross Enrolment Ratio in Classes I-V, VI-VIII and Combined, Rajasthan, 1992-2005

	Classes I-V (6-11 years) Primary			Classes VI-VIII (11-14 yrs) Middle			Classes I-VIII (6-14 yrs) Combined		
Year	Boys	Girls	Total	Boys	Girls	Total	Boys	Girls	Total
1992-93	119.5	60.9	91	76.8	28.9	53.9	NA	NA	NA
1994-95	124.5	67	96.9	79.3	28.7	55	NA	NA	NA
1996-97	114.5	71	94	76	33.3	56.2	NA	NA	NA
1998-99	125.52	75.68	101.82	78.57	33.6	57.56	NA	NA	NA
1999-2000	137.61	83.81	111.92	105.89	48.35	78.88	NA	NA	NA
2000-2001	138.29	83.44	111.99	103.87	47.84	77.45	125.28	70.25	99.06
2001-2002	139.07	83.17	112.5	102.01	47.47	76.19	124.84	69.74	98.48
2002-2003	101.6	92.43	97.25	68.93	40.78	55.67	89.83	73.98	82.33
2003-2004	120.18	109.41	115.07	74.3	47.22	61.54	103.65	87.19	95.87
2004-2005	125.4	116.66	121.24	84.82	54.8	70.67	110.42	94.06	102.67

Source : Selected Educational Statistics, Ministry of Human Resource Development, Government of India, 2002-03, 2003-04, 2004-05.

TABLE 3.6

Literacy Rate, Jaipur District, 1951-2001

(per cent)

Year		Male	Female	Total
1951	Total	18.32	4.11	11.52
1961	Total	27.48	8.35	18.47
1971	Rural	23.61	3.6	14.12
	Urban	57.06	33.42	46.13
	Total	33.82	12.4	23.72
1981	Rural	33.47	5.28	20.04
	Urban	62.14	38.39	51.12
	Total	44.11	17.18	31.4
1991	Rural	43.53	9.59	27.35
	Urban	65.56	44.56	55.78
	Total	53.69	25.37	40.34
2001	Rural	78.88	43.86	62.15
	Urban	86.54	67.13	77.46
	Total	82.8	55.52	69.9

Source : District Abstract, Directorate of Economics and Statistics, Government of Rajasthan, Jaipur, for relevant years.

In Jaipur district, there has been an increase in the accessibility of drinking water in the villages. The access to tap as an improved drinking water source in the villages of the district increased from 6 villages in 1971 to 247 villages in 1991 and further to 3643 in 2001 (table 3.7). This reveals that there are more than one water tap connections in some villages of the district. There were 137 tap connections per lakh of rural population in 2001 which was a major increase from 1991 (10 tap connections), table 3.8. There was no tap facility for water in any of the villages in 9 tehsils out of total 13 tehsils in Jaipur district in the year 1971 whereas there was no such tehsil existed in 2001 (table 3.7). This shows a tremendous improvement in the water supply facility over the period of three decades (1971-2001). The drastic increase in access to tap in the villages from 1991 to 2001 has led to rise in the rural female literacy rate during the same period because of saving of time in fetching water by women folk in rural areas.

TABLE 3.7
Drinking Water by Source in the Tehsils, Jaipur District, 1971-2001

(Number)

Tehsil	1971		1981		1991		2001	
	Tap	All other than Tap*	Tap	All other than Tap*	Tap	All other than Tap*	Tap	All other than Tap*
Kotputli	-	131	5	204	21	348	231	2121
Viratnagar	2	133	10	204	13	143	170	1437
Shahpura	-	-	-	-	16	148	158	1479
Chomu	-	-	-	-	29	189	144	1541
Phulera	1	208	13	243	39	373	354	3509
Dudu	-	186	3	256	10	346	244	2239
Phagi	1	248	2	306	16	415	297	2631
Sanganer	-	224	11	241	20	368	262	2243
Jaipur	-	116	-	113	15	208	131	1150
Amber	2	242	16	226	26	369	342	3007
Jamwa Ramgarh	-	315	12	407	17	479	443	3642
Bassi	-	215	4	279	11	396	390	3335
Chaksu	-	332	10	418	14	526	477	4197
Jaipur District	6	2350	86	2897	247	4308	3643	32531

Note : * includes Wells, Tubewells, Handpumps, Tanks, River, etc.

Source : Census of Jaipur District, 1971, 1981, 1991 and 2001.

Besides tap, there has been increase in other drinking water sources in villages during the period 1971-2001. The number of all other type of sources besides tap (such as, wells, tubewells, tanks, river, canal, etc.) increased by ten times during this period. There has been a radical expansion in the number of tubewells in the villages during the period. There were only 27 tubewells in 1971 which increased to 231 in 1991 and further increased to 3589 by the year 2001 (table 3.8). By 2001, all the villages of Jaipur district had access to some or the other type of drinking water source but not all have access to safe and improved sources of water.

TABLE 3.8

Drinking Water by Source in Rural Area, Jaipur District, 1971-2001

(Number)

	1971	1981	1991	2001
Total Number of Villages	2817	2706	2220	2077
Rural Population (lakhs)	17.37	21.70	28.56	26.59
Percentage of Rural Population	69.95	63.44	60.47	50.64
Types of Drinking Water Source				
Tap	7	109	291	3643
Well	2629	2571	2413	2184
Tubewell	27	78	231	3589
Tank	355	551	382	3902
River	180	396	271	4100
Canal	0	138	102	4131
Others	34	331	2662	4142
Handpump	NA	NA	NA	2188
Lake	NA	NA	NA	4146
Spring	NA	NA	NA	4149
Villages with more than one source	NA	1125	2359	NA
Villages with no drinking water facility of any kind	NA	10	9	NA

Note : Jaipur district includes the villages now in Dausa district from 1971 till 1991.

Source : Census of Jaipur District for relevant years.

Moreover, in Jaipur district, drinking water within premises through tap was accessible to 31.89 per cent households in 1991 which increased to 43.58 per cent households by 2001 (table 3.9). In rural areas, this percentage was 6.52 while in urban areas it was 64.42 in 1991. These percentages increased to 11.59 and 72.31 respectively in 2001. The percentage of households with access to safe drinking water from taps, handpumps and tubewells (combined) within premises increased from 33.28 to 44.85 during the 1991-2001. It shows a slight increase in the accessibility to both improved and safe drinking water sources but still rural–urban disparity continues in a prominent manner. Thus, in urban area more than 75 per cent households had access to improved sources of drinking water while in rural area this percentage was 13.18.

As reported in HDR (2006: 43), in Uganda, full two months of labour time was spent in fetching water, which could have been beneficially utilized for female education, for their income generation and for leisure. Similar result was drawn by SEWA (Self-Employed Women's Association), Gujarat which reports that reduction of one hour a day in water collection enables a woman to earn an additional $100 a year depending on the enterprise (HDR, 2006: 47-48).

The toilet facility in rural areas of Jaipur district is even worse. In 1991, only 2.70 per cent households had toilet facility within premises, this increased to only 6.40 per cent in 2001. Open defecation is still practiced in rural areas of Jaipur district. This causes all sorts of health hazards specially for women as they have to go either early morning or in late evening. The conditions are much better in urban areas but the coverage is still not 100 per cent. In 1991, percentage of urban households with toilet facility within premises was 65.03 which increased to 73.41 per cent in 2001 (table 3.9). Thus, rural-urban disparity with respect to toilet facility is quite prominent in Jaipur district, which causes all sorts of health problems for women.

The drainage facility in the rural and urban areas of Jaipur district was not satisfactory even till the year 2001. The bathroom facility within the premises in rural areas was for 13.22 per cent of the households while in urban areas it was 76.14 per cent in 2001 (table 3.10). Surprisingly, 23.86 per cent of urban households also do not have bathroom facility within the premises and 16.68 per cent have no toilet facility within the premises, and 21.71 per cent urban households do not have any drainage connectivity. The situation is even worse in rural areas where these percentages were 86.78, 88.28 and 77.62 respectively (table 3.10).

TABLE 3.9

Access to Drinking Water and Toilet Facility in Rural and Urban Households, Jaipur District, 1991-2001

(Number)

1991	Number of Households		All Sources		Tap		Handpump/Tubewell		Others *	
			Within Premises	Outside Premises	Within Premises	Outside Premises	Within Premises	Outside Premises	Within Premises	Outside Premises
Total	729975	Drinking Water	279545	450430	232800	77685	10130	164295	36615	208450
			(38.30)	(61.70)	(31.89)	(10.64)	(1.39)	(22.51)	(5.02)	(28.56)
		Latrine	219080	29280	198320	14940	4375	7380	16385	6960
			(30.01)	(4.01)	(27.17)	(2.05)	(0.60)	(1.01)	(2.24)	(0.95)
Rural	410100	Drinking Water	50950	359150	26745	30570	5535	141275	18670	187305
			(12.42)	(87.58)	(6.52)	(7.45)	(1.35)	(34.45)	(4.55)	(45.67)
		Latrine	11075	7390	8245	1870	780	3215	2050	2305
			(2.70)	(1.80)	(2.01)	(0.46)	(0.19)	(0.78)	(0.50)	(0.56)
Urban	319875	Drinking Water	228595	91280	206055	47115	4595	23020	17945	21145
			(71.46)	(28.54)	(64.42)	(14.73)	(1.44)	(7.20)	(5.61)	(6.61)
		Latrine	208005	21890	190075	13070	3595	4165	14335	4655
			(65.03)	(6.84)	(59.42)	(4.09)	(1.12)	(1.30)	(4.48)	(1.46)

Contd...

Contd...

2001	Number of Households		All Sources		Tap		Handpump/Tubewell		Others *	
			Within Premises	Outside Premises	Within Premises	Outside Premises	Within Premises	Outside Premises	Within Premises	Outside Premises
Total	785030	Drinking Water	391359	393671	342080	56062	9987	148741	39292	188868
			(49.85)	(50.15)	(43.58)	(7.14)	(1.27)	(18.95)	(5.00)	(24.06)
		Latrine	327367	60740	300916	23406	4767	17352	21684	19982
			(41.70)	(7.74)	(38.33)	(2.98)	(0.61)	(2.21)	(2.76)	(2.55)
Rural	371472	Drinking Water	65934	305538	43056	21507	5897	124447	16981	159584
			(17.75)	(82.25)	(11.59)	(5.79)	(1.59)	(33.50)	(4.57)	(42.96)
		Latrine	23786	19735	19860	3871	1588	8292	2338	7572
			(6.40)	(5.31)	(5.35)	(1.04)	(0.43)	(2.23)	(0.63)	(2.04)
Urban	413558	Drinking Water	325425	88133	299024	34555	4090	24294	22311	29284
			(78.69)	(21.31)	(72.31)	(8.36)	(0.99)	(5.87)	(5.39)	(7.08)
		Latrine	303575	41005	281056	19535	3179	9060	19340	12410
			(73.41)	(9.92)	(67.96)	(4.72)	(0.77)	(2.19)	(4.68)	(3.00)

Note: Figures in parentheses are percentages from respective number of households by rows. * Others include wells, tanks, river, stream, etc.

Source: Census of India, 1991 and 2001.

TABLE 3.10

Distribution of Households by Availability of Bathrooms, Type of Latrine within Premises and Type of Drainage Connectivity for Waste Water Outlet, Jaipur District, 2001

(Number)

	Number of Households	Households with bathroom facility within premises	Type of latrine within premises			No latrine within premises	Type of drainage connectivity for waste water outlet		
			Pit latrine	Water closet	Other latrine		Closed drainage	Open drainage	No drainage
Total	785030	363989	137423	170190	80488	396929	153527	253405	378098
		(46.37)	(17.51)	(21.68)	(10.25)	(50.56)	(19.56)	(32.28)	(48.16)
Rural	371472	49105	25338	6558	11625	327951	8377	74776	288319
		(13.22)	(6.82)	(1.77)	(3.13)	(88.28)	(2.26)	(20.13)	(77.62)
Urban	413558	314884	112085	163632	68863	68978	145150	178629	89779
		(76.14)	(27.10)	(39.57)	(16.65)	(16.68)	(35.10)	(43.19)	(21.71)

Note: Figures in parentheses are percentages from the number of households by rows.

Source: Census of India, 2001.

Though the sanitation facilities in the towns of Jaipur district have improved and increased during the post-Independence period especially in Jaipur city but the condition is not so encouraging in rural areas. The water-borne latrines in the towns have increased by 13 times during 1971-2001 (table 3.11). There are no more service latrines in the towns of Jaipur district by the year 2001. Moreover, there has been an increase in the number of other latrines by 118 times in the towns during the same period but these are quite less in number as compared to water-borne latrines. The latter ones are four times of the former in 2001 (table 3.11). Among the towns in Jaipur district, the Jaipur city improved tremendously as compared to rest of the towns. For example, it had 94 per cent of the total water-borne latrines in 2001 (table 3.11). The open surface drainage and pit system for the sewerage is widespread in the towns of Jaipur district. Proper infrastructure for waste water collection and its disposal is not developed. It is only in the Jaipur city, where sewer line has been laid down. Though there has been a change in the methods of disposal of night soil from basket, wheel barrow and headload to septic tank or pit system but still the method of disposal is confined to headload in towns like Viratnagar and Chomu of Jaipur district.

The importance of sanitation and safe drinking water for increasing life expectancy, as well as for human development and economic progress could be substantiated by the example of Great Britain where water reforms were introduced in 1850 while sanitation reforms were enforced in 1880-90. It was evident that with the introduction of sanitation reforms along with safe drinking water, the life expectancy in England increased after 1880 by 15 years with the reduction of about one-third in child mortality (HDR, 2006: 29-30).

The gap between water and sanitation facility has not declined as sanitation provision lags far behind access to water in the district. Actually, an increased supply of water, where drainage and human waste disposal provisions are inadequate, could exacerbate public health problems, especially in overcrowded towns and cities (HDR, 2006: 28-30). It would be a great setback for human well-being if provisions for water and sanitation are not simultaneously provided in development programmes.

3.2.4 Water Infrastructure

Water availability and accessibility is achieved through existence of water infrastructure. It includes water collection, storage, distribution network, waste water collection and disposal. In fact, accessibility to improved drinking water and sanitation facilities without proper

TABLE 3.11

Type of Sanitation Facility Available in the Towns, Jaipur District, 1971-2001

(Number)

Name of Town	Water Borne Latrines				Service Latrines				Others Latrines			
	1971	1981	1991	2001	1971	1981	1991	2001	1971	1981	1991	2001
Kotputli	NA	501	1286	2758	NA	754	-	0	NA	4	-	702
Viratnagar	-	6	195	384	-	190	65	0	-	-	-	370
Shahpura	-	50	600	1441	-	-	-	0	-	50	15000	381
Manoharpur	-	-	125	-	-	50	20	-	-	-	-	-
Chomu	-	273	700	2499	30	576	100	0	-	10	250	1840
Jobner	50	80	575	683	50	25	100	0	-	20	-	355
Kishangarh	-		70	1041	-	-	-	0	-	-	-	808
Renwal												
Naraina	-	30	400	-	-	60	5	-	-	-	-	-
Phulera	50	610	1619	2239	200	450	662	0	100	100	1080	899
Sambhar	-	291	1000	1744	14	300	1100	0	-	-	1000	632
Bagru	-	-	50	681	-	-	250	0	-	-	8	483
Jaipur	**19787**	**40198**	**60000**	**260995**	**8325**	**15400**	**9000**	**0**	-	-	**275**	**62100**
Sanganer	100	454	954	-	500	198	198	-	200	-	-	-
Amber	10	30	2000	-	200	73	-	-	100	8	-	-
Bassi	-	80	1000	-	-	310	1200	-	-	-	-	-
Chaksu	3	30	94	1252	-	-	-	0	180	145	114	293
Jaipur District	**20000**	**42633**	**70668**	**275717**	**9319**	**18386**	**12700**	**0**	**580**	**337**	**17727**	**68863**

Source: Census of Jaipur District, for relevant years.

infrastructure for waste collection, disposal and treatment could lead to pollution and public health hazards and high levels of risk for health. Water infrastructure also provides advantages for tourism, development of industry, flood control and in minimizing the adverse impacts of droughts. As a consequence, investments in water infrastructure lead to economic development. In an economy which is resilient to rainfall variability, as that of Rajasthan state as well as Jaipur district, improved water storage facilities would lead to economic development, as it makes the region and its population more adaptable to hydrological variability.

The provision of water storage for drinking water supply in the towns is provided in overhead tanks (OHT), service reservoirs (SR) and covered water reservoirs (CWR). The water storage capacity of these tanks and reservoirs is inadequate as compared to the growth of population of the towns (table 3.12).

In general, lack of water infrastructure creates adverse impact on the economic development. For instance, nations without improved access to water had an average annual per capita GDP growth of only 0.1 per cent, while nations with the same per capita income but with improved access to clean water and sanitation services enjoyed annual average growth of 3.7 per cent (Sachs, 2001; Sanctuary, 2005: 15). Therefore, improved water supply and sanitation, and water resource management can give a fillip to economic growth and increase annual average growth rate in a region. The economic benefits of improved water supply and sanitation in particular far outweigh the investment cost in its infrastructure (Sanctuary, 2005: 4). It is observed that productivity and production are augmented by economic, health and education gains both at individual and household levels.

The availability of water also maintains the ecological balance by creating possibilities for the development of fisheries, forest and recreational activities. It results in better climatic conditions for living. There are also some negative impacts of overexploitation of water resources which result in eventual climatic changes and have drastic effects on the lives of the people. These negative impacts arise due to water scarcity conditions but these can be minimized through the adoption of appropriate policy, proper management with well-planned and well-executed projects. These institutional factors and political will are the key components in the success of any attempt to address water issues. Therefore, the resultant impact of water on economic development of the region is the difference between these positive and negative impacts.

TABLE 3.12

Sources of Water Supply, System of Storage and Storage Capacity in the Towns, Jaipur District, 1971-2001

Name of Town	Source of Water Supply				System of Storage			Total Storage Capacity (000 litres)			
	1971	1981	1991	2001	1981	1991	2001	1971	1981	1991	2001
Kotputli	UC	W, TW	T, TW	T,TW	OHT	OHT	OHT		454.60	4540.00	1500
Viratnagar		W	T, W	TW	OHT	OHT	OHT		136.38	136.50	135
Shahpura		W, TW	TW	TW	OHT	OHT	OHT		227.30	225	499
Manoharpur		W, TW	T, TW		OHT	OHT			318.22	317.80	
Chomu	TW	TW, W	TW, W, T	TW, W,T	SR	SR	SR	300	1363.80	787.50	1723
Jobner	UC	TW	T, TW	T,TW	SR	SR	SR		613.71	340.50	340
Kishangarh Renwal			T, TW	TW,T		OHT	OHT, SR			249.70	944
Naraina		W	W, TW		SR	OHT			204.57	225	
Phulera	TW	W, TW	T, TW	TK	OHT. SR	OHT, CWR	OHT	300	795.55	915.07	915
Sambhar	TW	W	TW	TW,W	SR	OHT	OHT	300	909.20	950	1900

Contd...

Contd...

Name of Town	Source of Water Supply				System of Storage			Total Storage Capacity (000 litres)			
	1971	1981	1991	2001	1981	1991	2001	1971	1981	1991	2001
Bagru			TW, W	TW,T, W,TK		CWR, OHT	OHT			359.16	850
Jaipur	TK, TW	T, TW	T, TW, W	TW, TK,T	OHT, SR	OHT, SR, CWR	OHT, SR	14000	215671.33	219728.75	35980
Sanganer	TW	TW, W	TW, W		SR	SR, CWR		150	431.87	434	
Amber		TW, W	T, W		SR	OHT, SR			477.33	272.40	
Bassi		TW	T, TW, W		OHT	OHT			181.84	200	
Chaksu	UC	W	TW,W	TW,W	SR	SR, CWR	SR		795.55	782.50	1507
Jaipur District								15050	222581.25	230463.88	46293

Note : Sources of Water Supply and Storage: Uncovered (UC), Wells (W), Tubewell (TW), Tank (TK), Tap (T), Overhead Tank (OHT), Service Reservoir (SR), Covered Water Reservoir (CWR).

Source : Census of Jaipur District for relevant years.

3.3 WATER–ECONOMIC DEVELOPMENT INTERACTION: EMPIRICAL RESULTS

This section examines the interaction between water and economic development at empirical level for Jaipur district. For this, various indicators and indices have been calculated, such as, Hydrological Water Stress Indicator (HWSI), Social Water Scarcity Index (SWSI) and Water Poverty Index (WPI). These measures are based on the water availability, accessibility and human development parameters covering health, climate, economic welfare, environment and extent of sustainable development. Additionally, regression technique has been used to find the key determinants of Water Poverty Index (WPI).

3.3.1 Hydrological Water Stress Indicator (HWSI)

Hydrological Water Stress Indicator (HWSI), also known as **Falkenmark Water Stress Index,** measures the water stress through per capita water availability. It describes water stress in terms of physical water availability conditions in the region.

HWSI = per capita total renewable water resources

There are following four broad differentiating categories which describe water stress condition:

- **Water shortages occur irregularly,** if per capita water availability is more than 1600 m^3 per capita per year;
- **Water stress** appears regularly in the region, if water availability is between 1000 and 1600 m^3 per capita per year;
- **Chronic water scarcity** condition occurs, when per capita water availability is between 500 and 1000 m^3 per capita per year. This means water scarcity imposes a limitation to economic development and human health and well-being in the region; and
- **Beyond the 'water barrier' of manageable capability,** when water availability is less than 500 m^3 per capita per year. In this case water availability becomes a major constraint to the existence of life.

The HWSI was 1388.47 m^3 per capita per year for Jaipur district in 1991 which implies that the district was in the condition of "**water stress**" but in 2001, the condition deteriorated further and the district entered into **chronic water scarcity** condition. The HWSI was 914.16 m^3 per capita per year (table 3.13). Thus, there has been continuous deterioration in water availability in Jaipur district since 1971 and more so in the last decade.

TABLE 3.13
Various Indices: HWSI, SWSI, HDI and WPI, Jaipur District, 1971-2001

	HWSI	HDI	SWSI	WPI
1971	2188.78			
1981	2039.52			
1991	1388.47	0.607	4.57	
2001	914.16	0.778	2.35	60.019

Note: Hydrological Water Stress Indicator (HWSI), Human Development Index (HDI), Social Water Scarcity Index (SWSI), Water Poverty Index (WPI).

HWSI in cubic metres per capita per year.

HDI from Directorate of Economics and Statistics, Government of Rajasthan, Jaipur.

Source: Calculated.

3.3.2 Social Water Scarcity Index (SWSI)

Social Water Scarcity Index reflects the hydrological water scarcity in relation to the social condition of the region. It was developed by Ohlsson in 1999. It takes into account HWSI (Hydrological Water Stress Index) as the hydrological measure of water scarcity and Human Development Index (HDI) as a measure of social conditions prevailing in the region. The Human Development Index is a measure of social and economic development. It is calculated on the basis of life expectancy, literacy rate and per capita income.

The Social Water Scarcity Index (SWSI) is calculated as follows:

$$SWSI = \frac{HWSI}{\frac{HDI}{2}}$$

where, HWSI is the Hydrological Water Stress Indicator (in thousand m^3 per capita per year, i.e. 1388.47 m^3 per capita per year becomes 1.38847 thousand m^3 per capita per year)

HDI is the Human Development Index

The values are broadly grouped in four categories to define different stages of water availability. Lower value indicates better condition whereas higher value shows deterioration. The categories are as follows:

- below 5 indicates relative sufficiency;

- between 6 and 10 implies **stress conditions**;
- between 11 and 20 indicates **scarcity**; and
- more than 20 is **beyond the barrier** for existence of life.

For Jaipur district, the value of Social Water Scarcity Index (SWSI) was 4.57 for 1991 and 2.35 for 2001 (table 3.13). Both these values reflect **relative sufficiency** status of Jaipur district regarding water availability but it shows an improvement in its water sufficiency condition over the decade. This may be due to improvement in the Human Development Index. The HDI in 1991 was 0.607, which increased to 0.778 in 2001.

3.3.3 Water Poverty Index (WPI)

Water Poverty Index (WPI) is designed to identify and evaluate the relationship between availability of water resources and economic development. The purpose of this index is to measure the impact of water scarcity on the well-being of human population. It includes both physical and socio-economic factors associated with water scarcity. It was developed by Sullivan in 2002. The conceptual structure of the WPI incorporates some dimensions of each of the livelihood capital entitlements. The five key components of the index are Resource, Access, Use, Capacity and Environment. These are based on natural, social, physical, financial and human capitals. This allows monitoring of a combination of aspects affecting water management, including availability of water, access to water, human capacity for sustaining access, the use of water and environmental impacts. Hence, WPI provides a holistic perspective on water and economic development aspect with more efficient and equitable water management.

Water Poverty Index is a composite index. It is weighted average of the five major component indices. Each component index is made up of sub-components. The five key component indices are Resource Index (*R*), Access Index (*A*), Capacity Index (*C*), Use Index (*U*) and Environment Index (*E*). These are further defined as follows along with the variables used in the study to calculate the value of each component index for the 32 districts of Rajasthan (Appendix 3.1).

- **Resource Index** (*R*) : This component is a basic indicator of water availability in the region. It incorporates the net groundwater availability and the average annual rainfall.
- **Access Index** (*A*) : The access component measures the extent of accessibility to water for human use. Its sub-

components are percentage households with access to safe drinking water and toilet facilities, and percentage gross irrigated area.

- **Use Index** (*U*) : The use component includes domestic, agricultural and non-agricultural uses. All are positive variables assuming that the higher usage leads to better outcomes for human welfare. It includes domestic and industrial water use along with agricultural use.
- **Capacity Index** (*C*) : The capacity component measures the effectiveness of people's ability to manage water. Capacity to manage water resources is based on education, health and access to financing. The variables included are well-established health indicators, and closely related to access to clean water, i.e., per capita income, infant mortality rate, literacy rate and life expectancy at birth.
- **Environment Index** (*E*) : The environment component attempts to capture the environmental impact of water management to ensure long-term ecological integrity. It includes percentage forest area and percentage urban area.

The basic calculation for each sub-component index is based on the following formula:

$$\text{Sub-component Index} = \frac{X_i - X_{min}}{X_{max} - X_{min}}$$

where, X_i is the original values for district *i*,

X_{max} is the highest value district, and

X_{min} is the lowest value district.

Within each of the above-mentioned five components, the sub-component indices are calculated and then averaged to get the respective component index and weighted average of these gives the required composite index known as **Water Poverty Index** (WPI). The formula is as follows:

$$WPI = \frac{WrR + WaA + WcC + WuU + WeE}{Wr + Wa + Wc + Wu + We}$$

where, *R, A, C, U* and *E* are the component indices of Resources, Access, Capacity, Use and Environment respectively. *Wr, Wa, Wc, Wu,* and *We* are the respective weights of the components. For the present study these component weights are taken to be equal.

The scores of the Water Poverty Index range between 1 and 100. A lower score indicates higher water poverty whereas a higher score gives lower water poverty. The WPI was initially calculated for the 147 countries of the world by researchers from Keele University and Centre for Ecology and Hydrology, Wallingford, UK. India is in the category of **high water poverty** as the value of WPI is 53.2 (Lawrence, 2003:14). The internationally accepted classification of the values of the index is as follows:

Value of WPI	Water Poverty condition
• Below 35	Worse condition
• 35 - 47.9	Severe Water Poverty
• 48 - 55.9	High Water Poverty
• 56 - 61.9	Medium Water Poverty
• 62 - 67.9	Medium Low Water Poverty
• 68 - 78	Low Water Poverty (Best condition)

Table 3.15 gives the Water Poverty Index and the component indices for the 32 districts of Rajasthan for the year 2001 (figure 3.2). The WPI values vary in the range of 60.949 to 21.440 across the districts. WPI for Jaipur district is 60.019. This is in the **medium water poverty zone**. The other districts in this category are Alwar, Karauli and Kota. Jaipur district is very low on Environment Index but placed at high value in other sub-indices and HDI (table 3.15). The worst affected districts having WPI value below 35 are Churu, Jaisalmer, Rajsamand, Ganganagar. Most of the districts are affected by severe water poverty. There has been an improvement in the accessibility to drinking water and sanitation in Jaipur district during 1991 and 2001. The value of the Access Index improved from 12.674 in 1991 to 13.207 in 2001 as given in table 3.14. The rank of Jaipur district among other districts of Rajasthan State with respect to Access Index also improved from 6 to 3 during this period. Hanumangarh district is in severe water poverty zone. It is very low in Resources Index but high in other sub-indices, Access, Capacity and HDI, reflecting its progressive policies on accessibility and management.

TABLE 3.14
Access Index, Capacity Index and Environment Index, Jaipur District, 1991-2001

	Access Index	Capacity Index	Environment Index
1991	12.674 (6)	13.801 (5)	4.175 (16)
2001	13.207 (3)	13.187 (4)	4.148 (16)

Note: Rank of Jaipur district among the 32 districts of Rajasthan are given in parentheses.

Source: Calculated

The Climate Vulnerability Index (CVI) is used to assess vulnerability towards climate variations. In terms of water resources, vulnerability is not only influenced by the quantity of water available, but also by range of social, economic and environmental factors which affect the ability to cope with changing conditions. Climate Vulnerability Index (CVI) incorporates all these aspects. It is based on the sustainable livelihood approach similar to Water Poverty Index. It has six major components viz., resources, access, capacity, use, environment and geospatial. Thus, it incorporates all the five components of WPI and one additional component as geospatial. The geospatial component gives specific geographical characteristics of the region and includes variables, such as, population, land forms, slope, temperature, extent of urban area, etc. These are the variables which assess the influence of climate change on the capacity to manage water resources.

The identification of zones of vulnerability based on CVI provides a systematic rationale for deciding on priority areas where proactive measures to protect population should be taken. This needs further research. The position of India is in the **medium high zone** with respect to water resources and climate vulnerability.

3.3.4 Regression Results

This subsection deals with the regression results. Water Poverty Index and the Access Index are taken as dependent variables. Resource Index, Use Index, Environment Index, Human Development Index and Per Capita Income Index are taken as explanatory variables. Water Poverty Index (WPI) evaluates the relationship between water availability and economic development. This is affected by various factors such as water resources, its accessibility and use. The capacity to manage water as reflected by per capita income and environment. Access Index measures the extent of access to water for human use. This is also affected by factors, like water resources, its use and per capita income.

TABLE 3.15

Water Poverty Index (WPI) and its Components for the Districts of Rajasthan, 2001

S. No.	Districts	Resources Index	Rank	Access Index	Rank	Capacity Index	Rank	Use Index	Rank	Environ-ment Index	Rank	WPI*	Rank	HDI 2007	Rank
1	Ajmer	12.795	17	9.845	15	9.638	11	9.525	13	2.033	26	43.836	19	0.677	10
2	Alwar	18.056	1	12.191	5	10.906	8	13.054	6	3.545	17	57.752	3	0.744	6
3	Banswara	14.141	10	11.811	7	10.831	9	4.874	27	14.205	1	55.863	5	0.653	12
4	Baran	16.866	3	7.841	23	6.193	29	8.061	21	7.242	7	46.204	15	0.425	31
5	Barmer	6.512	29	2.504	32	8.996	16	8.900	18	10.242	4	37.154	27	0.578	21
6	Bharatpur	16.034	5	11.301	10	7.145	25	9.786	12	2.024	27	46.289	14	0.604	19
7	Bhilwara	13.669	14	9.166	21	9.003	15	8.604	20	2.267	22	42.709	20	0.633	15
8	Bikaner	6.678	28	6.764	27	13.363	3	9.425	15	2.899	20	39.129	23	0.779	3
9	Bundi	13.755	13	12.048	6	8.229	20	8.980	16	7.366	6	50.378	11	0.649	13
10	Chittorgarh	15.247	7	9.665	19	6.260	28	8.707	19	6.552	10	46.430	13	0.558	27
11	Churu	5.866	31	6.979	26	9.428	13	3.201	32	1.587	30	27.060	31	0.606	18
12	Dausa	12.346	19	10.583	13	8.716	17	8.921	17	3.275	18	43.842	18	0.576	23
13	Dholpur	13.354	15	10.620	12	4.944	31	7.508	23	3.085	19	39.511	22	0.497	30
14	Dungarpur	13.257	16	7.696	24	7.564	23	3.209	31	6.331	11	38.057	25	0.409	32
15	Hanumangarh	6.325	30	13.202	4	11.124	7	4.103	28	2.458	21	37.211	26	0.761	5
16	**Jaipur**	**15.634**	**6**	**13.207**	**3**	**13.187**	**4**	**15.918**	**3**	**2.074**	**25**	**60.019**	**2**	**0.778**	**4**
17	Jaisalmer	0.000	32	2.892	31	8.483	19	5.556	26	4.510	13	21.440	32	0.673	11

Contd...

Contd...

S. No.	Districts	Resources Index	Rank	Access Index	Rank	Capacity Index	Rank	Use Index	Rank	Environment Index	Rank	WPI*	Rank	HDI 2007	Rank
18	Jalore	11.220	22	6.223	28	6.573	27	12.135	8	3.841	15	39.992	21	0.527	29
19	Jhalawar	17.043	2	9.571	20	9.679	10	9.502	14	6.916	8	52.712	9	0.614	16
20	Jhunjhunu	8.960	24	7.244	25	9.628	12	10.550	11	1.868	28	38.249	24	0.686	9
21	Jodhpur	8.033	26	11.210	11	15.195	2	18.311	1	2.109	24	54.858	6	0.711	7
22	Karauli	14.848	8	9.691	18	8.692	18	12.629	7	10.774	2	56.635	4	0.566	25
23	Kota	16.401	4	14.198	2	12.772	5	10.667	10	6.911	9	60.949	1	0.787	2
24	Nagaur	12.443	18	6.099	30	9.082	14	17.356	2	0.723	32	45.703	16	0.61	17
25	Pali	12.025	20	6.222	29	7.401	24	7.984	22	2.158	23	35.789	28	0.547	28
26	Rajsamand	8.190	25	8.644	22	6.847	26	3.838	29	1.775	29	29.294	30	0.578	22
27	Sawai Madhopur	13.808	12	11.380	9	12.602	6	11.331	9	3.651	16	52.772	8	0.698	8
28	Sikar	10.572	23	10.274	14	7.667	22	15.142	4	8.964	5	52.619	10	0.645	14
29	Sirohi	11.864	21	16.227	1	16.083	1	5.800	25	3.871	14	53.845	7	0.809	1
30	SriGanganagar	6.902	27	11.667	8	6.081	30	3.595	30	5.474	12	33.719	29	0.561	26
31	Tonk	14.066	11	9.782	16	4.612	32	14.802	5	1.314	31	44.576	17	0.571	24
32	Udaipur	14.571	9	9.776	17	7.934	21	6.637	24	10.251	3	49.169	12	0.595	20

Note: WPI* is not divided by 100. HDI referred from Directorate of Economics and Statistics, Government of Rajasthan, Jaipur.
Source: Calculated.

Fig. 3.2 : Water Poverty Index Values Across Rajasthan State, 2001

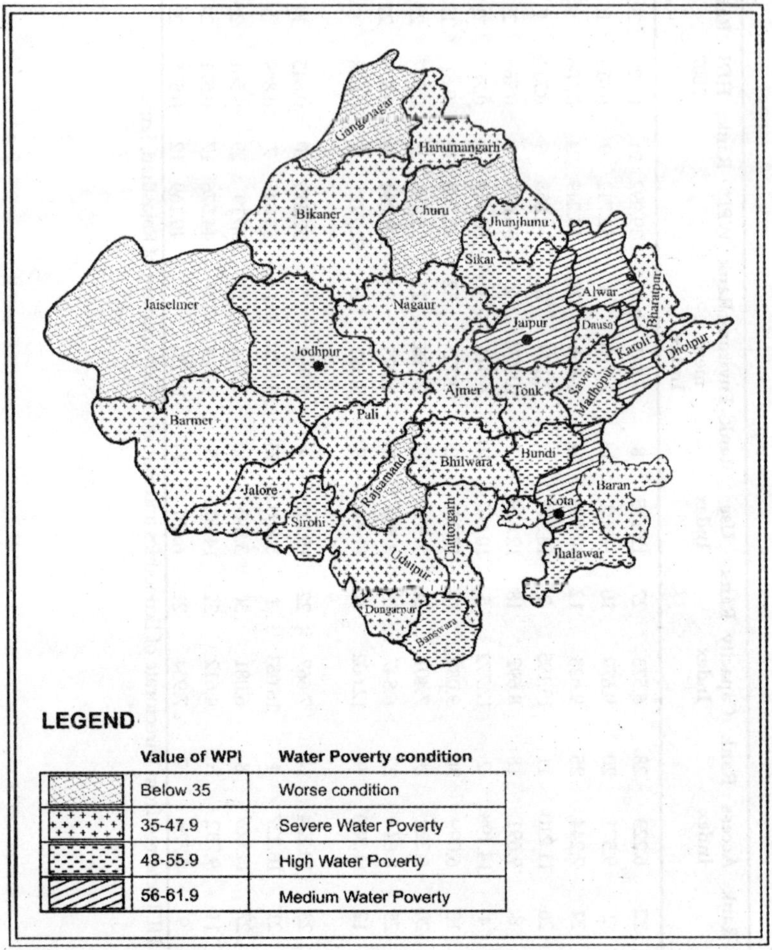

Source : **Calculated**

Six regression models have been used in the analysis. The functional relationship is as follows:

Model 1. WPI = *f* (Resource Index, Human Development Index)

Model 2. WPI = *f* (Resource Index, Per capita income Index)

Model 3. WPI = *f* (Resource Index, Human Development Index, Environment Index, Use Index)

Model 4. Access Index = *f* (Resource Index, Human Development Index)

Model 5. Access Index = *f* (Resource Index, Per capita income Index)

Model 6. Access Index = *f* (Resource Index, Human Development Index, Use Index)

All the dependent and explanatory variables are explained in the sub-section 3.3.3 which deals with Water Poverty Index and in Appendix 3.1. Regression results are given in table 3.16. Cross section data for 32 districts has been used for the year 2001.

Results

All the coefficients are statistically significant at 5 per cent level of significance and all have positive signs when WPI is regressed on Resource Index, Human Development Index (HDI), Environment Index, etc. The explanatory variables - Resource Index, HDI, Environment Index and Use Index explain 93 per cent variation in WPI (Model 3, table 3.16). The explanatory power of Model 1 improves when Environment Index and Use Index are added (Model 3) but it deteriorates when HDI variable is dropped (Model 2). The coefficient value of Resource Index and HDI deteriorates with addition of two explanatory variables Environment Index and Use Index. In all the three models, when WPI is taken as the dependent variable, the estimated coefficients have expected signs.

Models 4, 5 and 6 give results when Access Index is taken as dependent variable. All the coefficients are statistically significant at 5 per cent level of significance and all have positive signs except Use Index. HDI and Resource Index as explanatory variables explain 50 per cent variation in the dependent variable (Model 4) which improves to 57 per cent when Use Index is added to it (Model 6) but addition of Per capita Income Index lowers the explanatory power to 37 per cent (Model 5). The coefficient value of Resource Index and HDI improves with addition of Use Index (Model 6) but it deteriorates when HDI is dropped (Model 5). It seems that Use Index is an important determining factor of WPI and Access Index. Thus, regression results show that water resources, environment, use, income level, and HDI are important determining factors of WPI.

Correlation Results

Correlation matrix for the five indices and the WPI is given in table 3.17. Most of the correlation coefficients are small (less than 0.5) except few exceptions where the coefficient value is greater than 0.6. The correlation coefficient between access and capacity is only 0.40, although intuitively, a strong positive association between these two

TABLE 3.16

Regression Results related to Water Poverty Index and Access Index, 2001

	Dependent Variable	Intercept	Resource Index	Human Development Index	Index of Per Capita Income	Environment Index	Use Index	R^2	F-statistic	n
Model 1	**WPI**									
Coefficients		-6.973	1.92*	45.99*				0.77219	49.1502	32
Standard Error		6.426	0.212	8.787						
t-ratio		-1.085	9.036	5.234						
p-value		0.28679	<0.00001	0.00001					< 0.00001	
Model 2	**WPI**									
Coefficients		20.342	1.661*		9.702*			0.6256	24.2289	32
Standard Error		3.691	0.274		4.209					
t-ratio		5.511	6.053		2.305					
p-value		<0.00001	<0.00001		0.0285				< 0.00001	
Model 3	**WPI**									
Coefficients		-11.8339	1.49705*	42.2792*		1.01979*	0.790418*	0.93132	91.5314	32
Standard Error		3.78915	0.133546	5.26473		0.156089	0.135942			
t-ratio		-3.1231	11.21	8.0306		6.5334	5.8144			
p-value		0.00424	<0.00001	<0.00001		<0.00001	<0.00001		< 0.00001	

Contd...

Contd...

	Dependent Variable	Intercept	Resource Index	Human Development Index	Index of Per Capita Income	Environ-ment Index	Use Index	R^2	F-statistic	n
Model 4	**Access Index**									
Coefficients		-5.40951	0.40131*	16.2416*				0.50565	14.8313	32
Standard Error		2.93151	0.0969106	4.00844						
t-ratio		-1.8453	4.141	4.0519						
p-value		0.07523	0.00027	0.00035					3.66e-005	
Model 5	**Access Index**									
Coefficients		3.87875	0.297751*		4.47227*			0.37779	8.80407	32
Standard Error		1.47371	0.109525		1.68022					
t-ratio		2.632	2.7186		2.6617					
p-value		0.01346	0.01095		0.01254				0.00103	
Model 6	**Access Index**									
Coefficients		-5.88534	0.474688*	18.7485*			-0.21154*	0.5733	12.5401	32
Standard Error		2.78093	0.098024	3.97234			0.100397			
t-ratio		-2.1163	4.8426	4.7198			-2.107			
p-value		0.04334	0.00004	0.00006			0.0442		2.23e-005	

Note: n = 32, * Significant at 5 per cent level.

Source: Calculated

components is to be expected. Similarly, a strong negative correlation between resources and use is expected because the more scarce the resources, the better use is made of them but the correlation coefficient is 0.31 (table 3.17). A strong negative association is expected between resources and environment as the more scarce the resources, more attention is generally paid for its conservation. Here, the correlation coefficient is positive and low (0.2).

The table 3.17 shows the correlation between the WPI and its sub-indices and HDI. There is a strong positive association between the HDI and capacity (0.82), as the capacity index is partly based on the HDI variables. The other sub-indices are not strongly correlated with the HDI, and, overall, there is a moderately positive correlation between the WPI and HDI (0.36) which shows that water issues are distinctively different to general development status as measured by HDI. The relationship between the WPI and access (0.66), WPI and resources (0.75) is much stronger as compared to the correlation between the WPI and the HDI.

This empirical analysis suggests that in the long run, there may not be any such thing as physical water scarcity. It is also explained by the SWSI values for the Jaipur district which puts the district at relative sufficiency level. However, it can be concluded that economic development plays a vital role in the water accessibility and precisely in water poverty of the region. It is the critical 'adjustment variable' in the process by which societies reduce their 'water poverty'. Societies 'manufacture' water scarcity with the growth of population and development. It could be gradually adapted through restructuring the economic systems to use the natural resource endowments properly. Tushaar Shah emphasized similar view (Shah, 2007: 308-309).

Moreover, the low-income districts have little or no scope to improve their water resources management, and economic development is the only way to reduce their water poverty. In order to be effective in water poverty alleviation, water resources management strategies should be efficient and region specific.

Table 3.17

Correlation Matrix for WPI and its Components, 2001

	WPI	Access Index	Environment Index	Resources Index	Capacity Index	Use Index	HDI
Access Index	0.6595	1					
Environment Index	0.3349	0.0206	1				
Resources Index	0.7463	0.4752	0.2	1			
Capacity Index	0.445	0.4044	-0.0782	-0.071	1		
Use Index	0.5674	0.062	-0.1817	0.31	0.2089	1	
HDI	0.3616	0.4619	-0.1879	-0.1316	0.8212	0.2415	1
PCI Index	0.3906	0.4682	0.0456	0.1779	0.4293	0.074	0.6698

Source: Calculated

Appendix 3.1

Definitions and Data Source for the Variables included in various Subcomponent Indices of Water Poverty Index (WPI) for the Districts of Rajasthan

S. No.	WPI Component	Definition	Data Used	Data Source
1	Resource Index	The resource component is a basic indicator of water availability in the region.	• Net Ground Water Availability (MCM) (2004) • Average Annual Rainfall (cm)	• State Ground Water Department, Government of Rajasthan, Jaipur. • Census of India, 2001
2	Access Index	The access component measures the extent of access to water for human use. It evaluates as to how well provisioned the population is, including domestic and industrial use and irrigation.	• Percentage Households with Access to Safe Drinking Water (2001) • Percentage Households with Access to Toilet Facilities (2001) • Percentage Gross Irrigated Area (2001)	• Directorate of Economics and Statistics, Government of Rajasthan, Jaipur.
3	Use Index	The use component includes domestic, agricultural and non-agricultural use. All are positive variables assuming that the higher usage, the better outcomes for human welfare.	• Domestic and Industrial Water Use (MCM per capita) (2004) • Agricultural Use (MCM) (2004) • Per Capita Income (Rs.) (2004-05)	• State Ground Water Department, Government of Rajasthan, Jaipur.

Contd...

Contd...

S. No.	WPI Component	Definition	Data Used	Data Source
4	Capacity Index	The capacity component measures the effectiveness of people's ability to manage water. Capacity to manage water resources is based on education, health and access to financing. The variables included are well-established health indicator, and closely related to access to clean water.	• Infant Mortality Rate (per 1000 live births) (2002-04) • Literacy Rate (per cent) 2001 • Life Expectancy at Birth (years) 2001	• Directorate of Economics and Statistics, Government of Rajasthan, Jaipur.
5	Environment Index	The environment component attempts to capture the environmental impact of water management to ensure long-term ecological integrity.	• Percentage Forest Area (2001) • Percentage Urban Area (2001)	• Directorate of Economics and Statistics, Government of Rajasthan, Jaipur. • Census of India, 2001.

□□□

4

Water Management and Institutional Framework

Effective water management is the need of the day. It is required for increasing the efficiency in water use and water supply in the domestic, industrial and agricultural sectors. There is inequality in water supply, inaccessibility and inappropriate water tariff in urban and rural areas in proportion to population, which once again emphasises the need for better management of water resources. Additionally, over the years, the annual per capita availability of renewable fresh water in Jaipur district has shrunk alarmingly from over 5000 cubic metres in 1951 to below 1000 cubic metres in 2001. It indicates that the region has fast moved to a 'water emergency' zone, as below 1000 cubic metres of annual per capita water availability is considered critical for human survival.

In the process of growing population, urbanization, industrialization and economic development, it is only through efficient management that the challenge of scarcity of water resources could be appropriated. It is true that the efficiency of management cannot be put to test in abundance of water situation but it can be in its shortage, as rightly pointed out by Benjamin Franklin, "When the well is dry then we know the worth of water" (Lal, 1972). The United Nations Water Conference in May - June 1976 emphasized that the major objectives and guidelines for management of water resources for all developing countries are to provide access to safe and ample water supply for drinking and hygienic waste disposal.

This should receive priority with a view to achieve measurable, qualitative and quantitative targets serving all the population by 1990 (Biswas, 1978: 971).

There are multifaceted problems in water sector. A significant percentage of people do not have access to drinking water and proper sanitation facilities. On the other side, fresh water sources are drying up faster than their replenishment, while the existing sources of fresh water are being damaged by pollution. These observations have also been highlighted in the debates at the World Water Forums (WWF). There are three sets of practices which have blighted national efforts in India to tackle the water crisis: (a) inefficient and wasteful use of water in agriculture, industry and households; (b) pollution of water resources and (c) unsustainable extraction of groundwater. The solutions to all these problems are related to extraction, storage and distribution of water according to demand keeping in view the priorities of human development and health, instead of pure supply-side approach related to 'production' of water (United Nations Report, 2006). Hence, proper management of both demand-side and supply-side aspects is required.

The predominant challenges to water management in Jaipur district are scarcity and unequal distribution of water. The supply of water to the inhabitants of this district has become a great challenge due to unplanned urbanization, increased dependency on groundwater resources to fulfill the demand and the ignorance of the people towards these issues. In the arid and semi-arid regions of the district, the situation is all the more critical due to overexploitation of groundwater and paucity of surface water resources. In the present situation another challenge is the disparity in the supply of water owing to the allocation of water by default rather than design. This problem is attributable to total institutional failure in tackling the issues related to efficiency, equity and sustainability of water resources.

4.1 INSTITUTIONAL FRAMEWORK

In India, the institutional framework for development programmes of water resources includes the Central and State Government departments which allocate, monitor and manage the water supply, along with planning and implementation of various schemes. Besides, it encompasses active participation of non-government organizations (NGOs), water users and media.

4.1.1 Infrastructure at National Level

The Ministry of Water Resources of Government of India has been assigned the work of overall planning and development of groundwater resources and formulation of the national water development policy. It also attends to strategies of creating awareness for artificial recharge of groundwater, maintaining water balance of different basins and sub-basins for possible inter-basin transfers. Besides, it provides technical guidance and monitors the irrigation, flood control and other multi-purpose projects (major and medium) of the States. This Ministry is responsible for laying down policy, guidelines and programmes for the development and regulation of country's water resources. Moreover, there are other departments of Central Government, such as, Central Water Commission, Central Ground Water Authority, Central Ground Water Board, Water and Power Consultancy Services, which supervise nationwide surveys and allocation of grants to states and also give them directions in matters of water conflicts (GOI, 2003). Some of them are as follows:

Department of Drinking Water Supply

In 1999, Department of Drinking Water Supply (DDWS) was formed by the Government of India under the Ministry of Rural Development (MoRD), to strengthen rural water supply as well as sanitation. It is a nodal department in the Ministry of Rural Development for providing scientific, technical, and financial assistance in drinking water and sanitation sector to the states.

Central Water Commission (CWC)

The Central Water Commission is a premier technical organization under the Ministry of Water Resources of Government of India since 1945. In consultation with the state governments, it carries out its responsibilities of initiating, coordinating and furthering schemes for control, conservation and utilization of water resources for the purpose of flood control, irrigation, navigation, drinking water supply and hydro-power development. In fact, the main concern of Central Water Commission is to implement the National Water Policy.

Central Ground Water Authority (CGWA)

The CGWA was constituted under "Environment Protection Act 1986" for effective regulation and management of groundwater resources in the areas where groundwater has been overexploited to the limit of exhaustion. The CGWA also looks into the projects of roof top rain water harvesting. It has constructed 11 artificial recharge structures around the urban areas of Jaipur city like Raj Bhawan, Chief Minister's residence, Secretariat building, High Court, Malviya National Institute of Technology (MNIT), Reserve Bank of India, Office of Central Ground Water Board at Jhalana Doongri, etc. It has arranged training programmes to educate the masses at grassroots level about the techniques of rain water harvesting for artificial recharge in major cities of Rajasthan. The training programmes were organised at Jaipur, Mathania (Jodhpur district), Jodhpur, Alwar and Udaipur. Along with this, it created mass awareness about water harvesting through posters, electronic and print media.

Central Ground Water Board (CGWB)

The CGWB, a subordinate office of the Ministry of Water Resources, is responsible for carrying out nationwide surveys of groundwater resources and guiding the States in scientific and technical matters relating to groundwater. Besides, it has taken up artificial recharge studies in the dark and overexploited blocks of Rajasthan and other States. It has also worked out the feasibility, construction and cost-benefit ratio of roof top rain water harvesting methods under experimental recharge studies. Moreover, it has constructed recharge injection wells and piezometers. Further, it has initiated the regulation for the cities to have water harvesting on Government and other buildings by utilizing surplus monsoon run-off through artificial recharge techniques. It has assessed that 36 BCM surplus monsoon run-off can be harvested through artificial recharge techniques in subsurface reservoirs for increasing agricultural production, for checking decline in water levels and for improving groundwater quality and developing congenial environment.

The CGWB has developed models of artificial recharge systems in association with State Government organizations. These models are suited to different hydro-geological and agro-climatic situations, which could be adopted by States and other public and private organizations.

The CGWB has also initiated building bylaws to facilitate the implementation of water harvesting systems. It has organized 150 mass awareness training programmes in rural and urban areas to educate people and to seek their active cooperation in groundwater management. These training courses provide information about the benefits of rain water harvesting and the innovative and economical techniques to implement it in urban environment. It has undertaken 11 blocks as notified areas in Rajasthan. The block of Jhotwara in Jaipur district is one of them. According to the notification, groundwater abstraction structures in the "Notified Areas" could be built with the permission of the CGWA. It is now made mandatory for future construction of any groundwater withdrawal structures.

4.1.2 Infrastructure at State Level

The water sector in Rajasthan state is managed by a number of departments, each having its own programmes, territory and mandate. The Government of Rajasthan, on the lines of the Central Government, has divided the operation and maintenance of water sector into various departments, such as, State Ground Water Department, Public Health Engineering Department (PHED), Irrigation Department, Indira Gandhi Nahar Project and Command Area Division Department, Watershed Development Department, Water Conservation and Wasteland Management Department and Water Pollution Control Board. These departments cater the needs of water supply and development of water resources in an integrated manner (Vyas, 2005).

Irrigation Department

The main activities of the Irrigation Department include survey, investigation, design and planning of surface water schemes, hydrological and meteorological studies, and optimal utilization of available surface water resources. The department also carries out the construction and maintenance of major, medium, and minor irrigation schemes and implements flood control measures.

State Ground Water Department

This state department works in accordance with the CGWB. Its main activities include planning, development, exploration and utilization and checking exploitation of groundwater resources. It conducts periodic surveys of available groundwater supplies in different blocks and also examines the quality of groundwater. It monitors the water table and groundwater withdrawal and recharge. It has also designed and undertaken construction of rain water harvesting structures, artificial recharge and injection wells in the state. Besides, it facilitates and provides guidance for implementing these structures at individual and community levels.

Indira Gandhi Nahar Project and Command Area Development Department

The Indira Gandhi Nahar Project (IGNP) receives water from the Ravi-Beas rivers through interstate water agreements. This life line of western Rajasthan is one of the major national projects. IGNP has the overall responsibility of this project.

Watershed Development Department

It is responsible for construction of water harvesting structures, such as, anicuts, bunds, etc., and also for management of the watershed catchment area of the river basins.

Water Pollution Control Board

It is responsible for controlling pollution of land and water resources. At several places, water bodies are polluted as municipal waste water and industrial effluents are discharged into them without proper treatment. The Board is supposed to ensure enforcement of pollution control laws.

Public Health Engineering Department (PHED)

The PHED of Government of Rajasthan was established in 1965, and emerged as an independent unit as a result of the expansion of Public Works Department (PWD). It includes two units: (i) Rajasthan Water Supply and Sewerage Management Board, and (ii) Public Health Engineering. This department is responsible for planning and execution of drinking water supply schemes for urban and rural areas. Surface and ground water is used as per availability in a particular area and supplemented, when necessary, by outside sources. It looks after water supply and sewerage management, departmental policy formulations, sanction of mega projects and funds. In view of the importance of the first unit, it has been manned by representatives of Finance, Planning, Panchayati Raj and Rural Development. Accordingly, it has two major functions: (i) production and distribution of water, and (ii) assessment and realization of revenue.

The objective of PHED is efficient management of the regular supply of drinking water, maintenance of its infrastructure and orderly solution of the water problems of the state of Rajasthan. Further, it maintains a record of minute details of work and its distribution to officers' in-charge, water production, supply and distribution, revenue collection and other related issues. It has no water resources of its own but it works as an agency for providing water from the irrigation projects, dams, anicuts, canals and other groundwater resources of the district under its jurisdiction. Its primary function is to supply drinking water and provide handpumps and tubewells to satisfy the popular demand of water. Its management of water resources reveals that it has no consideration for the quality and regular supply of groundwater.

Apart from these departments, there are a number of side-line departments and agencies which are involved in development, management and utilisation of water in the state. A number of NGOs and Voluntary Organisations are also involved in these tasks. PRI bodies have an increasing role in water management. The 73rd Amendment of the Indian Constitution has provided a three tier local government structure in the rural areas, having Gram Panchayats (GPs) at grassroots level, Panchayat Samitis (PSs) at the block or middle level and Zila Parishads (ZP) at the district level. Its broad objective is to transfer all projects along with concerned functionaries and funds to the Panchayat Raj Institutions (PRI), and to ensure people's participation in these projects.

Many activities of these departments, agencies and institutions overlap, and sometimes clash with each other, which has an adverse impact on the welfare of the people and development of the state economy. At present there is no effective linkage between these departments, resulting in lack of coordinated approach to development and management of water resources. For example, the same groundwater aquifer may be used for irrigation as well as urban and rural drinking water supply in certain regions without any agency coordinating the efforts. As a consequence, as soon as a tubewell or a hand pump is installed by PHED or Rural Development Department for supply of drinking water, a number of public and private tubewells sprang up for supplying water for irrigation in the same area and from the same aquifer. As the withdrawal of water for irrigation is much greater, the level of groundwater aquifer goes down, drying up the handpumps and tubewells installed for drinking water. The concerned departments sink even deeper wells to mitigate this situation. The vicious circle continues and the supply of water is sustained neither for irrigation nor for drinking water.

There is provision under Irrigation System Act, 2000 for Water Users' Association (WUA), Village Ground Water Committees (VGWC) and Farmers' Organisations (FO) to ensure participation of farmers in water management. This provision is either partially implemented or has an inherent conflict of interest among different water providers and water users, as it does not indicate well-defined objectives or set of priorities. So also, it is not equipped to deal with multi-sector uses of water resources, nor does it show any plans to manage the state's total surface and groundwater resources. The other uses of water like domestic, industrial and environmental are neglected or are kept on low priority. Moreover, there is no provision for separate departments for looking after development, management and regulation of water supplies. As a result, the management and planning of water on sustainable basis is neglected. Hence, it is essential that departments of policy and planning which require expertise should be separated from the department of resources development, conservation, recharge, etc.

In addition to the above, other committees, working groups, task forces, etc., at state, district and panchayat levels also deal with water-related issues. It is evident from the constitution of these bodies that the roles, responsibilities and objectives of most of them overlap. There is also duplication in the tasks assigned to these committees. Further, there is lack of co-ordination among the committees and no feedback is passed on from one to other committee. In any event, hardly any committee meets with a regular agenda and a work plan.

4.1.3 Role of NGOs in Water Management

The effective water management calls for defining the role and responsibility of water managers and partners including policy planners, Central and State organizations, Non-Government Organizations (NGOs), Voluntary Organizations (VOs), Research Institutes, Public Representatives, Industries and common people.

The NGOs act as facilitator and catalyst for promoting the partnership of the rural community with the corporate houses and government in the implementation of Government projects of rural development. These agencies have been mobilized to take the initiative to construct the water conservation units with community participation, for the development programmes of the Government (Joseph, 2006).

The NGOs working for water resources development and conservation in Rajasthan are Cecoedecon, Tarun Bharat Sangh (TBS), SWRC Tilonia, Sadguru Foundation, etc. These NGOs have evolved a working model with the objectives of fulfilling the requirements and overall development of the villagers. Cecoedecon has been engaged in addressing the issue of water for over twenty years, beginning from grassroots level, with a long term perspective. Besides, in association with other organizations, it has initiated resolutions, such as, Phalodi Declaration (1997), Shahbad Action Plan (1998), Lakshmangarh-Charlu (2001) and the Pani Utsav (2004). Among these, the Pani Utsav was organized at Jaipur from 16 March to 22 March, 2004 to create awareness against reckless exploitation and pollution of groundwater causing threat to human life and biodiversity. Tarun Bharat Sangh (TBS) had initiated rainwater conservation with the active assistance of the villagers of Nimbi, 30 km from Jaipur which resulted in overall prosperity within six years. At the time of installation of this project in 2001, there was no water in wells and *baodis* (stepwells) and the villagers were forced to migrate to Jaipur city for livelihood. The organization collected Rs. 1.5 lakhs for Ghatwara check dam to retain water and to prevent soil erosion in the fields. Consequently, the water level in the wells and the moisture in the soil increased resulting in high yield of crops and fodder in Nimbi village. This improvement generated employment to the extent that labour from other villages was employed by the farmers of this village.

The *Sambhagiya Jal Abhiyan Samiti* also associated itself with the government project of water conservation. It proposed that 10,000 houses in Jaipur district will be geared to adopt water harvesting system by June 2006. Further, it was also envisaged that community centres of the colonies will also have this system with the help of Municipalities and Municipal Corporations.

The management of water in rural areas should be entrusted to local NGOs and voluntary organizations (VOs), as these have direct linkages with community and can play as a bridge between government and community. These can play a lead role in guiding Village Water Sector Committees (VWSC) in planning, project formulation and its implementation. For instance, the dedication and commitment of NGOs in the areas of their location have led to the successful implementation of the Aapni Yojana through community participation. Such projects cannot be handled alone either by government machinery or by the Panchayati Raj Institutions (PRIs). The selection of NGOs for water management in rural areas is made at the district level by District Water Sector Committees (DWSC) and

Zila Parishads (ZP), where the process for empanelment of local NGOs was enforced at the end of 2006. The Rajasthan Government also proposed a crash programme for NGOs through short training courses in order to equip them for better performance in social mobilization campaigns under SJD and TSC programmes.

The UNICEF is one of the major institutions working in development sector, especially in the areas of child health and education, which are interrelated with health, environment, sanitation, safe drinking water, nutrition, education and family planning. It provides coordinated services in developing countries to achieve its objectives. So also, it has extended support to Government of Rajasthan for the development of various models of rain water harvesting wherein water can be collected and used by the community or recharged into the ground for sustaining the groundwater table. In the district of Jaipur, UNICEF is actively assisting Gram Vikas Nav Yuvak Mandal (GVNML) of Lapodia village in Dudu block for making water conservation structures, developing pasture land and pond farms known as *chowka* system. The project was started as a sample unit and after evaluating the positive results, it has been installed on a large scale. In this project, the whole pasture land is treated for growing grass, shrubs and trees so that it can conserve humidity in soil and prevent the overflow of rain water to enable it to seep in ground for recharge.

The whole project depends on natural process and is economical, as it involves no expenditure except labour of villagers. It has brought favourable results in Lapodia with increase in the level of groundwater and production of milk, etc. The village has been able to sell milk of Rs. 35 lakhs during the consecutive four droughts (2001-2005) in Dudu. It has also educated the people in favour of community participation in maintaining the pasture land and removing encroachments. Consequently, this process has started in 20 villages and all encroachments have been pulled out. Besides, the UNICEF has funded Centre for Science and Environment in the same village of Dudu block with the cooperation of GVNML to revive traditional methods to conserve rain water, such as, *kundi*. It has also given financial support to the programmes of community development covering health, Swajaldhara projects of drinking water and sanitation to Scouts and Guides for making water harvesting structures in schools and dairies. Similar financial grant is provided for making anicuts and dams, and also development of integrated model for fluorosis mitigation involving domestic de-fluoridation through activated alumina filters. This model has been tested and shown noteworthy results. These concrete examples of the contribution of NGOs could be adopted in other parts of the Jaipur district for the successful management in the water sector.

4.1.4 Role of Corporates

The Corporates in Rajasthan have made rapid strides and gained new momentum while undergoing several structural changes during the past several years. Earlier confined only to urban pockets, the movement has spread to rural areas of the State. There are some MNCs like, Indian Tobacco Company (ITC), Jamshedpur Utility Services Company (JUSCO), and Ambuja Cement Foundation (ACF) which are working in Maharastra, Jharkhand and Gujarat respectively. The experiences of these MNCs can be beneficially adopted as guidelines for the management of water resources in Jaipur district. For instance, the ITC under its project 'Sunhera Kal' in Maharastra focuses on natural resource management, covering wasteland, watershed and agricultural development specially to create livelihood for tribals and rural communities by recycling 90 per cent of solid waste water. It has constructed over 1,200 reservoirs and has helped in the irrigation of 15,000 hectares of land. The Tata Iron and Steel Company of Jamshedpur provides the municipal services of drinking water, electricity, relief assistance and recycled water to 700,000 residents of Jamshedpur on subsidized rates.

4.1.5 Role of Media in Community Participation

The role of media has been emphasized as a representative of masses and as active partner in India's economic development. A.P.J. Abdul Kalam, former President of India, in his *Vision 2020*, has highlighted the importance of media and expected that the journalists should interact with grassroots social reformers and highlight their core competence, dedication and experience in serving rural communities. The media should always be guided by the value system drawn from cultural heritage while propagating issues related to economic and human development (Kalam, 2006).

The print media in Rajasthan is growing towards the direction of developmental politics. In order to achieve this target, it is essential to have research wings in academic institutions to carry out research on topics of national interest and provide solutions to medium and long term problems. All types of media - electronic, print and newspapers in coordination with socio-political organizations must work in concurrence following similar approach. The cooperation of socio-political organizations, such as, Bharat Jagriti Manch, Rajasthan Jan Manch, Mohalla Vikas Samiti, Jan Jagriti Samiti, Bharat Uday Sansthan and other associations can be achieved through media in organizing water conservation projects in the villages of Jaipur district and other parts of Rajasthan state.

The mission of creating awareness, activating community participation and organizing voluntary labour for rejuvenation of traditional water resources and implementation of water conservation techniques was taken up by *Rajasthan Patrika* in a project named Amritam Jalam in 2003. Under this project the traditional system of water supply of Jaipur city and its environs were highlighted and restoration of decaying water bodies was initiated through community participation in rural and urban areas of Jaipur district. Along with this, other problems of water resources, such as, the recharge of groundwater, harvesting rain water, tree plantation and conservation of pasture land as a long term plan for water conservation were organized by initiating people and social organizations. Media can encourage and attract corporate sector for investing for remedial and capacity building measures for the rejuvenation of traditional water bodies in Jaipur city. The *Rajasthan Patrika* had received a contribution of Rs 5.18 crores towards renovation of traditional water sources in Jaipur city and its environs from MPs and MLAs. This reveals that the print and electronic media can play a leading role in creating awareness and bringing about attitudinal change among people and also mobilizing Corporate Sector towards the conservation of water resources.

The Panchayats can be an auxiliary to the media for providing information on water use, water policy and programmes of the government in rural areas of Jaipur and other districts of Rajasthan State. They can also encourage the people's participation through media in the process of effective and proper water management. The success of many micro participatory projects justifies that local initiatives can maximize water availability. It is specially because the community participation is based on four factors: (i) control, (ii) operation and maintenance, (iii) ownership and (iv) contribution of cost of water supply system. The essence of community management lies in control rather than operation and maintenance; because control covers the decision making powers that puts a community truly in charge of the system.

4.2 VARIOUS PROGRAMMES AND SCHEMES OF THE GOVERNMENT

The efforts of State Government are supplemented by Central Government by providing financial assistance and guidelines under the various centrally sponsored schemes and financial support in the form of special assistance. The existing programmes and schemes for the supply of drinking water in Rajasthan are as follows:

4.2.1 Accelerated Rural Water Supply Programme (ARWSP)

The Accelerated Rural Water Supply Programme (ARWSP) was implemented in Rajasthan in 1972-73 with 100 per cent grants and aid to cover drinking water supply. According to this programme (ARWSP), the target of providing water for basic needs per capita per day was fixed as 40 lpcd for human beings, and 30 lpcd for cattle in rural areas. Besides, one hand pump for 250 people and a source of water within the range of 1.6 km in plains and 100 metres in hilly areas was sanctioned. The term safe water was defined as free from contamination both biological (cholera, typhoid, etc.) and chemical (excess arsenic, fluoride, salinity, iron, nitrates, etc.) (GOI, 1986).

In 1986, the entire programme was given a mission approach with the launching of the Technology Mission on Drinking Water and Related Water Management. This Technology Mission was renamed as Rajiv Gandhi National Drinking Water Mission (RGNDWM) in 1991-92. In 1999, new initiatives in water sector were introduced through Sector Reform Project (SRP).

4.2.2 Sector Reform Project

The Government of India initiated reforms in different sectors of water supply in rural areas to institutionalize community participation to ensure sustainability of systems and resources. The Rural Water Supply Programme represented a paradigm shift from supply-oriented approach to demand-driven approach based on empowerment of villagers. It aimed at gradual change in government's role from provider to facilitator and concentrated on conservation measures for sustained supply of water through rainwater harvesting and groundwater recharge. It was proposed that minimum contribution from the villagers must be 10 per cent of the capital cost of the project ensuring at least 40 litres per capita per day (lpcd) water to all users. The remaining 90 per cent would be borne by Government of India. The quantity of water may be increased subject to the availability of water. The contribution of villagers could be either in cash, kind, land or labour. The Sector Reforms Project was launched on pilot basis in the districts of Jaipur, Alwar, Sikar and Rajsamand with a view to involve the community in preparation, planning, execution, operation and maintenance of such schemes by the beneficiary community (Srivastava, 2005).

4.2.3 Swajaldhara Project

The Swajaldhara Project of Government of India was launched on 25 December, 2002 in the state of Rajasthan on pilot basis through Sector Reform Project. The fundamental reform principles with terms of demand- responsive approach and community participation were adhered to by the state Government. Swajaldhara has two streams: (i) Swajaldhara-I which will have Gram Panchayat as the lowest unit for implementing reform initiatives; and (ii) Swajaldhara-II which will have the district as the unit for implementation (GOI, 2004). In Jaipur district the scheme was launched in 29 villages of Phulera, 10 of Dudu, 4 of Amber and 6 villages of Chaksu tehsils. An amount of Rs. 96.74 crores was sanctioned for 1338 schemes in Rajasthan state by November 2004, out of these 401 schemes about 30 per cent have been completed and handed over to the community for maintenance. In Jaipur district, 391 schemes were sanctioned and out of which about 45 per cent schemes have been handed over to the community for maintenance.

The operational part of water supply schemes under Sector Reforms Project revealed several lacunae, which required rectification to achieve the goals of the reform programme. The results of the schemes indicated that financial and technical inputs to rural water supply have not been commensurate with the huge investments made in this sector. As a result, water scarcity persisted. The removal of these lacunae entailed a change in the perception of the rural people and convinced them to the idea that water is a social right to be provided by the Government, free of cost.

4.2.4 Financial Support

The Government of India has been providing special assistance and funds since the beginning of the First Five Year Plan (1954) to States to establish special investigation divisions for identifying the problems of water in rural areas. The Rajasthan State Government selected PHED, Rural Development Department, Panchayati Raj Department, Municipal Boards, Corporations or Development Authority as the agents for implementation and disbursement of funds for water projects. However, the objectives of the programme could not be attained due to insufficient funds while the issues of water scarcity in villages not only persisted but also proliferated. Consequently, Rajasthan Government focused its efforts on augmenting water supply through installation of hand pumps on tubewells and borewells in rural areas. However, the availability of potable drinking water in rural areas, especially during the summer months, could not achieve satisfactory standards. Even after the completion of twenty years, these programmes have suffered from several primary flaws, such as, poor maintenance, non-involvement of people in operations and maintenance and neglect of management of traditional water resources.

The Government of Rajasthan made efforts to rectify these flaws while formulating new policy for management of water in the state. The Government specified its decision to control over-extraction of groundwater, providing more funds for repairs and rehabilitation, promoting people's participation and reserve 20 per cent funds for states' patronage to sector reforms. Above all, it treated water as a socio-economic good and stressed for creating stronger links with watershed development programmes.

4.2.5 Projects of Government of Rajasthan

The Government of Rajasthan had started three projects in the year 2005 for development of rural areas in Jaipur district : (i) Upkhand Uday, which looks after health, education and cooperative needs at block level; (ii) Shri Sthala; and (iii) Shri Sarovar, for the maintenance of rural and urban lakes and step-wells with an objective to promote tourism.

The Rajasthan Urban Infrastructure Development Project (RUIDP) is related to the development of infrastructure for water supply specially in urban areas. It is funded by Asian Development Bank which has specified its scope of work in areas where adequate water supply is not available. The project aims at proper distribution of water from all sources to improve water supply in the Jaipur city. For instance, it plans to construct 7 surface reservoirs of fresh water, 13 overhead water tanks and one new pumping station. Besides, it proposes to replace damaged and junk pumping machinery of 63 pumps at various pumping stations. The areas specified under the project are new colonies in Jaipur city viz., Mahesh Nagar, Vidyut Nagar Zone, Kalyan Nagar Zone, Jhotwara North Zone, Jhotwara Centre, West and South, Sanganer, Jagatpura Zone I and II, Maharani Farm, Singhdwara Yojana, Phus ka Bangla and Vidyadhar Nagar. In 2005, it was proposed to install 11 tanks and 109 tube wells in 296 colonies with estimated cost as 2485.39 lakhs (table 4.1). Another project under RUIDP plans to establish infrastructure of waste water treatment plant at Delawas in Jaipur city. The treated water from this plant would be collected at the dam of Ramachandrapura and supplied to Amanishah Nallah from where it would be used for irrigation. It would also help to increase the level of groundwater and compensate the shortage of drinking water.

TABLE 4.1

Water Infrastructure Installation under Rajasthan Urban Infrastructure Development Project (RUIDP), 2005-06

Number of Colonies covered	Area covered	Infrastructure to be installed	Estimated Cost (lakh Rs.)
53 Colonies	Mahesh Nagar (North & South)	20 Tubewells, 2 Overhead Tanks, 1 Clear water tank	541.81
27 Colonies	Vidyut Nagar Zone	12 Tubewells, 1 Overhead Tank, 1 Clear water tank	377.88
28 Colonies	Kalyan Nagar Zone	8 Tubewells, 1 Overhead Tank, 1 Clear Water Tank	184.26
5 Colonies	Jhotwara North Zone	12 Tubewells, 1 Overhead Tank, 1 Clear Water Tank	198.98
33 Colonies	Jhotwara Centre, West and South	24 Tubewells, 3 Overhead Tanks, 1 Clear Water Tank	672.49
23 Colonies	Sanganer	3 Tubewells, 1 Overhead Tank, 1 Clear Water Tank	308.23
53 Colonies	Jagatpura Zone–I & II	28 Tubewells, 2 Overhead Tanks, 1 Clear Water Tank	744.94

Contd...

Contd...

Number of Colonies covered	Area covered	Infrastructure to be installed	Estimated Cost (lakh Rs.)
17 Colonies	Maharani Farm	2 Tubewells, 1 Overhead Tank, 1 Clear Water Tank	193.36
35 Colonies	Singh Dwara Yojana	1 Tank and Pipeline	46.22
15 Colonies	Phus ka Bangla	1 Tank and Pipeline	46.22
17 Colonies	Vidhyadhar Nagar	1 Overhead Tank and 1 Clear Water Tank	71.00

Source : Annual Report, Rajasthan Urban Infrastructure Development Project, Jaipur, 2005-2006.

The Rajasthan Water Sector Restructuring Project (RWSRP), aided by World Bank, has the basic objective to raise the standard of social and economic life of farmers through their own participation. Better water management would ensure both an augmented inflow of water and upgradation of agriculture. The traditional sources of water would be renovated on a large scale to improve the availability of water during the periods of scarcity. The Rajasthan Water Sector Restructuring Project (RWSRP) has taken a lead in proposing for the first time to form Farmer's Organisations in a phased manner to cover total irrigated area of Jaipur district. The proposal is a major step in this direction under which rehabilitation and modernisation of 94 major, medium and minor projects covering 5 lakh ha and a total of 2 lakh farmers will be benefitted and additional 80 thousand ha is envisaged to be irrigated annually (GOR, 2005).

The **Wasteland Development Programme** is under operation in the Jaipur district from 1999. At present (2007), it is conducting successfully six projects of Government of India in Amber, Chaksu, Jamwa Ramgarh, Bassi and Shahpura tehsils of Jaipur district. The total cost is Rs. 1979.54 lakhs and the area proposed to be covered is 38,534 ha of wasteland. There is another project under the **Desert Development Programme.** It covers Dudu block of Jaipur district. The evaluation of the work of these projects is still to be carried out (GOR, 2006).

The objective of all these projects of Jaipur district is to provide favourable use of natural resources like soil, water and vegetation for creating congenial environment and for generating employment and self-reliance among the rural population. These projects in Jaipur district are jointly implemented by Zila Parishad and Zila Jal Grahan Samiti devolving to Gram Sabhas, Jal Grahan Samitis and Self Help Groups.

The Rajasthan State Government had launched a project of **Jal Abhiyan** on 10 December, 2005. The project aimed at constructing 80,000 water harvesting structures and renovation of 25,000 traditional water bodies before the onset of monsoon. Under this project, the State Government also planned a **Jal Chetana Yatra** at its headquarters in Jaipur and other districts in Rajasthan from 15 May, 2006. It resolved to generate awareness among the people for conservation of water and to popularize new techniques of protecting groundwater and rain water harvesting through audio-visual media and personal contact. In the Jal Chetana Yatra, 305 chariots were used. The itinerary of one chariot was two villages including Panchayat headquarters and one major village. Panchayats were assigned the work of constructing 40,000 anicuts and check dams. Besides, the Water Resource Department was entrusted to build 1500 anicuts and the Education Department was advised to build 5000 roof top conservation structures in school buildings. In addition to this, the Rural Development Department was given the responsibility to build 1500 roof top rain water harvesting structures. The target of the Jal Abhiyan and Jal Chetana Yatra was to build 1 lakh water harvesting structures within three months by 30 June, 2006 (GOR, 2006).

4.3 WATER SUPPLY FRAMEWORK IN JAIPUR DISTRICT

The PHED manages and operates complete water supply in Jaipur city and other urban areas of the district, but it covers the water supply partially in rural areas.

4.3.1 Rural Water Supply

There are 2131 villages in Jaipur district, out of them 2127 are inhabited. Among these, 143 villages are supplied water through pipeline scheme, 142 through Jal Pradaya Yojana, 119 through Pump and Tank (P&T) project, 7 through Traditional Source Scheme (TSS) and 356 through Janta Jal Yojana (JJY) while 1360 are supplied water through handpumps. This water supply is not able to sustain itself regularly during summer season. Hence, 436 villages and 523 hamlets are supplied drinking water through tankers during four months of summer as given in table 4.2. The total number of tanker trips is 224010, which reveals that the main source of supply of drinking water is through tankers as the local sources of water are either unsafe for drinking or are insufficient to supply the required quantity of water. It also indicates that it is the groundwater that is supplied through tankers. The Government spends Rs. 3.71 crore on water transportation through PHED, which maintains the Jaipur Water Supply Scheme under Government of Rajasthan. The transportation through tankers is used in all tehsils of Jaipur district except in towns of Phulera, Sambhar and Naraina, where train with 25 bogies supplies drinking water. This supply amounts to 4.5 lakh litres daily to Sambhar and Phulera and 3 lakh litres to Naraina. Among all tehsils of Jaipur district, viz., Phulera, Dudu, Phagi, Chaksu, Amber and Bassi are worst hit with water scarcity during the four months of summer.

TABLE 4.2

Water Supply in Rural Areas through Tankers, Jaipur District, 2006

S. No.	Name of Tehsil	Number of Villages	Number of Hamlets	Number of Tanker trips				
				April	May	June	July	Total
1.	Phagi	60	55	3810	5970	5970	5970	21720
2.	Sanganer	3	8	0	540	540	540	1620
3.	Dudu	95	100	3330	12390	12390	12390	40500
4.	Phulera	135	150	11070	15120	15120	15120	56430
5.	Chaksu	45	60	2010	5100	5100	5100	17310
6.	Amber	18	28	2100	3960	3960	3960	13980
7.	Bassi	15	29	1320	3480	3480	3480	11760
8.	Chomu	8	12	510	1410	1410	1410	4740
9.	Jaipur	8	17	1950	3930	3930	3930	13740
10.	Jamwa Ramgarh	22	28	2490	7410	7410	7410	24720
11.	Kotputli	8	15	420	1710	1710	1710	5550
12.	Shahpura	7	14	150	750	750	750	2400
13.	Viratnagar	12	7	720	2940	2940	2940	9540
Total		436	523	29880	64710	64710	64710	224010

Source : Public Health Engineering Department (PHED), Government of Rajasthan, Jaipur.

4.3.2 Water Supply System in Jaipur City

The first piped water supply system was commissioned in 1874 in the walled city of Jaipur. It was reorganized in 1933 by adding 10 million litres of water per day from Ramgarh lake. In the post-Independence period due to increase of population and expansion of the city outside the walled enclosure the Jaipur water supply was supplemented, time and again, and at present (2007) the Jaipur water supply scheme has a capacity of supplying 292.5 MLD of water from ground and surface sources including (i) Ramgarh lake which has a capacity of 65 million cubic metre and (ii) 744 tubewells in the city. The PHED has set-up two control rooms one at Ajmeri Gate and other at Gandhi Nagar for quick disposal of water problems. The department has chalked out plans to meet the water demand in the city and reduce its dependence on groundwater resources. It will supply 360 MLD water to Jaipur city and 40 MLD to rural areas covering Malpura, in the first phase by the end of 2008 from Bisalpur-Jaipur Water Supply Project. It is also proposed to bring surface water from the Chambal Scheme to Jaipur and Ajmer Cities costing Rs. 166.50 crore. Presently, Jaipur city is divided into two parts; (i) walled city (North Jaipur), and (ii) outside walled city (South Jaipur). The dividing line between the two is the Mirza Ismail Road.

The drinking water scheme presently covers 22.15 lakh population of Jaipur city out of the total population of 26.15 lakhs (PHED). During summer the average supply per person is 149 litres per day and the total requirement is of 4000 lakh litres per day while the total water supplied from different sources is 3390 lakh litres. Thus, there is a shortage of 610 lakh litres of water for the people. According to the PHED this shortage would be covered through 1250 tubewells and 1803 hand pumps and 600 tankers. The problem of PHED is loss of 40 per cent and above water in transportations and distribution (T&D) in Jaipur city and at other centres. There is no centralized and reliable system for the collection of data by the department pertaining to leakages, amount of production of water, consumption of power and asset maps. These shortcomings are highlighted in the consultancy report of May 2000, jointly prepared by the French-based Sureca Engineers and the Tata Consultancy Engineers. There is a need to restructure PHED organizationally to enable it to perform an efficient consumer care system.

The water supply in the colonies of the Rajasthan Housing Board in Jaipur city viz., Jawahar Nagar and Malviya Nagar is managed by the Line Department of PHED. The design of water supply scheme in these colonies was initially according to the norms of PHED. However, there is a shortage of water supply for the residents of these colonies due to unauthorized squatters and slums cropping up in the adjoining areas. The same problem exists for other colonies in Jaipur city developed by JDA, and private developers and builders.

4.4 MANAGEMENT STRATEGIES

In view of the failure of government policies to resolve water scarcity in all sectors, it is essential to specify the management options of water use. These options could be pinpointed as measures of conservation of water, augmentation of groundwater by artificial recharge and equitable supply of water. The efficiency of utilization in all the diverse uses of water should be improved with minimal wastage and the awareness should be created among people about its scarcity. Their realization for conservation of water and active participation in water management could be further promoted through education, regulation, incentives and penalties. Besides, reform in the prevailing institutional set-up could be initiated through orientation and training programmes to confront challenges.

The overexploitation of groundwater, decline in water table, total loss of water in tube wells and hand pumps has resulted in increased concentration of dissolved salts in water, making it unsuitable for drinking. As a result, the number of habitations previously getting safe or quality drinking water has gradually reduced or they receive degraded quality of water. This grim situation could be resolved by shifting the source of water supply from groundwater to surface water and initiating the development, conservation and renovation of existing surface water sources.

(i) In Jaipur district the surface water is available in various river basins, community tanks, and canals which could be further procured by construction of new reservoirs to conserve water. (ii) The supply of surface water could be ensured by changing the norms of equitable distribution to the areas according to specific demand. (iii) Lastly, the water supply could be ascertained by rain water harvesting and by educating people for systematic use of water for drinking, agriculture and industries. Thus, the management of water could be made effective by conservation of surface water, rejuvenation of traditional water resources, and augmentation of groundwater from recharge and equitable supply of water according to national priorities and cultural values. For the effective and well planned management following strategies are required.

4.4.1 Conservation of Water

All efforts should be directed to save and store every drop of precipitation. This could be achieved by adopting a holistic approach of watershed programme, covering afforestation, soil conservation, livestock management, disposal of sewage along with conservation of surface water and recharge of groundwater. The programme of watershed management is a technique of water conservation in the regions of low rainfall. The villages can achieve self-sufficiency in drinking water through watershed management covering, (i) management of excess flowing water, (ii) proper use of conserved water and (iii) raising the level of groundwater. These processes could be fulfilled by water harvesting which has received acceptance everywhere.

The design of water harvesting structures is transformed according to the regional variations and needs of people. Hence, it requires ingenuity of the NGOs or Government agency and willingness of the community to improvise its design, structure and maintain its operation. In the words of Sunita Narain, "On our part we have to make it work", as "water harvesting is a life and death programme" (Agarwal, 1997).

Watershed Management in Rural Areas

The watershed management programmes in rural areas consist of techniques to check the flow of rain water by making contours and to divert it with the objective of conservation, recharge and preventing erosion. These objectives are achieved by planting trees parallel to contours. So also, check dams, anicuts and a series of square ponds connected with drains are built to check overflow in the plain region to store water. Moreover, in rural areas watershed could also be developed from water collected from roof of public buildings, such as, Chaupal Bhawan, post offices and schools and diverted to dried wells for storage. But the conservation of roof top rain water is advisable only in pucca houses. In kuchcha houses large amount of water is absorbed by its sandy structure (Reddy, 2000).

The watershed has achieved importance in the semi-arid regions of Jaipur district. It is adopted as a measure for improving socio-economic condition, stabilizing productivity of irrigated agriculture and striking a balance in the existing disparity between *rabi* and *kharif* crops. The sustainable crop production could only be attained through dry land farming and conserving rain water for future use in agriculture.

Different programmes of watershed development at national and state levels have been initiated in Jaipur district. The **National Watershed Development Programme** (NWDP) was implemented in Amber, Jamwa Ramgarh, Bassi, Govindgarh, Dudu and Viratnagar blocks of Jaipur district under the Tenth Five Year Plan to cover an area of 8685 ha at a cost of Rs.303.90 lakhs. It has spent Rs. 269.65 lakhs covering 7704 ha land till March 2007.

Rain Water Harvesting in Urban Areas

The target of the Government is to conserve 80 per cent of rain water in the form of surface and groundwater resources. The State Groundwater Department in association with Central Ground Water Board has prepared many conceptual plans and designs for roof top rain water harvesting. These plans which are executed in many government buildings (table 4.3) are very costly and occupy large parts of land. Hence, the State Ground Water Department has also prepared designs of low cost structures occupying small areas to facilitate its implementation in every house of the urban area. The rain water could be stored from roof tops by making drains and underground tanks.

The individual household can become self-sufficient in domestic need of water by adopting the measure of roof top rain water harvesting as justified by table 4.4. It indicates the availability of surplus rain water run-off from different plot sizes in case of normal rainfall. The estimation of water utilization, by each family comprising six members is calculated as, 120 litres water consumption per capita per day. Based upon these considerations, percentage of water likely to be harvested in each house against the water consumption would range from 6.08 per cent for smallest plot size i.e., 50 sq. m to 30.82 per cent for the biggest plot size i.e., 250 sq. m. These results justify the adoption of roof top harvesting by individual families to become self-sufficient in domestic needs for water.

Rejuvenation of Traditional Sources

It is a general consensus that potable drinking water can be procured from traditional sources, such as, *baodi* (stepwells), *tanka*

TABLE 4.3
List of Government Buildings and Institutions where the Roof Top Harvesting has been installed, Jaipur City, 2005-06

S No.	Name of Building	Year of construction	No. of structures	Run-off area (sq. metre)	Run-off water with rainfall of 30 mm per hour (cubic metre per hour)	Quantity of water available for annual recharge (cubic metre)	Quantity of water available for recharge in 20 years (cubic metre)	Cost of the construction (lakh Rs.)	Cost of water recharged (Rs. per litre)
1.	Ground Water Department	2000-01	3	1050.00	26.77	457.00	9139.00	3.13	0.012
		2004-05		371.00	9.45	164.00	3280.00	0.13	0.004
		2004-05		190.00	4.83	83.88	1677.60	0.06	0.003
2.	Secretariat	2000-01	2	4319.00	90.70	1548.00	30960.00	2.75	0.008
		2000-01		4209.00	88.37	1508.00	30160.00	3.25	0.010
3.	Vitta Bhawan	2000-01	1	4167.00	87.51	1493.45	29869.00	4.50	0.015
4.	MREC Campus	2000-01	1	5348.00	136.37	2328.00	46560.00	1.96	0.004
5.	Chief Minister house	2000-01	1	2546.00	60.38	230.70	18614.00	5.70	0.030
6.	State High Court	2000-01	1	4420.00	92.82	1584.00	31680.00	3.02	0.009
7.	Central Ground Water Board	2000-01	1	1250.00	42.50	544.00	10880.00	2.17	0.019
8.	Raj Bhawan	2000-01	2	869.00	22.16	378.00	7560.00	4.87	0.034
				729.00	18.59	333.65	6673.60		
9.	Irrigation Department	2002-03	1	5200.00	176.80	2261.00	45220.00	4.90	0.010
10.	Nehru Bhawan	2002-03	1	7626.00	173.00	2964.00	59280.00	11.11	0.018
11.	Viduyt Bhawan	2002-03	2	3413.00	133.29	1482.00	29640.00	8.80	0.014
				3965.00	158.52	1487.00	29740.00		
12.	Jal Bhawan (New)	2003-04	1	2784.00	83.52	1472.74	29455.00	2.21	0.007
13.	Collectorate	2003-04	1	5088.00	153.00	2691.55	53831.00	9.18	0.017

Source: State Ground Water Department, Government of Rajasthan, Jaipur, 2006.

(tanks), lakes and wells. Hence, these sources must be revived, protected, and excavated to store rain water by making drains along the natural slope. These traditional water sources be fitted with modern equipments of pumping and pipeline to facilitate water supply to individual households.

TABLE 4.4

Availability of Surplus Rain Water Run-off from different Plot Sizes

S. No.	Total Plot Size (m3)	Built-up/ Roof Top Area (sq.m)	Run-off area (90 per cent of Roof Top area) (sq.m)	Availability of surplus rain water run-off which can be harvested (cubic metre per year)	Water likely to be harvested by each house against water consumption. (per cent)
1	50	30	27	16	6.08
2	100	60	54	32	12.16
3	150	90	81	49	18.64
4	200	120	108	65	24.73
5	250	150	135	81	30.82

Note : Availability of surplus rain water run-off in case of normal rainfall.

Source : P.N. Mishra, Unpublished data, State Ground Water Department, Jaipur, 2006.

4.4.2 Augmentation of Groundwater

The augmentation of groundwater is necessary for agricultural development in the Jaipur district. Agriculture is possible only when water table is between 0.5 and 1 m below ground level. If it drops too low, no crops can be grown without irrigation or rainfall. Hence, it is necessary to ensure recharge of groundwater in critical and overexploited blocks through construction of appropriate structures. The excessive run-off rain water in the villages can be impounded jointly or separately at a place nearest to the source of water. Necessary recharge of the groundwater may be carried out at these sites through recharge structures which can be an integral part of new schemes. The construction of sub-surface barriers in *nallas*, streams, and seasonal rivers may be undertaken. The tubewells and recharge structures should be located at the same sites.

It has been estimated by State Ground Water Department that if 10 per cent of rainwater is conserved in Jaipur city with its average mean annual rainfall of 600 mm, it would be sufficient to meet the demand of drinking water for 94 days in the city as given in table 4.5. This table shows that conservation of 40 per cent of rain water by the construction of different artificial recharge structures could meet demand of 25 lakhs people for one year approximately. This additional water supply could be achieved by artificial recharge.

TABLE 4.5

Quantum of Water available from Rain Water Harvesting, Jaipur City, 2006

Rainfall Conserved (per cent)	Quantum of Water Conserved (in mcm.)	No. of Days for which domestic water demand can be fulfilled.
10	28.2	94
20	56.4	188
30	84.6	282
40	112.8	376

Note : Quantum of water conserved during normal rainfall.

Source : P.N. Mishra, Unpublished data, State Ground Water Department, Jaipur, 2006.

The drainage of rain water from roof tops and roads could be directed into abandoned dug wells or tube wells for artificial recharge. The concept plan and design of artificial recharge from storm water, roof top or pavement run-off has been prepared on experimental basis. The points near Police Memorial Circle, Narayan Singh Circle, Rambagh Circle, Ravindra Manch and Takhtesahi Road areas of Jaipur city (table 4.6) have been identified through a preliminary survey where rain water accumulates during rainy season due to inadequate drainage system, which can be conveniently developed as artificial recharge pits. The table 4.6 indicates that by construction of four storm water harvesting structures about 31384 cubic metre per year of water can be recharged to the groundwater resources.

4.4.3 Institutional Changes

There is a need for the formation of a central planning organization in Rajasthan State for efficient management and integrated development of water resources in domestic, industrial and agricultural sectors. This could be achieved by raising the PHED as the nodal department for integrated development of water resources and for monitoring the implementation of water policy of Rajasthan state. In this capacity, the PHED would coordinate and supervise the working of the line departments in the execution of various programmes and ensure equitable water supply in rural and urban areas of the district. It would also implement appropriate water tariff rates to cover the operation and maintenance costs of water supply. This transformation of the PHED as the apex body would coordinate State and Central Government's water resources programmes. Besides, it would facilitate the working of the programmes of Swajaldhara and Total Sanitation Campaign under the Panchayats in rural areas. It could be further strengthened by associating the NGOs in carrying out the programmes of Information, Education and Communication (IEC) about drinking water and sanitation in the villages. It is through NGOs that the villagers would have a better understanding of the water schemes for smooth execution, operation and maintenance.

TABLE 4.6

Summary of the Concept Plans prepared for Storm Water Harvesting, Jaipur City, 2006

Concept Plan Component	Police Memorial Circle	Narayan Singh Circle	Rambagh Circle	Takhteshahi Road
Pavement / Road Areas (Sq.m)	17,064.00	11,697.00	11,235.00	12,312.00
Availability of Surplus run-off for recharge (m^3/hr at 30 mm/hr rainfall intensity)	512.00	351.00	337.00	369.00
Optimum storage of the capacity of system (m^3)	230	230	230	230
Availability of surplus run-off which can be harvested (m^3/year)	10,238	7,018	6,741	7,387
Anticipated Life of the Project	20 Years	20 Years	20 Years	20 Years
Quantum of Recharge during the life span (m^3)	2,04,760	1,40,360	1,34,820	1,47,740

Source : P.N. Mishra, Unpublished data, State Ground Water Department, Jaipur, 2006.

(i) Equitable Water Supply : The equitable supply of drinking water in rural areas is to be planned and executed through District Water and Sanitation Mission and the Village Water Supply and Sanitation Committees constituted under Gram Panchayats. There are two types of schemes viz., (i) individual village schemes, such as, Traditional Source Scheme (TSS), Jawahar Jal Yojana (JJY), Handpump and Tubewell Scheme (P&T) and Piped Schemes, and (ii) Regional Schemes covering many villages falling in more than one block.

(ii) Water Tariff : The present rate of water tariff collected by PHED is subsidised. It is less as compared to the tariffs of other states and in view of the expenditure on the services, operation and maintenance of water supply incurred by the department. The Rajasthan Government is paying more than 74 per cent subsidy for the maintenance of drinking water supply schemes. During the decade of 1991-2000, the PHED spent three times more than its revenue in Jaipur district for meeting the rising demand of drinking water. It could initially collect water tariff only from consumers having house connections as per prevalent practice. Hence, it could collect water tariff to the extent of 8 percent of the total expenditure incurred on maintenance.

The water rates have been doubled recently but these are still meagre and do not reflect the economic price and the scarcity value of water. In the Jaipur city the domestic rate per 1000 litres to 15000 litres is Rs.1.25 and from 15000 to 40000 litres is Rs. 2.40 and above 40000 litres is Rs. 3.20 (table 4.7). So also, the minimum charges of water per month for domestic category are Rs. 16 for 15 mm service line and Rs. 96 for 20 mm service line, and these gradually increase according to the thickness of service line. The rates for industry are Rs. 8.80 per 1000 litre and increase according to the consumption of water. Similarly, the charges for fresh connections and metre service begin from a minimum of Rs. 15 and increase on the same ratio. The charges for sewerage are calculated according to the consumption of water. These are 20 per cent of the charges of water supply, wherever the sewerage system exists and an extra 13 per cent, when it would be connected to the sewerage treatment plant.

A thorough revision of current rates of water supply to cover the operation and maintenance cost, and linking the cost recovery with quality of service is a pre-requisite to the improvement of the overall performance of agricultural and the urban water sectors. The water rates may be raised and the system of operation and maintenance be handed over partly to Farmers' Organizations. Gradually, tariff should be increased and sustained efforts be made for its collection in phased manner both in urban and rural areas.

TABLE 4.7

Comparative Statement of Water Tariffs of PHED, Jaipur, 1987–97

(Rupees per kilo litres)

S. No.	Category of Consumers	1987 Gross	1987 Net	1994 Gross	1994 Net	1997 Gross	1997 Net
A	**Domestic**						
1	Upto 15000	1.25	1	1.25	1	1.56	1.25
2	Above 15000 to 40000	1.5	1.2	1.5	1.2	3	2.4
3	Above 40000 to100000	1.5	1.2	1.5	1.2	4	3.2
4	Above 100000	2	1.6	2	1.6	4	3.2
6	Minimum Charges (15mm)	22	18	25	21	40	35
B	**Flat Rate**						
1	For 15 mm per family up to two taps	20	16	20	16	25	20
2	For each additional tap	5.5	4.4	5.5	4.4	7.25	5.8
C	**Commercial (Non-domestic)**						
1	Upto 15000	2.5	2	3.75	3	4.68	3.75
2	Above 15000 to 40000	3	2.4	6.25	5	8.25	6.6
3	Above 40000 to 50000	3	2.4	10	8	11	8.8
4	Above 50000 to100000	3.75	2.7	10	8	11	8.8
5	Above 100000	4.5	3.6	10	8	11	8.8
6	Minimum Charges (15 mm)	20	16	20	16	71	60
D	**Industrial**						
1	Upto 15000	5	4	10	8	11	8.8
2	Above 15000 to 40000	6	4.8	12.5	10	13.75	11
3	Above 40000 to 50000	6	4.8	15	12	16.5	13.2
4	Above 50000 to100000	6.75	5.4	15	12	16.5	13.2
5	Above 100000	9	7.2	15	12	16.5	13.2
6	Minimum Charges (15 mm)	20	16	20	16	120	111
E	**Sewerage charges**						
1	without treatment plant	20 per cent of bill		20 per cent of bill		20 per cent of bill	
2	with treatment plant	33 per cent of bill		33 per cent of bill		33 per cent of bill	

Source : Public Health Engineering Department (PHED), Government of Rajasthan, Jaipur.

Installation of proper water metres in households and industries, auditing of water balance from distribution systems and progressive water tariff structure are some of the essential measures for efficient water management. The use of secondary and tertiary water (recycled water) should be encouraged in industries and in irrigation by providing incentives like subsidy, tax rebate, tax holiday, etc. Similarly, in agricultural sector, implementation of water rates on volumetric basis to cover the expenditure on operation and maintenance of water resources should be implemented. The use of treated sewage water for non-edible crops and saline water for tolerant crops should be introduced in agriculture.

(iii) Privatisation : Water is a socio-economic good, but it should not be considered as a commodity. Total privatisation is not desirable as it would give rise to inequality and environmental problems. The Central Government is encouraging the entry of international private companies in the water sector. The five companies entering the water market today are basically construction companies - Suez Lyonnaise des Eaux (French), Bechtel Enterprises (American), Vivendi Environment (a French company now called Veslia), RWE and Thames Water (German) and Saur (French). They are known to build canals and sewage systems, but have also developed interest in the water markets for huge profits. There are several foreign funding agencies, MNCs and other corporate houses as well, working with projects of rural development, such as, European Commission, Asian Development Bank, World Bank, Corporate Houses, KFW, EEC, OECF and SIDA.

The government must limit these companies and funding agencies to provide funds for the various water resources projects. These agencies should only be allowed for the maintenance and operation of water supply system and should not be given complete control over the water resources. The government must control the tariffs. The collection of tariff can be out sourced. These measures would ensure better management, additional revenue, efficient maintenance and operation of the supply system.

Thus, it can be stated that strong, accountable and transparent institutional framework is the key factor for adoption of water management strategies to increase water use efficiency. The issue is not primarily of shortage of water, but also absence of proper mechanisms for conservation, distribution, and efficient use of water.

The demand-oriented water management, increasing water use efficiency through water pricing and technology, water conservation through watershed, augmentation of water through rain water harvesting and recharge of water are some of the measures to cover the shortage of water. Moreover, improved water management could be achieved by initiating attitudinal change among people regarding conservation, crop selection, irrigation practices and reuse of water. These management strategies can be practiced only with the support of a comprehensive water policy, effective legislation and responsive institutional set-up.

❑❑❑

5

Water Policy and Legislations

The policy of Government is like a captain of the ship, which steers it through difficult, conflicting and complex situations and leads it to its ultimate aim of social welfare of the masses. This is equally true for the water policy of Rajasthan state. Water is socially indispensable and economically essential for growth and development of the state. A well-integrated and region-specific water policy governs sustainable development of water resources for the fulfillment of present and future needs, and smoothens its optimum utilization. Besides, the policy highlights the objectives of economic development and equitable supply of water to all users. Accordingly, the water policy should stipulate for development, conservation and proper usage of water as its guiding principles.

The term 'policy' means general directives or guidelines for decisions in specific cases. Hence, the water policy for Rajasthan has to recognize water as a national scarce resource. It should be able to minimize the negative impacts of overuse and misuse of water. Further, it should cover regional watershed projects, locations of polluting industries, agro-climatic zones, and areas of different population density in towns. It should be able to accommodate patterns of rainfall, surface water bodies and groundwater, and frame its own region specific water policy, reflecting the regional requirements as well as national goals. In the last few decades, a number of challenges have emerged in the development and management of water resources. There is water crisis due to accelerated growth of population leading to reduction in the availability of water per capita, and deterioration in its quality due to overuse and pollution.

The formulation of a comprehensive water policy must address to all these issues, as these are essential prerequisites for proper assessment of its adequacy and completeness. Besides, the water policy must be linked for sustainable development to programmes of other sectors, viz., public finance, agriculture, energy, industry and commerce, health, human settlement, transport and environment (figure 5.1) (UNEP, 1989: 225-251). In view of various facets of use of water, the water policy should be based on the interrelationship of three factors viz., natural water resources, human activity, and water resources management (figure 5.2). The **natural resources** include policy for achieving a scientific understanding of the hydrologic continuum of the region, its use for the development of natural and artificial water resources, and its assessment and planning. The **human activity** is of three types; (a) comprising irrigation, domestic, industry and entertainment; (b) natural water hazards; and (c) degrading quality of water. The policy should take into consideration all these aspects of human activity for promoting appropriate use of water, safeguarding its adverse impact on the natural water resources and minimizing its economic and social losses from natural hazards (Munasinghe, 1990: 33-48). The **management of water resources** encompasses equitable supply, development and conservation of water for social and economic well-being, planning and implementation of programmes and strategies. The fulfillment of these objectives of efficiency, equity and sustainability would strike a balance in supply and demand of water.

Munasinghe (1990: 33-48) has discussed the different aspects of water policy in details, and emphasizes on the need of analyzing the links between water and other sectors of the economy, and illustrates a conceptual framework as indicated in figure 5.1. A comprehensive water policy should strive to establish harmony between national objectives and regional priorities for water resources management. It should be able to resolve the conflicts between national economic growth and self-sufficiency as well as environmental quality and sustainability of the water resources. Moreover, the policy should provide guidelines for developing international agreements on water management, for making investments and budget provisions, for developing water resources, and for involvement of public in planning and execution of projects. These guidelines would create a balance between a new and systematic use of existing water facilities as well as between centralization and decentralization of water planning and implementation. These goals and objectives of the water policy could be achieved with the support of legislation. Water policy and water laws interact and influence each other as the latter also reinforce water management in the state (Hufschmidt, 1993: 60-69).

Fig. 5.1 : Policy Overlaps : Water Resources and Other National Sectors

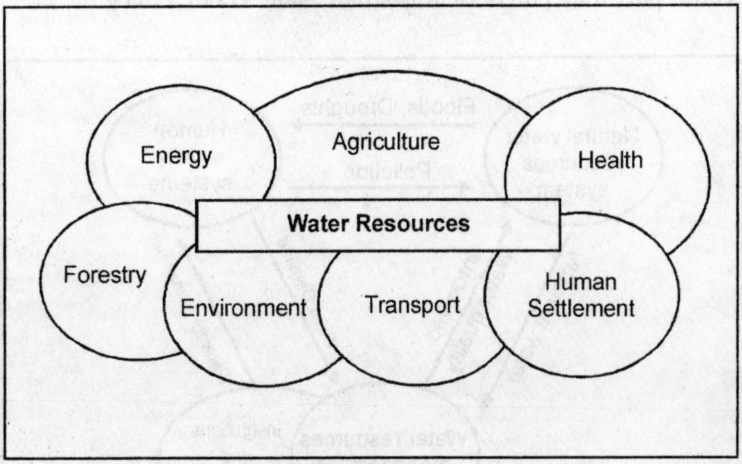

5.1 WATER POLICY : INDIA

The issue of water in India was associated with irrigation and agriculture under the Ministry of National Resources and Scientific Research till 1985. After the bifurcation of the departments of Agriculture and Irrigation and their upgrading as separate ministries of the Central Government, the Ministry of Water Resources emerged as a separate ministry in 1985. As a result, the National Water Resources Council was constituted and a National Water Policy was adopted in September 1987 to review the decline in the water resources of the country.

The objective of the National Water Policy (1987) provided a general set of propositions for development of water resources in the states, so that the latter may formulate a policy and action plans according to their specific needs. This policy only gave a brief description of official functioning in water sector and underscored the issues, like environment, and equitable, adequate and sustainable supply of drinking water on priority. Moreover, its objectives remained confined to paper and holding of meetings by the officials of the Central Government. Surprisingly enough, no sincere efforts were made either by the Centre or States for its revision till 2002. The draft of the National Water Policy, 2002 was prepared by the Government of India in 1999 and was adopted without any change by the Rajasthan State in the same year. Thus, the National Water Policy became part and parcel of Rajasthan State Water Policy.

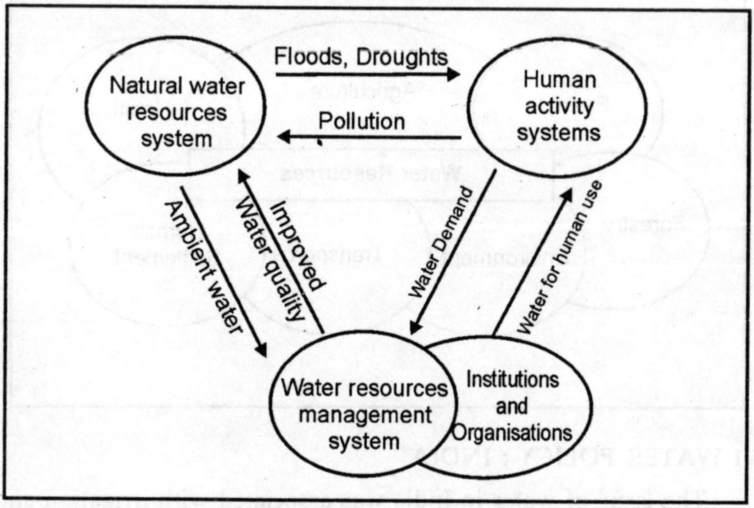

Fig. 5.2 : Interrelationship of the Three Systems-Framework for Policy Analysis

5.2 WATER POLICY: RAJASTHAN STATE

The State Water Policy of Rajasthan, which first came into existence in 1999, has been revised and its draft prepared in 2005 is awaiting approval. The document of the water policy of 1999 has 19 sections covering various aspects of water availability, its use in different sectors and its management. The preamble of the policy specially mentions issues pertaining to the increase in demands for water for drinking, food and power-generation owing to population growth and economic changes. In fact, the policy emphasizes the need of building good database, paradigm shift from groundwater to surface water for improving supply of water, implementation of basin-wise planning and draws attention to drought proofing. The policy has stressed on reorientation and creation of new institutions in water sector. It introduces rotational water distribution system and volumetric water allocation in irrigation sector and highlights need to increase the rate on water charges to cover the cost of operation and maintenance of systems. Besides, it also encourages a change in priorities of financial allocation to ensure a balance between the needs of development, operation and maintenance.

The Rajasthan State Water Policy aims at developing maximum possible extent of all utilisable water resources including surface water, groundwater, waste water and water from other states through canals for optimal economic development of the state. It proposes to initiate integrated multidisciplinary approach to planning, implementation of projects of irrigation, river basin and management of surface and ground water. It seeks to develop information system, maximize water availability, project planning, institutional reforms, construction of structures and implementation of legislation.

5.2.1 Appraisal of State Water Policy

The water policy of Rajasthan state pays only a desultory attention to the development of water resources except irrigation dams and large water structures like canals and tanks. The rejuvenation of traditional system of water harvesting with the cooperation of community has been neglected in the policy. Hence, the State should focus its attention to the rejuvenation of traditional water systems and strengthening these by financial and technological assistance (Editorial *EPW*, 2002)

The policy has some innovative ideas like integrated water resources management (IWRM) and participatory irrigation management (PIM). Apart from this, it emphasizes on multi-sector and multi-disciplinary approach instead of inter-disciplinary and holistic approach. It lays stress on community management of common pool resources, people's participation and water harvesting, but it does not elaborate it properly. Hence, it cannot be implemented completely to reap results of water resource conservation. This is the main reason for its failure, especially in relation to the issues of water harvesting and community management of water resources. For example, the policy provides for integrated water resources management but does not specify guidelines for water allocation and the implementation of IWRM. The implementation of the principles of IWRM makes it necessary to create river basin authorities for managing intrastate and interstate river basin.

Moreover, the important issues of water, such as, commodity versus basic right and the necessity of water have been ignored in the policy. It mentions institutional mechanism, rain water harvesting, inter-basin transfer and desalination of brackish water, but does not specify the measures for achieving the targets relating to the nature of orientation and restructuring of institutions. Of course, the policy focuses on the priority of drinking water. However, it does not cover its ancillary subjects, such as, sanitation, washing, cooking needs of human beings, besides water demands of livestock and wild life. Though the policy gives top priority to drinking water but in practice, preference is given to industrial and agricultural use.

Ambiguity in Water Policy

There is ambiguity in the water policy about private and public participation, which has resulted in the formation of a proposal for handing over the water supply system to multinational companies. This move is in violation of the spirit of the Indian Constitution and against the orders of Supreme Court. The policy has recommended participatory approach in the process of management of supplying drinking water to everyone, but the effort of the government institutions and the wordings of the statement do not convey the spirit of mutual interaction. The decision making rights rest with the government and the community is only involved as stakeholders, and not as owners in the process of management. The role of the people is confined to their looking after the water sources, which would certainly dampen their enthusiasm for participation in planning, development and management of water resource projects. The contention of the government in restraining people from participation in the decision making process of water policy is that it has ample sources and plenary powers to introduce innovative ideas, pool general financial resources and initiate corporate management in water policy without any shackles.

Lack of Practical Approach

The water policy of Rajasthan Government requires coherence

and vision of grassroots democratic society (Iyer, 2002). Therefore, it is essential for the State government for adopting a practical approach in initiating new strategies according to specific situation and requirements of a region. The targets of the policy are justified and well-defined but do not elaborate the issues of institutional reforms, democratic pattern of working and formation of water user associations. The goals are appreciable but the strategies for achieving them have not been worked out (Ballabh, 2002). For instance, the policy harps on the mega projects started with external financial help. These projects of external agencies often face resistance because of their vested interests. In place of these, promotion of small projects under the management of local institutions would prove less expensive and their decentralized management would be acceptable to community. Therefore, the water policy should provide for decentralized schemes which should be devolved in self-governing institutions that are well-posted with rural areas and local needs. The participation of people is also one of the major factors for the successful implementation of any water policy. It was erroneous on the part of the government to exclude the people from controlling the supply of water resources, and depriving them from participation in decision making process and limiting their participation only to conservation and maintenance of water resources. Hence, this water policy needs modification to the extent that it should take into consideration the participative role of the Village Panchayats to decide for the type of structure of water conservation and measures for irrigation of their fields. Further, it also refers to the reclamation of waterlogged and saline affected land but it does not specify the measures to handle the problem in future. Of course, the policy stresses on the optimal productivity per unit of water by suggesting conjunctive use of ground and surface water. It advocates for a well developed information system regarding water availability, accessibility, use and free exchange of information between various agencies. But there is no provision for data compilation and the system of its collection requires updating. There is no open access to the database. Hence, these gaps in water policy require rectification.

Laxity in Implementation

There is another cause of delay in the implementation of water policy and water projects by the State. There is **no legislation** related to water resources and its use and nor is there any water law in the state. There is slackness in efforts and laxity in legal control over the groundwater resources, as Rajasthan State Government could neither form a policy to exercise control over groundwater use, nor could it enact the Ground Water Bill. The state has not adopted the laws passed by the Central Government. For instance, in 1970, 1992 and in 1996, the Ministry of Water Resources circulated to states a model Bill of Ground Water to regulate and control their development of groundwater. It has not been adopted by Rajasthan state, though Maharastra, West Bengal, Pondicherry and Gujarat have passed a Bill specifically for groundwater, while Goa, Tamil Nadu, Lakshadweep, Kerala and Andhra Pradesh have enacted it in some form of legislation. Another instance is related to the circulation to the States the Comprehensive Flood Control Master Plan by Central Government, and the Bill on flood plain zoning by Central Water Commission in 1975. Manipur is the only state to enact this as legislation.

The water policy draft of 2005 of Rajasthan State does not indicate any specific change in the spirit of its water policy of 1999. However, in general the changes suggested in the water policy draft of 2005 are superficial and confined to jugglery of words and idealistic approach. Of course, some additions are made in to the policy draft on some issues like integrated water resource management (IWRM) and participatory irrigation management (PIM). These instances are enough to reveal that there is a need for revision in the water policy and finalization of several legislative proposals for improved water management in Rajasthan State.

5.2.2 Appraisal of Water Legislation

The role of judiciary is to protect, interpret and regulate the encroachments on rights of man and society. The Supreme Court has stated in its order that 'drinking water is a fundamental right and State is duty bound to provide safe drinking water to every citizen'. The State can protect this right of man by providing water where there is none. In order to ensure adequate and requisite supply of water in all sectors according to the spirit of Constitution, the Government of India has passed legislations for the advancement of human and economic development and to safeguard the rights of people. The legislation empowers the actions, and safeguards the basic rights of the people. It helps to resolve anomalies and inequities in case of disputes and conflicts. The Constitution of India has made specific provisions regarding the individual rights of water. It recognizes that the access to water is equal for all, as it is indispensable for life.

The Articles 15 (2), 21 and 37 of the Indian Constitution explicitly state the fundamental rights, right to life and ownership and control of society on material resources. The Article 15 (2) clearly states that no citizen shall, "on grounds only of religion, race, caste, sex, place of birth or any of them be subject to any disability, liability, restriction or condition with regard to use of wells, tanks, and bathing ghats". The Article 21 provides the right to life which indirectly refers to water as essential for life. The Article 37 also recognizes the principle of equal access to material resources of the community. Similarly, Article 39 (b) refers that State shall (in particular) direct its policy towards securing the ownership and control of material resources of the community in such a way as to subserve the common good. Article 51-A (g) deals with the fundamental duties of the citizens to improve the natural environment and protect forests, lakes, rivers and wildlife and show compassion for living creatures.

Further, the Constitution of India has recognized the need of a decentralized structure of self-governance. It emphasizes self-governance at village level through Gram Panchayat which comprises the elected members of a village and is empowered to prepare plans for economic development and social justice. The Eleventh Schedule of the Constitution includes minor irrigation projects, water management and watershed development (Entry 3), drinking water (Entry 11), waterways (Entry 13), health and sanitation (Entry 23), public distribution and maintenance of community assets (Entry 28 and 29), etc. But these provisions and schemes of decentralization of power are yet to be executed by the State.

It is clearly stated in the Constitution that water related to interstate rivers and river valleys comes under the Union List (Article 246, Entry 56), and water in relation to agriculture, water supplies, irrigation, canals, drainage, sewage, embankment and water storage is enlisted in State List (Article 246, Entry 17). The Government of India has provided general guidelines for passing legislation in support of the water policy and water management. In turn, the Government of Rajasthan has adopted the laws passed by the Central Government from time to time, pertaining to irrigation, water sharing from rivers and big irrigation projects, conservation and water pollution. It has adopted some of the resolutions of the former Princely States but by and large, State Water Policy is governed by the provisions of Central Government Acts, as indicated below (Vyas, 2005).

The Rajasthan Irrigation and Drainage Act, 1954

The Act was passed to ensure irrigation and safeguard catchment areas of water bodies. The Act is mainly concerned with the control of irrigation but it also regulates its associated subjects, such as, restrictions on encroachments and dumping garbage in catchment areas of water bodies. On the other side, the Irrigation and Drainage Act, 1954 of the Rajasthan Government should be revised as it does not take into account the groundwater, which fulfills 90 per cent requirement of drinking water supply and 60 per cent of irrigation in the state.

Water (Prevention and Control of Pollution) Act, 1974

The Act was passed by the Central Government for 12 states including Rajasthan. It ensures the quality of water, provides for the prevention and control of water pollution and maintenance of quality of water. It made provision for exercising control on factories, outlets or channels carrying sewage or any other form of stagnant water which causes pollution from discharge of effluents and sewage, emission from factories rendering the water injurious for health and life of humans and animals, plants and aquatic beings. Water sources include river, water course, inland water, subterranean water, sea or tidal water. The Act made provisions to enact these through Boards to control the abstraction of water, discharging sewage, restriction on outlets and discharge.

In the face of the Acts for Prevention of Pollution and Protection of Environment, there are industries which are polluting surface and groundwater sources. Such industries are allowed to work as these are major foreign exchange earners for the Government. In such a pathetic situation the role of the Judiciary becomes important to signify that industry has no right to destroy the ecology, degrade the environment and pose health hazards.

Water (Prevention and Control of Pollution) Cess Act, 1977

The Act was enforced to augment water resources and initiate self-reliance in water services. It provides for the levy and collection of cess on the consumption of water by persons carrying on industry with a view to augment the resources of the Central Board. The collection is entrusted to local authority or any other body with the duty of supplying water. It provides meters for assessing consumption of water.

The Environment (Protection) Act, 1986

The Act provides for the protection and improvement of environment and for matters connected therewith. The decision to formulate the legislation was taken after the UN Conference on Human Environment in June 1972. The Act is related to protection and improvement of environment and prevention of hazards to human beings, other living creatures, plants, property, etc. It has defined environment which includes water, air and land and the interrelationship which exists between water, air, land and human beings, living creatures, plants, micro-organism and property. The Act extends to whole of India.

The role of Government does not end by making legislation until it is effectively implemented and its violation is seriously penalized. The catchment areas of water bodies are the property of the water resource but they are not protected against encroachments. For instance, in the Jaipur city the catchment of the Amanishah Nalla, Gullar Dam and Talkatora have been acquired by land mafias, and out of these catchment areas land has been provided for residential colonies and road. In this case, the Court of Law should enforce the legislation. Similarly, the legislation of ownership of water resources and local self-government units should be strengthened to penalize the violators. So also, there should be bylaws for sharing social responsibility by external agencies and business houses.

Besides these Central Government Acts, there are legislations passed by the State Government of Rajasthan which are indirectly related to water. These legislations could be listed as Rajasthan Minor Irrigation Act, 1943; Rajasthan Forest Act, 1953; Rajasthan Irrigation and Drainage Act, 1954; Rajasthan Land Revenue and Tenancy Acts, 1956; Rajasthan Municipalities Act, 1959; Rajasthan Soil and Water Conservation Act, 1964; Rajasthan Water Supply and Sewerage Corporation Act, 1979; Rajasthan Panchayati Raj Act, 1994; and Rajasthan Farmers Participation in Irrigation Systems Act, 2000.

The Land Regulation Act, 1990 of Rajasthan State not only prohibits conversion of any water body as a private property of an individual, group or trust, but it also treats it as an encroachment. The Rajasthan State has also formed a legislation on extraction of groundwater known as Ground Water Act more than a decade ago (1996), but it is awaiting endorsement of the Rajasthan State Legislative

Assembly. This Ground Water Bill, was initially framed by the Central Government containing directions on issues of licensing and registration for boring wells. The State Government should add significant clauses to resolve this problem by fixing the limit of the depth and the amount of extraction from the boring wells. In fact, the root cause of decrease in water level is overexploitation and low recharge. Hence, this should be kept in mind while finalizing the Bill of Ground Water.

Thus, the spate of water legislations of Central and Rajasthan State governments have emphasized judicious, equitable and sustainable distribution of water, management for utilization of water, and fixing water charges for agriculture, industrial and drinking water. Further, the introduction of autonomous bodies, such as, Water Corporation, Water Users' Associations and Ground Water Authority has also been incorporated in the Rajasthan State Water Policy. Along with these organizations, these Acts have emphasised collection of strong database on groundwater, grant of permit to extract groundwater, and legislations for construction of rain water harvesting structures.

5.3 WATER POLICY: JAIPUR DISTRICT

There is a need for adoption of a specific water policy in case of Jaipur district to meet its local geophysical variations and specific issues of water resources, but within the parameters of State Water Policy. The geographical environment of Jaipur district forewarns the scarcity of water, and indicates the necessity for the formulation of a comprehensive water policy centering on water scarcity. The scarcity of water should be accepted as a natural phenomenon and it be made a pivot for all action plans and projects. The projects of water must be guided by the consideration that Jaipur district has arid or semi-arid land where pastures can flourish more than irrigated agriculture because of lesser rain fall. The water management policy should be directed towards measures of saving water in domestic, industrial and agriculture sectors as the scarcity is both natural and man made (Mehta, 2005). The policy should have provision of equitable supply of drinking water in urban and rural areas. The amount of supply must include all domestic needs of human population and livestock. There should be efficient blockwise water resource planning aiming at converting all the available water into potable water. The state must adopt an interdisciplinary and holistic approach (figure 5.2) to revise and frame its policy, covering water quality, accessibility to water resources, their hydrological renewal, use and equitable access, water infrastructure of storage, harvesting, recycling and recharge of water, distribution network, maintenance, information system and institutional framework.

5.3.1 Augmentation of Water Resources

The water policy dwells on maximizing water availability to the state and on assessment and comprehensive maintenance of all surface and groundwater resources. Hence, surface and groundwater resources must be treated as unitary resource. In order to conserve and augment the existing water resources, the government must adopt measures for maximizing retention and minimizing losses of water. The changes in hydro-meteorological phenomenon affect the availability of water resources. For this reason, the objectives of the policy must be to conserve all water resources physically and economically as far as possible, and minimize all harmful elements. The policy should be framed according to the use of water resources and as complementary to physical factors of the region, such as, river basins and sub-basins, old water reservoirs and wells, tube wells and bore wells. An integrated water resources planning should be adopted at the river basin and sub-basin levels. There should be a detailed list of all water resources blockwise along with their water capacity. This list should also include all possible recharge structures, common buildings and pasture land which could be utilized for water harvesting and conservation. All the water reservoirs and dams should be properly defined along with their capacity and catchments. There should be a proper accounting of all water resources, water supply and proposed development projects. This information must be accessible to all institutions dealing with supply, development and maintenance of water resources. The projects of conservation, recycling and development of water resources and river basins should be prepared according to the regional needs. The budget allocation in different sectors for development of water resources, infrastructure for its storage and supply should be according to the economic, social and fiscal priorities.

It may also be pointed out in regard to application of State Water Policy in Jaipur district that annual de-silting of the lakes and step-wells, construction of walls on embankments, and beautification by growing trees and construction of check dams, developing islands for the breeding of birds in the lakes, and electrification for water supply be undertaken as a maintenance measure. The traditional water sources which have become non-functional may be renovated and recharged with the organized voluntary efforts on community level. The process of renovation and purification should be methodical and sustainable. The catchment areas of water bodies should be demarcated, cleaned and repaired. Besides taking care of urban and rural demands of water, safeguarding the life of river systems and other water bodies should be an important objective of planning. This includes maintaining minimum water flows, prevention of pollution from industry and agriculture and control of sand extraction from river bed to ensure the preservation of aquatic life and other ecological factors.

The Rajasthan State policy is silent over the rights of the individuals, community and state on water resources. In regard to Jaipur district, it may be suggested that the groundwater should be treated as a common property resource and not as owned by individuals occupying the over lying piece of land. The right to control and monitor the use of groundwater should rest with the community organizations for ensuring the use of groundwater within permissible limits. Development of groundwater resources should be maintained for recharging possibilities of water for ensuring social equity. The overexploitation of groundwater and its pernicious effects on environment should be prevented by legislation which should be effectively enforced by local self-government bodies, the WUAs and Gram Sabhas. Moreover, the Government should transfer the authority for regulating groundwater use to the lowest level, i.e., to the Gram Sabha in rural areas and Water Associations in towns. It should manage this situation by laying down the rules and regulations and monitoring its implementation. In case of default the Gram Sabha or Water Associations be penalised and in turn be authorized to recover it from individuals or groups as necessary. Further, the excessive use of groundwater should be discouraged by supplying electricity and diesel at the market rates and not on subsidised rates. The subsidies meant for the marginal and poor farmers must reach them and its misuse should be checked. This should not be given to affluent farmers.

5.3.2 Water Quality

The water policy of Rajasthan State has laid down the principles of maintaining water quality of both surface and groundwater and has stressed on a regular monitoring of water quality. On this subject it may be suggested that the drainage must be connected with sewer lines and to sewerage treatment plants. The connection of sewer lines to the lakes should be closed. The water of sewerage plant should be purified, bio-remediated and oxygenated through compressed air. Similarly, the chemicals and polluted effluents must be treated and made free of nitrogen and phosphorus before draining them in the water bodies. The quality of water must be regularly checked and kept free from pollution and acids before supply. Water quality is a major part of water policy for potable water. The water quality could be ensured by prevention of pollution of water bodies and by introduction of penalties through "polluter pays principle". Besides, improvements in existing strategies and support of new techniques based on science and technology will be necessary to eliminate the pollution of surface and groundwater resources. The recycling and re-use of water are important measures to improve water quality. Moreover, the open water bodies such as wells, tanks and lakes must be fitted with pipeline and filter so that the quality of water comes under safe category for drinking and domestic use.

The legal provision in the present policy of Rajasthan State against obstructing the flow and pollution of natural water resources can also be adopted beneficially in Jaipur district to maintain quality of water. For example, the scattered waste of open stone quarries on land in Jaipur district more often obstructs the natural flow of water to the reservoirs and dams. Thus, the quarries pollute and create shortage of water by stagnating water at inappropriate places. Similarly, pollution through industry and chemical waste is illegal. The enforcement of the legal actions and penalties needs to be strengthened to deter the defaulters.

5.3.3 Water Charges

The water policy of Rajasthan State could also be applied in Jaipur district on the issues of water tariff with slight modification. Reasonable and proportional charges for water should be levied on users but the cess should be decided in proportion to the use of water and socio-economic conditions of that area. The imposition of fees for the use of water would encourage a rational attitude for using water. The rate of water should be classified according to the user group, such as, domestic, agriculture, hotels and other commercial activities. Separate tax should be levied on large scale usage, such as, multi-storeyed complexes, swimming pools and entertainment parks and retail usage. This would inculcate among the users a sense of value for water and help in generating revenue for financing the water services, coverage of operation, maintenance expenditure and other possible interventions provided in the water resource plans.

5.3.4 Information System

The Jaipur district water policy should also elaborate on information system. On this point it may be suggested that the Government Departments should coordinate and hold meetings with representatives of water management and users of all sectors of water, such as, agriculture, industry, and society. The PHED should be made a nodal agency to coordinate with all other water departments. The assistance of media is important, as it would create consciousness of water programmes and rope in legislative members to activate political will. Besides, proper database for projects should be maintained. It would be helpful for generating awareness among the people as well as coordinating with all concerned agencies.

The effective information system in Jaipur district would integrate various agencies to avoid duplication in their work and avail of correct statistics and data to generate trustworthiness. The information regarding the availability of water, its actual use, future scarcity and demand is useful for planning and implementation of projects. The policy must make a provision for establishment of one centralized information centre at district and state levels, where the database should be pooled from all the departments. This system of information should maintain a uniform standard for coding and classification and a regular method for processing data.

5.3.5 Composition of Project

The water policy of Jaipur district also needs elaboration on people's centered water projects. These projects must focus on socio-economic benefits to the community covering development of human resources, conservation of water resources and modernization of water infrastructure along with river basin development. These projects should generate employment and contribute to food production, water security, health and sanitation and self-sufficiency in water (UNICEF, 2005). The projects should be designed on the directions of the State Water Policy according to the requirements of the water zones in Jaipur district, such as, watershed protection, flood affected areas, groundwater depletion zones, etc. The projects should be planned in three stages. First, it should focus on the positive synergies between poverty reduction, economic efficiency, and environmental protection. Secondly, it should be developed with the participation of beneficiaries. Thirdly, it should be based on an integrated approach to planning and management of natural resource in consonance with an Environment Action Plan.

5.3.6 Integrated Approach

The integrated approach envisages long term projects for educating the people and creating awareness among them for participation in all processes of planning, restoration, conservation, maintenance and use of water. The development of all water resources for Jaipur district requires the implementation of integrated, planned and multipurpose projects of irrigation, water conservation and river basin development. The Jaipur district should undertake a comprehensive exercise in water sector and prepare a Water Sector plan according to the State Water Policy (Joshi, 2006). One of the important elements of the new water policy of the district should be demand-oriented management and equal responsibility of all the sections of society in the process of development of water resources. The leading corporate houses like Tata, Wipro, Reliance, Birla, etc., can be encouraged to invest in the development of water sector in Jaipur district. The corporate houses can adopt a village or a Panchayat which can become a role model for others. In fact, these water issues can only be resolved mainly by participative development at grassroots level through grassroots democracy (Vyas, 2005).

There should be integrated planning for maximising water usability in Jaipur district. This can be planned in an integrated manner by taking into account the following types of integration: (i) between rainfall, surface water and groundwater; (ii) between different sectoral uses and environmental requirements; (iii) between structures i.e., water harvesting structures for use of water and recharge of groundwater to the high dams on the main rivers; (iv) between water to be supplied from the bigger structures to the smaller structures when required during drought or lean period; (v) between institutions at the community level, NGOs and the government; and (vi) between different types of land use like agriculture, forestry, wetlands, non-agricultural uses, flood buffer zone, etc.

The availability of usable water in Jaipur district could be increased through recycling of water, using water saving techniques of irrigation, desalination of brackish water and inter-basin transfer of water. Co-ordinated development of surface water and groundwater and its conjunctive use should be envisaged right from the initial stage of projects. The management of the water resources should be done by adopting a participatory approach between various governmental agencies, the users and other stakeholders in all processes of planning, development and management of the water resources in the district. Necessary legal and institutional changes should be made at various levels to ensure the implementation of the specified objectives. The WUAs and the local bodies, such as, municipalities and Gram Panchayats should particularly be involved in the operation, maintenance and the management of water infrastructures and other facilities. All projects that seek to conserve water or generate power should make the Environmental Impact Assessment (EIA), the Social Impact Assessment (SIA) and Cost Benefit Analysis.

5.3.7 Demand-oriented Management

The supply of water should be allocated according to the demand of water in different sectors of water use. The PHED, which would be working as a nodal department, should decide the priority of allocation of water according to the demands in different sectors of Jaipur district. Efforts should be made to generate consciousness for water saving through education, regulations, incentives and disincentives in different sectors in the following manner.

Domestic Sector : The water saving devices may be introduced in domestic uses of water, such as, installation of water meters to all consumers, introduction of progressive water tariff structure, auditing of water balance on each water distribution system and provision of separate pipelines for treated sewage water and potable water.

Industrial Sector : The industrial sector should include measures of progressive water tariff, water recycling facilities and treated urban sewage water for cooling and other processes.

Agriculture Sector : The agriculture sector should introduce revised water rates on volumetric basis on an appropriate level to yield enough revenue for maintenance costs, treated sewage water for non-edible crops and saline water for tolerant crops. Moreover, efforts should be made to initiate use of innovative irrigation practices, such as, pressure irrigation, drip and sprinkler systems for improvement in irrigation with reduced water loss. The WUAs should be made responsible for collection of water charges and to use it for maintenance. The treatment of sewage before disposal, prevention of pollution from pesticides in agriculture should be initiated through the use of bio-fertilizers and bio-pesticides. The management of river basin should be promoted in integrated manner by involving afforestation and soil conservation and livestock management.

5.3.8 Empowerment of Local Self-Government

In order to achieve successful results in demand-oriented management, it is essential to empower the local governance system. Hence, the Water Corporations should be formed in Jaipur district at grassroots level. The Government should provide funds to PHED for water infrastructure and to train its existing official staff for working in the new set-up. The constitution of Water Corporations must be based on democratic pattern with representatives of the people elected from the Water User Groups. All the necessary legal, administrative and financial provisions should aim towards the empowerment of local self-governing units and Panchayats. Access to safe water must be key indicator of all national development plans (Kathpalia, 2002).

5.4 WATER LEGISLATIONS

In order to ensure efficient management and successful implementation of water policy in Jaipur and other districts of Rajasthan State, the existing water laws must be strengthened or revised. Provision of recharge be made compulsory for the large scale water users by legislation. The ordinance must be issued and its implementation should be through community and voluntary organizations. The pending draft bill on groundwater of Rajasthan State needs to be revised in consultation with NGOs, CSOs and public forums in order to eradicate deficiencies, and should be passed at the earliest.

The legislative system of India has adopted in principle the doctrine of '**public trust**' as part of its jurisprudence. According to it, the State is a trustee of all natural resources and is under a legal obligation to protect the natural resources. The conflict of private ownership could be resolved by legislation. The issues of ownership and control of State versus village level administrative units on distribution of groundwater, and conservation of rain water also needs explanation by legislation. Similarly, the issue regarding equal access to water at the community level faces challenge in the prevalent caste structure of rural society (Ramnathan, 1992: 1-6).

There is also need for a legislative provision for regulating sewage collection system and for providing treatment to control water borne diseases. The rural and suburban towns have been lacking access to drinking water and sanitation facilities. The prevalent system of manually collecting and carrying garbage and excreta from the houses should be stopped by legislation. Besides, the legislation should also contain remedial measures for sewage collection and treatment.

The State Pollution Control Board of Rajasthan State can extend its nominal cess on extracting of groundwater by domestic and other commercial users like industrial units. The laws governing ownership of groundwater on private land and water assets should be reviewed and restrictions be imposed on the ownership of a farmer's well in his field and also on reservoirs and other water assets belonging to community. On this count, the exploitation of groundwater by a large number of well owners engaged in supply of groundwater to private colonies in the suburbs of Jaipur city and for agriculture also requires immediate prohibitory measures by legislation. The 73rd Amendment has provided self-governance which entails the strengthening of the WUAs and VWSCs by active legal support. The Acts must specify a decisive role to WUAs in the distribution of water and setting up of allocation priorities. A comprehensive change in existing legislation on water is a prerequisite for the implementation of community participation.

The Rajasthan State is also involved with the neighbouring states of Punjab and Haryana on the issue of distribution of river water. So also, there are instances of disputes between the States owing to extraction of groundwater and public and private water supply system. For immediate resolution of such interstate water disputes, an independent commission should be constituted comprising affected parties, local community, subject specialists and independent person of high repute in public life. Cross-sectoral water sector agreements, framing of policies and their implementation should ensure that subject experts are incorporated at every stage. It should be ensured that all water resources available within the boundaries of the State, whether surface or groundwaters, regional waters or rivers are considered State owned property. Of course, there is a law for selling of water but it is not strictly enforced. As a result of this, a water market in the form of domestic water sale by trucks from private wells is practised. Illegal water markets between farmers and well owners are in operation in some areas without the sanction of the concerned Authority.

In a nutshell, the water policy of Rajasthan state needs review and practical approach for its implementation and should have support of well defined legislation to succeed in achieving its objectives of bringing about social and economic development of the Jaipur district.

❑❑❑

6

Conclusion

The water resources play an important role in economic development and social progress of a country. This relationship between water and economic development is becoming complex due to ecological, social and demographic changes leading to depletion of water level, pollution, salinity and degraded quality of water, which are also potential health hazards. This complexity would tend to rise if water is not managed properly with respect to its demand and supply. The issues related to water scarcity, distributional inequality, neglect and ignorance of community about its conservation have to be dealt with serious thought and concern.

There is a natural water scarcity in Rajasthan state as well as Jaipur district due to physiographical features and gradual advancement of the region towards chronic water scarcity conditions with the growth of population. There are ample possibilities for conservation and development of water resources in the district. Proper conservation of rain water, protection of forest cover and environment, and renewal of groundwater within reasonable limits would facilitate economic development of the region.

It is essential to manage, protect and develop traditional as well as other water resources. There is lack of surface water resources and the status of groundwater in Jaipur district is also in semi-critical and overexploited stage. It is not only because of environmental changes but also due to patterns of human activities, and extended use of groundwater in municipal, industrial and agricultural sectors. The assessment of total water availability has led to several issues, such as deficiency of surface water resources, increase in encroachments in catchment areas, groundwater depletion, natural resources as common property, poor water quality, etc.

Availability and accessibility to safe and clean water is essential for economic development as it generates economic, health and various other benefits, which sequentially increases productivity and efficiency of the people. Improved access to water provides better irrigation facilities, which in turn increases agricultural productivity and promotes the use of new technology, HYV seeds, crop diversification leading to increase in crop yield. Improved water supply, sanitation and water resources management boosts economic growth and contributes substantially to health and poverty alleviation. Reliable and sufficient water availability and accessibility increase opportunities for education, employment and other productive activities. Increase in water storage capacity is essential to overcome the negative effects of rainfall variability in the region. Physical water scarcity could be overcome through integrated water management and economic development as it leads to better adaptive capacities to climate variability and improved ecosystem.

The Jaipur district is heading towards chronic water scarcity conditions. It is in a much better condition in water poverty and water accessibility as compared to other districts of the state as it is in medium water poverty condition. Most of the districts of the state are in high water poverty conditions. They lack in water distribution provision and accessibility. The water poverty conditions indicate poor water infrastructure in the state, especially with respect to access to drinking water and sanitation.

Institutional framework for management consists mainly of government departments. The participation of NGOs, Corporate houses and media in management process is marginal and confined to limited areas. Presently, it does not inculcate self-sufficiency and cohesion in the community for water projects. The management practices are not focused on targets of equitable supply, optimum use of surface water, augmentation of groundwater, conservation of water, watersheds and self-sufficiency in managing water projects.

The water distribution system in the urban areas of the district is faulty. There is no provision to minimize losses during transport of water and leakages. The control cells have been set-up to work round the clock in urban areas to attend promptly to complaints, yet these are not streamlined. The rural areas of the district are not well connected to water supply network and still depend on sources other than tap. The PHED supplies water for domestic and industrial uses. It has not been able to raise sufficient funds of its own due to low revenue generation. The water charges are neither revised nor recovered and thus, the department is bearing continuous loss.

The water supply in the urban areas does not ensure regular supply of good quality water. There is no provision of waste water recycling for reuse of water especially in domestic and industrial sectors. There is lack of coordination among related departments, viz., water supply, sanitation and waste collection and disposal of sewerage.

The water policy of Rajasthan state has not been formulated in view of the growing water scarcity in the region. It is an adaptation of the National Water Policy under the directives of the central government. In principle, the water policy of Rajasthan state encompasses equitable supply, maximum use of surface water, development and conservation of water resources, self-sufficiency in water projects involving local-self governance. In practice, the policy lacks clarity, regional specificity, practical approach to problems of management of water resources, implementation of irrigation projects and support of water legislation.

The revised Rajasthan water policy of 2005 is still in the stage of draft and is awaiting approval of the government. So also, the Ground Water Bill is awaiting approval of the Rajasthan State Legislative Assembly. There are Acts pertaining to water pollution, drainage, and environment but there is laxity in their implementation and execution.

SUGGESTIONS

Several corrective measures could be suggested to resolve the emerging issues to achieve a balance between demand and supply of water. These issues cover rain water harvesting, artificial recharge methods, watershed structures, rejuvenation of surface water resources, restoration and renovation of supply network.

(i) The surface water may be utilized for water supply after the onset of monsoon till its end. The use of groundwater during this period may be minimized and stepped up thereafter. This will conserve precious groundwater resources for use during the lean period.

(ii) Structural shift from water-intensive agriculture and industries should be promoted as it would decrease economic vulnerability due to water scarcity.

(iii) The water supply services in domestic sector should primarily be focused on drinking water and sanitation. A basic minimum supply of drinking water must be ensured to the disadvantaged sections of society at subsidized rates.

(iv) The use of software technology must be encouraged to share the information. The information of meteorological forecasts and satellite images from remote sensing should be made available to farmers to guard against flood and drought. Information regarding the total water requirements including village-wise data of water supply and list of water deficient villages should be regularly updated for showing the percentage of water requirement.

(v) The water sector needs institutional reforms in order to improve its efficiency in irrigation, rural and urban water supply and sanitation. The government should seek advise from a group of experts on all water issues. This would facilitate in creating public opinion and awareness among people on water issues. In this strategy of gradual and sequential reforms, the role of public education and consensus building is extremely important.

(vi) Special attention should be given to ensure supply of potable water to all schools especially in rural areas through PHED, PRI, PWD or Education Department. The government should provide adequate funds to the Education Department for this purpose and authorize it to coordinate with concerned departments.

(vii) The major challenges in the development of water infrastructure in Jaipur district are – maintenance, operation and management. The water apparatus must include the key factors of management i.e., participation of community, incentives by government, water entitlements, transparency, entry of private sector, competition, accountability, financing and environmental quality. Attitudinal change among the functionaries of the water-related departments is essential to deal with the problems of water in an integrated manner. They should prepare time-bound plans for the implementation of management strategies.

(viii) In order to increase irrigation efficiency it is advisable to adopt a comprehensive approach covering demand-oriented water supply, new irrigation techniques requiring less water, agronomic reforms and management of medium and minor irrigation projects.

(ix) The reuse of domestic waste water, recycled water and treatment of sewage and industrial waste water should be encouraged by the government by installing sewage treatment plants in urban areas. The industrial sector should be encouraged for the use of recycled water and for the installation of their own plants of water recycling.

(x) The treated water could also be utilized for irrigation of non-edible crops, development of gardens, fire fighting, washing of roads and flushing of sewer lines through dual pipe lines.

(xi) There is a need for the formation of a central planning department and also restructuring of the government institutions for integrated development of water resources. This would facilitate the management of equitable supply of water, water tariff to cover operation and maintenance, and to counter privatization efforts from external agencies.

(xii) The cost of operation and maintenance of water supply should be gradually recovered from the people with the provision that this could be in cash or service in rural areas.

POLICY IMPLICATIONS

The following are the policy implications :

(i) The Rajasthan state should develop a comprehensive water sector plan for the development of its water resources with the objectives of providing safe and clean drinking water on priority along with irrigation requirements.

(ii) The government should pay adequate attention to rural water supply and sanitation facilities. It should implement its special programmes in the districts having scarcity and difficulty in accessibility of water for drinking and sanitation services.

(iii) The government should plan a campaign to recharge groundwater and harvest the surface run-off in areas with untapped potential expeditiously. A long term programme must be enforced to check deforestation, mining and soil conservation activities for water conservation.

(iv) The river basin organizations (RBOs) should be developed at district and state levels. This organisation must comprise experts in water supply, quality, management and economic development at state level to provide specific guidelines for planning and management of river basins and sub-basins along with other water resources.

(v) The administrative set-up in all the water related departments of the state government, such as Ground Water Department, the Irrigation Department, the PHED and other line departments may be organized under one umbrella. A central organization is required for water management in the district to monitor and coordinate at the decentralized level and to implement various strategies and schemes.

(vi) The State Government should prepare a White Paper on water policy. The work and duties of the institutions should be clearly spelled out at the time of their formation and accountability must be ensured.

(vii) The Rajasthan State Water Policy should be based on hydrological cycle of the region. It should curtail human activities responsible for pollution, wastage, exploitation of water and promote favourable human activity to conserve water, plantation of vegetation and forest. It should follow the spirit of the Indian Constitution that water is a common property resource and a fundamental right.

(viii) There should be a comprehensive water law for the management and rational use of surface water, groundwater; and to prevent encroachments in catchment areas, pollution and interstate river water disputes.

(ix) The issues of ownership of land over groundwater should be clearly defined as common pool resource. These issues should be resolved through formation of organizations of (i) owners of land, and (ii) users of water and (iii) by experts having technical information of groundwater.

(x) The legislations must direct the industries to avoid pollution through industrial effluents into water bodies and instruct them to install treatment plants for polluted discharge. Besides, there should be incentives for industries which have made efforts to treat and recycle their polluted water.

(xi) The Rajasthan Groundwater (Regulation) Bill 1997 should be passed and executed in the light of present groundwater scenario. However, it should be preceded by creating a mass awareness among the people strict for regulation over extraction of groundwater.

(xii) A Water Regulatory Agency should be established for the approximation of progressive cost of water when it is used as an economic good, as has been proposed in Maharashtra. Its organization could be modelled after the existing autonomous Rajasthan State Power Regulatory Authority.

Thus, it could be concluded from the present study that the major issues regarding water scarcity and disparity in distribution of water are not only the result of negative impacts of nature and ecological factors, but are also mostly man made and could be avoided through efficient management, comprehensive State Water Policy, and supportive and active legislations for water resources. In order to ensure economic development and efficiency in water distribution and its optimum utilization for the advancement of human life, sustainable efforts should be made in the direction of the restoration of local-self governance through extension programmes and education of women and children. Though these are all long term measures and the results would not be visible immediately but they would prove sustainable in local-self governance, generating awareness and harnessing responsible water uses. All this would certainly lead to efficient management and economic development in Rajasthan state and Jaipur district.

❑❑❑

Bibliography

I. Books and Articles

Acharya, Shabd S. and M.S. Rathore, (2005), "Emerging Issues in Water Management: The Question of Ownership", *Institute of Development Studies* (IDS), Jaipur.

Agarwal, A. and Sunita Narain, (eds.), (1997), *Dying Wisdom: India's Environment, A Citizens' Report*, Centre for Science and Environment, New Delhi.

Agarwal, Anil, James Kimondo, Gloria Moreno and Jon Tinker, (1981), *Water, Sanitation, Health - for All?* (Prospects for the International Drinking Water Supply and Sanitation Decade, 1981-90), Earthscan Publications, London.

Agarwal, Anil, Sunita Narain and Indira Khurana, (eds.), (2001), *Making Water Everybody's Business: Practice and Policy of Water Harvesting*, Centre for Science and Environment, New Delhi.

Aitken, C. K., et.al., (1994), "Residential Water Use: Predicting and Reducing Consumption", *Journal of Applied Social Psychology*, Vol. 24, 16 January, pp. 136-158.

Alam, Jayanti, (2004), "Water, Not for Private Ownership", *EPW*, July 24, pp. 3351-3352.

Alexander, K.C., "Economic Development and Social Change", *Journal of Rural Development*, Vol.1, No. 6.

Allen, Adriana, Julio Davila, and Pascale Hoffman, (2006), "Governance of Water and Sanitation Services for the Peri-Urban Poor: A Framework for Understanding and Action in Metropolitan Regions", University College London, Development Planning Unit, London.

Anand, Sudhir and Amartya Sen, (1994), "Human Development Index: Methodology and Measurement", Occasional Paper 12, United Nations Development Programme, Human Development Report Office, New York.

Appasamy, Paul P., (2004), "Managing Conflict in the Bhavani River Basin", in Vaidyanathan, A. and H.M. Oudshoom, (ed.), *Managing Water Scarcity: Experiences and Prospects,* Manohar Publishers, New Delhi.

Bajpai, Peeyush and Laveesh Bhandari, (2001), "Ensuring Access to Water in Urban Households", *EPW,* September 29, pp. 3774-3778.

Balak, Ram, N. Singh, and J.S. Chauhan, (1995), "Mapping of Khadin–A Typical Farming System of Thar Desert", *Indian Cartographer,* Vol. 15, pp. 45-49.

Ballabh, V. and Katar Singh, (1997), "Competing Demands for Water in Sabarmati Basin: Potential and Future Conflicts", *IDPAD Seminar on Managing Water Scarcity: Experiences and Future Prospects,* Amersfort, Netherlands, Oct. 11-17.

Ballabh, V., (2002), "Emerging Water Crisis and Political Economy of Irrigation Reforms in India", *Workshop on Asian Irrigation in Transition Responding to the Challenges Ahead,* Asian Institute of Technology, Bangkok, 22-23 April.

Ballabh, V., Dinesh Kumar and Jayesh Talati, (1999), "Food Security and Water Management: Institutional Challenges for Early 21st Century", *National Symposium on Building and Managing Organizations for Rural Development,* Institute of Rural Management, Anand, December 13-14.

Ballabh, Vishwa, (2003), "Politics of Water Management and Sustainable Water Use", *Indian Journal of Agricultural Economics,* Vol. 58, No. 3, July-September, pp. 467-476.

Bandyopadhyay, J. and B. Mallik, (2003), "Population and Water Resources in India: Crucial Gaps in Knowledge for Sustainable Use in Future", in Sengupta, R. and A.K. Sinha, (eds.), *Challenge of Sustainable Development: The Indian Dynamics*, CDEP-IIMC, Kolkata and Manak Publishers, New Delhi, pp. 81-111.

Bandyopadhyay, Jayanta, (2009), *Water, Ecosystems and Society : A Confluence of Disciplines*, Indian Institute of Management, Calcutta.

Barbier, Edward B., (1989), *Economics, Natural Resources Scarcity and Development: Conventional and Alternative Views*, Earthscan Publications Ltd., London.

Bardhan, Pranab and Dilip Mookherjee, (eds.), (2007), *Decentralization and Local Governance in Developing Countries: A Comparative Perspective*, Oxford University Press, New Delhi.

Bell, Frances, and Robert Millward, (1998), "Public Health Expenditures and Mortality in England and Wales, 1870-1914." *Continuity and Change*, Vol. 13, No. 2, pp. 221–49.

Bell, S. and S. Morse, (1999), *Sustainability Indicators: Measuring the Immeasureable*, Earthscan, London.

Bhandari, L.M., T.N. Bhargava, A.D. Purohit, and I.C. Gupta, "Potability Classification of Ground Waters in Arid Zone of Western Rajasthan", *Annals of Arid Zone*, Vol. 9, pp. 221-223.

Bhati, Vinita M., (ed.), (1996), *Water Resources and their Utilization*, Vigyan Prakashan, Jodhpur.

Bhatia, Ramesh, (2007), "Water and Economic Growth", in Briscoe and Malik, (eds.), (2007), *Handbook of Water Resources in India: Development, Management and Strategies*, The World Bank, Oxford University Press, New Delhi, pp. 99-136.

Bhowmik, K.L., (ed.), (1988), "Ecology and Human Development", *Current Anthropological and Perspectives*, Vol. 5, Inter India Publication, New Delhi.

Birkenholtz, Trevor, (2004), "Tubewell Institutions in Rajasthan", *Rajasthan Studies Centre*, Jaipur.

Biswas, A.K., (1976), *Systems Approach in Water Management*, Tata McGraw Hill, Tata Publishing Company, New Delhi.

Biswas, Asit K. and Juha I. Uitto, (eds.), (2001), *Sustainable Development of the Ganges-Brahmaputra-Meghna Basins*, Oxford University Press, New Delhi.

Biswas, Asit K., (ed.), (1978), *Water Development and Management, Proceedings of the United Nations Water Conference*, Vol. I, Part 4, Robert Maxwell, Pergamon Press, Oxford.

Biswas, Asit K., Ceasar Herrarpa Toleda, Hector Ganduno Velasco and Cecilia Tortajadz Quiroz, (1997), *National Water Master Plans for Developing Countries*, Oxford University Press, New Delhi.

Biswas, Asit K., Mohammad Jellali and Glenn Stout, (eds.), (1993), *Water for Sustainable Development in the Twenty First Century*, Water Resources Management Series: 1, Oxford University Press, Delhi.

Black, Maggie and Talbot, (2005), *Water – A Matter of Life and Health*, UNICEF and Oxford University Press, New Delhi.

Briscoe, John and A. Garn Harvey, (1995), "Financing Water Supply and Sanitation Under Agenda 21", *Natural Resources Forum*, Vol. 19, February, pp. 59-70.

Briscoe, John and R.P.S. Malik, (2006), *India's Water Economy Bracing for a Turbulent Future*, Oxford University Press, New Delhi.

Briscoe, John and R.P.S. Malik, (eds.), (2007), *Handbook of Water Resources in India*, The World Bank, Oxford University Press, New Delhi.

Bromley, Daniel W., (1982), "Land and Water Problems: An Institutional Perspective", *American Journal of Agricultural Economics*, Vol. 64, December, pp. 834-44.

Bromley, Daniel W., (1989), "Property Relations and Economic Development: The Other Land Reform", *World Development*, Vol. 17, No 6.

Bromley, Daniel W., (1989), *Economic Interests and Institutions: The Conceptual Foundations of Public Policy*, Basil Blackwell, New York.

Bromley, Daniel W., (1993), "Reconstituting Economic Systems: Institutions in National Economic Development", *Development Policy Review*, Vol. 11.

Cahill, Michael and Pattrick Tony Fitz, (eds.), (2002), *Environmental Issues and Social Welfare: Broadening Perspectives on Social Policy*, Blackwell Publishing Company, U.K.

Cairncross, Sandy, (1987), "Benefits of Water Supply", *Developing World Water*, Grosvenor Press International, Hong Kong, pp. 30-33.

Calla, S.N., (2006), "Water Crisis in Urban Rajasthan", Briefing Paper in Joshi, Sharad, (ed.), (2006), *Rajasthan Pani Utsav*, Cecoedecon, Jaipur.

Camara, Antonie S., (2002), *Environmental Systems: A Multidimensional Approach*, Oxford University Press, London.

Carley, Michael, and Ian Christie, (1992), *Managing Sustainable Development*, Earthscan Publications Ltd., London.

Carney, D., (ed.), (1998), *Sustainable Rural Livelihoods: What Contribution Can We Make*? DFID, London.

Carruthers, I.D. and J.A. Morrison, (1992), *Institutions and Social Conflict*, Cambridge University Press.

Carruthers, I.D. and J.A. Morrison, (1996), "Institutions in Water Resources Management: Insights from New Institutional Economics", in Howson, P. and R.C. Carter, (eds.), (1996), *Water Policy: Allocations and Management in Practice*, Proceedings of International Conference on Water Policy, E&FN Spon, London, pp.205-12.

Carter, Richard C., (1998), "Water Policy and Policy Implementation", *Water Lines*, Vol. 16, No. 3, January, pp. 2-8.

Chatterji, P.C., N.S. Vangani and M.L. Sharma, (1985), "Unmanaged Drinking Water Sources in Arid Area of Rajasthan: A Case Study of Nagaur District", *Annals of Arid Zone*, Vol. 24, pp. 47-55.

Chattopadhyay, S.K. and H.S. Sharma, (1998), *Sustainable Development: Issues and Case Studies*, Concept Publishing Company, Delhi.

Chaturvedi, M.C., (1976), *Water in Second India* – Second India Studies, Ford Foundation, Macmillan.

Chaturvedi, M.C., (1987), *Water Resources Systems, Planning and Management*, Tata McGraw Hill Publishing Company Ltd., New Delhi.

Chopra, (2001), *Migration, Common Property Resources and Environmental Degradation: Interlinkages in India's Arid and Semi-Arid Regions*, Sage Publications, New Delhi.

Chopra, K. and B. Goldar, (2000), *Sustainable Development Framework for India: The Case of Water Resources*, Report prepared for the United Nations University, Tokyo, Institute of Economic Growth, New Delhi.

Chopra, Kanchan and Gopal K. Kadekodi, (1993), "Watershed Development: A Contrast with NREP/JRY", *EPW*, June 26.

Chopra, Kanchan, C.H. Hanumantha Rao and R.P. Sengupta, (eds.), (2003), *Water Resource, Sustainable Livelihoods and Eco-system Services*, Concept Publishing Company, New Delhi.

Chouhan, T.S., (1995), *Indian Desert: Resources and Perspective Development*, Printwell Publishers, Jaipur.

Chouhan, T.S., (1996), "Water Resources of India: Appraisal, Conservation and Management", in Bhati, Vinita M., (ed.), (1996), *Water Resources and their Utilization*, Vigyan Prakashan, Jodhpur, pp. 18-64.

Churchill, A., (1987), *Rural Water Supply and Sanitation: Time for a Change*, The World Bank, Washington DC.

Cleaver, Frances, (1998), "Incentives and Informal Institutions: Gender and the Management of Water", *Agriculture and Human Values*, Vol. 15, No. 4, pp.347-60, also in Saleth, Maria, (ed.), (2002), *Water Resources and Economic Development*, Edward Elgar Publishing Ltd., Cheltenham, U.K.

Cosgrove, W. and F.R. Rijsberman, (2000), *World Water Vision: Making Water Everybody's Business*, Earthscan Publications Ltd., London.

Cullet, Philippe, (2006), "Water Law Reforms: Analysis of Recent Developments", *Journal of Indian Law Institute*, Vol. 48, No. 2, pp. 206-231.

Cullet, Philippe, (2009), *"Water Law, Poverty and Development: Water Sector Reforms in India"*, Oxford University Press, New York.

Custodio, E. and A. Gurgui, (eds.), (1989), *Development in Water Science: Ground Water Economics*, Vol.39, Elsevier Science Publisher, Amsterdam.

Dalal, K.L., (1991), *Human Development: An Indian Perspective*, Vikas, New Delhi.

Das, Binayak and Ganesh Pangare, (2006), "In Chattisgarh, a River becomes Private Property", *EPW*, February 18, pp. 611-612.

Dastance, N.G., (1970), "Water Management Research in India", *Indian Journal of Agronomy*, Vol. 25, No. 4.

Deolalikar, Anil B., (2005), *Attaining the Millennium Development Goals in India*, The World Bank, Oxford University Press, New Delhi.

Desai, M., (1995), *Poverty, Famine and Economic Development*, Edward Elgar, Aldershot, U.K.

Deshpande, R.S., (2005), "Community Management of Water: Experience and Issues", *Institute of Development Studies*, Jaipur.

Dhawan, B.D., (1982), *Development of Tubewell Irrigation in India*, Agricole Publishing Academy, New Delhi.

Dhawan, B.D., (1993), *Indian Water Resource Development for Irrigation,* Commonwealth, New Delhi.

Dhawan, B.D., (1999), *Studies in Indian Irrigation Problems,* Commonwealth Publishers, New Delhi.

Dhawan, B.D., (2002), *Technological Agriculture: A Study of Water Saving Method,* Commonwealth, New Delhi.

Dhillon, Paul Singh, (1988), *Water Resources Development and Management in North-West India,* CRRID Publication, Chandigarh.

Dixon, John A., (1992), "Analysis and Management of Watersheds" in Dasgupta, Partha and Karl-Goran Maler, (eds), (1992), *The Environment and Emerging Development Issues,* Vol 2, Clarendon Press, Oxford.

Driscoll, Fletcher G., (1987), *Ground Water Wells,* Johnson Division, St. Paul, Minnesota, U.S.A.

Dubash, Nauroz K., (2002), *Tubewell Capitalism: Ground Water Development and Agrarian Change in Gujarat,* Oxford University Press, New Delhi.

Dutta Roy, B. and R.P. Athaparia, (eds.), (1999), *Water and Water Resource Management,* Omsons Publications, New Delhi.

Eckstein, Gabriel and Yoram Eckstein, (2003), "A Hydrological Approach to Transboundary Ground Water Resources and International Law", *Eckstein Finished. Doc,* Internet based International Water Law Project available at http://www.internationalwaterlaw.org, pp. 201-258.

Editorial, (2002), "Water Policy: Many Loose Ends", *EPW,* April 6.

El-Hinnawi, Essam and Manzur H. Hashmi, (1987), *The State of the Environment,* United Nations Environment Programme (UNEP), Butterworths, London.

Evans, P. and B. Appleton, (1993), "Community Management Today: The Role of Communities in the Management of Improved Water Supply Systems", Occasional Paper 20, IRC, The Hague.

Falkenmark, M. and C. Widstrand, (1992), "Population and Water Resources: A Delicate Balance", *Population Bulletin,* Population Reference Bureau, Washington.

Falkenmark, M., J. Lundqvist and C. Widstrand, (1989), "Macro-scale Water Scarcity Requires Micro-scale Approaches: Aspects of Vulnerability in Semi-arid Development", *Natural Resources Forum,* Vol. 13, No. 4, pp. 258-267.

Falkenmark, Malin and Gunnar Lindh, (1993), "Water and Economic Development", in Peter H. Gleick (ed.), *Water in Crisis: A Guide to the World's Fresh Water Resources,* Chapter 7, Oxford University Press, New York, pp. 80-91.

Falkenmark, Malin, (1999), "Forward to the Future: A Conceptual Framework for Water Dependence", Ambio, Vol. 28, No. 4, June, pp. 356 – 61, also in Saleth, R. Maria, (ed.), (2002), *Water Resources and Economic Development,* Edward Elgar Publishing Limited, Cheltenham, UK, pp. 3-8.

Faroda, A.S. and Manjit Singh, (eds.), (1998), *Fifty Years of Arid Zone, Research in India,* Central Arid Zone Research Institute, Jodhpur.

Faroda, A.S., N.L. Joshi, S. Kathjee, and Amalkar, (eds.), (1999), *Management of Arid CCD System,* CAZRI, Scientific Publishers, Jodhpur.

Feder, G. and G. LeMoigne, (1994), "Managing Water in Sustainable Manner", *Finance Development,* Vol. 31, June, pp. 24-27.

Fonesca, Catarina and Eveline Bolt, (2002), *How to Support Community Management Water Supplies: Guidelines for Managers,* IRC, International Water and Sanitation Centre, Netherlands.

Foster, Stephen, Adrian Lawrence and Brian Morris, (1998), "Ground Water in Urban Development: Assessing Management Needs and Formulating Policy Strategies", *World Bank Technical Paper No. 390,* The World Bank, Washington DC.

Gadgil, Sulochana and Siddhartha Gadgil, (2006), "The Indian Monsoon, GDP and Agriculture", *EPW,* November 25, pp. 4887-4895.

Garn, M., (1998), "Managing Water as an Economic Good: The Transition from Supply-Oriented to Demand-Responsive Services", New York. *World Bank Water and Sanitation Programme.*

Ghosh, Gouri Shankar, (1995), *Water Supply in Rural India: Policy and Programme,* Ashish Publishing House, New Delhi.

Gleick, P, (2000), *The World's Water 2000-2001: The Biennial Report on Freshwater Resources,* Island Press, Oakland California.

Gleick, P.H., (1997), "Human Population and Water: Meeting Basic Needs in the 21st Century", in Pachauri, R.K. and Lubina F. Qureshi, (eds.), *Population, Environment and Development,* TERI, New Delhi.

Gleick, P.H., (2000), *The World's Water, 2000-2001: The Biennial Report on Freshwater Resources*, Island Press, Washington DC.

Gleick, Peter H., (1993), "Water in the 21st Century", in Gleick, Peter H., (ed.), (1993), *Water in Crisis: A Guide to the World's Freshwater Resources*, Oxford University Press, New York, pp. 105-113, also printed in Saleth, R. Maria, (ed.), (2002), *Water Resources and Economic Development*, Edward Elgar Publishing Limited, Cheltenham, U.K., pp. 9-17.

Gleick, Peter H., (1997), "Basic Water Requirements for Human Activities: Meeting basic Needs", *Water International*, Vol. 21, No. 2, June, pp. 83 – 92, printed in Saleth, R. Maria, (ed.), (2002), *Water Resources and Economic Development*, Edward Elgar Publishing Limited, Cheltenham, U.K., pp. 496-505.

Gleick, Peter H., (1998), "Water and Human Health", in Peter H. Gleick (ed.), *The World's Water: The Biennial Report on Fresh Water Resources*, Chapter 2, Island Press, Washington DC, pp. 39-67.

Gleick, Peter, (1999), "The Human Rights to Water", *Water Policy* I, Elsevier Science Publishers, Amsterdam.

Goldar, (2003), "Water Use in India: Industry Estimates of Value of Water and Price and Elasticity of Demand", in Chopra, (ed.), *Water Resources, Sustainable Livelihoods and Eco-System Service*, Concept Publishing Company, New Delhi.

Guha, Ramchandra, (ed.), (1994), *Social Ecology*, Oxford University Press, New Delhi.

Gupta, Avijit and Mukul G. Asher, (1998), *Environment and the Developing World: Principles, Policies and Management*, John Wiley and Sons., New York.

Gupta, N.L., (ed.), (1994), *Urban Water Supply*, Rawat Publication, Jaipur.

Gupta, S.K., (2000), *Sustainable Development Framework for India: The Case of Water Resources*, Institute of Economic Growth, New Delhi.

Hansen, S., and R. Bhatia, (2004), "Water and Poverty in a Macroeconomic Context.", paper commissioned by the Norwegian Ministry of the Environment in preparation for the United Nations Commission on Sustainable Development , New York.

Harold, Thomas E., (1951), *The Conservation of Ground Water: A Survey of the Present Ground-Water Situation in the United States*, McGraw Hill Book Company, Inc., New York.

Hassan, J. A., (1985), "The Growth and Impact of the British Water Industry in the Nineteenth Century", *The Economic History Review*, New Series, Vol. 38, No. 4, pp. 531–47.

Heidecke, Claudia, (2006), "Development and Evaluation of a Regional Water Poverty Index for Benin", *Environment and Production Technology Division*, Discussion Paper 145, IFPRI, Washington DC.

Holland, Sjolander Ann Christin, (2006), *The Water Business – Corporation versus People*, Books for Change, Bangalore.

Holmberg, Johan, (ed.), (1992), *Policies for a Small Planet*, International Institute for Environment and Development, Earthscan Publication Ltd., London.

Hooja, R., G. Pangare and K.V. Raju, (eds.), (2002), *Users in Water Management: The Andhra Model and Its Replicability in India*, Rawat Publications, New Delhi.

Hooja, Rakesh and Rajendra Joshi, (eds.), (1999), *Desert, Drought and Development: Studies in Resource Management and Sustainability*, Institute of Rajasthan Studies, Rawat Publications, Jaipur.

Hooja, Rakesh, (2006), *Management of Water for Agriculture: Irrigation, Watersheds and Drainage*, Rawat Publications, Jaipur.

Hooja, Rakshat, (2005), "Participatory Planning / Implementation and Promoting Collective Action: A Case Study of the Methods used by Tarun Bharat Sangh for undertaking Water Harvesting Projects in Rajasthan", IDS, Jaipur.

Hord, R. Michael, (1986), *Remote Sensing: Methods and Applications*, John Wiley & Sons., New York.

Hufschmidt, Maynard M., (1993), "Water Policy for Sustainable Development", in Biswas, Asit K., Mohammed Jellali and Glenn E. Stout, (eds.), (1993), *Water for Sustainable Development in the Twenty First Century*, Chapter 6, Oxford University Press, New Delhi, pp. 60-69, also in Saleth, R. Maria, (ed.), (2002), *Water Resources and Economic Development*, Edward Elgar Publishing Limited, Cheltenham, U.K.

Hussain, Intizar, Liqa Raschid, Munir A. Hanjra, et.al., (2002), "Wastewater Use in Agriculture: Review of Impacts and Methodological Issues in Valuing Impacts", Working Paper 37, *International Water Management Institute*, Sri Lanka.

Indian Tobacco Company (ITC), (2006), "Transforming Lives and Landscapes: ITC's Community Development Philosophy at Work", *Sunehara Kal*, available from ITC website.

Inoguchi, Takashi, Edward Newman and Glen Paoletto, (eds.), (1999), *Cities and the Environment: New Approaches for Eco-Societies*, United Nations University Press, Tokyo.

Iyer, Gopal K., (1996), *Sustainable Development: Ecological and Socio-Cultural Dimensions*, Vikas IV, New Delhi.

Iyer, Ramaswamy R., (1994), "Federalism and Water Resources", *EPW*, March 26, pp. 733-736.

Iyer, Ramaswamy R., (2001), "Water: Charting a Course for the Future", *EPW*, April 14.

Iyer, Ramaswamy R., (2002), "The New National Water Policy", *EPW*, May 4.

Iyer, Ramaswamy R., (2003), *Water: Perspectives, Issues, Concerns*, Sage Publications, New Delhi.

Iyer, Ramaswamy R., (2006), "Water Resource Management: Some Comments", *EPW*, November 4, p. 4623.

Iyer, Ramaswamy R., (2007), *Towards Water Wisdom: Limits, Justice, Harmony*, Sage Publications, New Delhi.

Iyer, R.R. (ed.), (2009), *Water and the Laws in India"*, Centre for Policy Research, New Delhi.

Jairath, Jasveen, (2001), *Water User Associations in Andhra Pradesh–Initial Feedback*, Centre for Economic and Social Studies, Hyderabad, Concept Publishing Company, New Delhi.

James, A. J., Joep Verhagen, Christine van Wijk, Reema Nanavaty, Mita Parikh, and Mihir Bhatt, (2002), "Transforming Time into Money Using Water: A Participatory Study of Economics and Gender in Rural India", *Natural Resources Forum*, Vol. 26, No. 3, pp. 205–17.

James, L.D. and R. Lee, (1971), *Economics of Water Resources Planning*, McGraw Hill Publishing Co., Bombay.

Janakrajan, S., (2004), "Conflict over the Use of Ground Water: Some Evidence from Tamil Nadu", in Vaidyanathan A. and H.M. Oudshoom, (eds.), *Managing Water Scarcity – Experiences and Prospects*, Manohar Publishers, New Delhi.

Jansky, Libor and Juha I. Uitto, (eds.), (2006), *Enhancing Participation and Governance in Water Resources Management: Conventional Approaches and Information Technology*, Bookwell, New Delhi, First published in 2005 by the United Nations Press.

Jensen, J.R., et.al., (eds.), (1996), *Watershed Development: Emerging Issues and Framework of Action Plan for Strengthening a Learning Process at All Levels*, Watershed Development Coordination Unit (WDCU), Publication No.1, New Delhi.

Joachin, Blatter and Ingtan Helen, (eds.), (2001), *Reflections on Water: New Approaches to Transboundary Conflicts and Cooperation*, MIT Press, Cambridge, Massachusetts.

Jodha, N.S., (1994), "Common Property Resources and the Rural Poor", in Guha, Ramchandra, (ed.), (1994), *Social Ecology*, Oxford University Press, New Delhi, pp. 150-189.

Jodha, N.S., (1995), *Sustainable Development in Fragile Environment: An Operational Framework for Arid, Semi-Arid and Mountain Areas*, Environment and Development Series, CEE, Ahmedabad.

Johnstone, Nick, Libby Wood and Robert Hearne, (1999), "Private Sector Participation in Urban Water and Sanitation: Realizing Social and Environmental Objectives in Developing Countries", *Natural Resources Forum*, Vol. 23, November, pp. 287-303.

Joseph, A.D., (2006), "Groundwater Scenario, Issues and Management Strategies in Rajasthan", Briefing Paper, in *Rajasthan Pani Utsav*, Cecoedecon, Jaipur.

Joshi, B.M., (1999), *Development of Agricultural Economics through Water Management*, Raj Publishing House, Jaipur.

Joshi, Sharad, (2006), "'Rajasthan Pani Utsav': An Interface between the Government; Corporate and Private Sector; Civil Society Organizations and The Communities", Briefing Paper, *Rajasthan Pani Utsav*, Cecoedecon, Jaipur.

Joshi, Sharad, (2006), "Governance and Policy in Water Management: A Dialogue with Government Officials, Political Leaders and Civil Society Members", Briefing Paper, *Rajasthan Pani Utsav*, Cecoedecon, Jaipur.

Kalabernattn, John M., (1983), *Appropriate Technology for Water Supply and Sanitation*, (VI), The World Bank, Washington DC.

Kalam, A.P.J. Abdul, (2006), "Media as a Partner in National

Development", *The Hindu*, November 27, adapted from President Kalam's address at the Press Council of India, November 16, 2006, during the celebration of National Press Day.

Kallolikar, S. and P.M. Natarajan, (2004), *Rainwater Harvesting – New Approaches for Sustainable Water Resources Development*, Pudukottai.

Kanmony, J. Cyril, (2003), "Drinking Water in Kanyakumari", *EPW*, August 30, pp. 3633-3636.

Karanth, K.R., (1987), *Ground Water Assessment: Development and Management*, Tata McGraw Hill Publishing Company Ltd., New Delhi.

Kashwan, Prakash, (2006), "Traditional Water Harvesting Structure: Community behind Community", *EPW*, February 18, pp. 596-598.

Kasperson, Roger E. and Jeanne X. Kasperson, (1987), *Water Re-Use and the Cities*, Academic Publishers, Jaipur.

Kathpalia, G. N. and N. S. Vardan, (1971), *Need for a National Water Policy*, CBIP, Publication No. 113, November, New Delhi.

Kathpalia, G.N. and Rakesh Kapoor, (2002), *Water Policy and Action Plan for India 2020*: An Alternative, Alternative Futures, Development Research and Communications Group, New Delhi.

Kaushik, Kusum, (2000), *Water Management Strategy for Semi Arid Lands with special reference to Jaipur District*, Unpublished Thesis, University of Rajasthan, Jaipur.

Khan, M.A., (1989), "Upgraded Village pond-nadi to ensure improved Water Supplies in Arid Zone", *Water and Irrigation Review*, Israel, Vol. 19, pp. 20-23.

Khan, M.A., (1996), "Inducement of Ground Water Recharge for Sustainable Development", in *28th Annual Convention, Indian Water Works Association*, Jodhpur, pp. 147-150.

Khan, M.A., (1996), "Sustainable Development of Water Resources to Augment Rural Water Supply and to Improve Biomass Production in Arid Ecosystem of Rajasthan", in *Proceedings of III Water Congress*, Indian Institute of Technology, New Delhi, p. 136.

Khan, M.A., (1998), "Rainwater Management", in Faroda, A.S., Manjit Singh, (eds.), (1998), *Fifty Years of Arid Zone Research in India*, Central Arid Zone Research Institute, Jodhpur, pp. 167-174.

Knapp, K. C. and L. J. Olson, (1995), "The Economics of Conjunctive Ground Water Management with Stochastic Surface Supplies",

Journal of Environmental Economic Management, Vol. 28, May, pp. 340-356.

Kolarkar, A.S., K.N.K. Murthy and N. Singh, (1980), "Water Harvesting and Run-off Farming in Arid Rajasthan", *Indian Journal of Soil Conservation*, Vol. 8, pp. 44-49.

Kolarkar, A.S., K.N.K. Murthy and N. Singh, (1983), "'Khadin'-A Method of Harvesting Water for Agriculture in the Thar Desert", *Journal of Arid Environments*, Vol. 6, pp. 59-66.

Krupanidhi, K.V.J.R. and S.K. Doshi, (1986), "Ground Water Management in the Arid and Semi-Arid Tracts of Western Rajasthan", Proceedings of International Seminar on *Water Management in Arid and Semi-Arid Zones*, Vol. II, Agricultural University, Hissar, pp. 89-101.

Kumar, M. Dinesh, (2003), "Food Security and Sustainable Agriculture in India: The Water Management Challenge", *Working Paper*, 60, International Water Management Institute, Sri Lanka.

Kumar, M. Dinesh, (2007), *Groundwater Management in India: Physical, Institutional and Policy Alternatives*, Sage Publications, New Delhi.

Kumar, M. Dinesh, A. Patel, R. Ravindranath, and O.P. Singh, (2008), "Chasing a Mirage: Water Harvesting and Artificial Recharge in Naturally Water-Scarce Regions", *EPW*, 30 August, pp. 61-71.

Kumaram, P., C.N. Bhargava and T.S. Bhakuni, (1971), "Fluoride in Ground Water and Endemic Fluorosis in Rajasthan", *Indian Journal of Environmental Health*, Vol. 13, No. 4, pp. 316-324.

Lal, Deepak, (1972), *Wells and Welfare*, Development Centre of the Organization for Economic Cooperation and Development (OECD), Paris.

Larson, B. A. and D. W. Bromley, (1990), "Property Rights, Externalities, and Resource Degradation: Locating the Tragedy", *Journal of Development Economics*, Vol. 33, October.

Lawrence, Peter, Jeremy Meigh and Caroline Sullivan, (2002), "The Poverty Index: An International Comparison", *Keele Economic Research Papers*, Vol. 19, Staffordshire, UK.

Lee, (1994), "Urban Water Supply and Sanitation in Developing Countries", in Nickum, James E. and K. William Easter, (eds.), *Metropolitan Water Use Conflicts in Asia and the Pacific*, Chapter

2, East-West Centre and United Nations Centre for Regional Development, Boulder, Westview Press, San Francisco and Oxford, pp. 19-35.

Lee, N and F. Walsh, (1992), "Strategic Environmental Assessment: An Overview", *Project Appraisal,* Vol. 7, No. 3, pp. 126-136.

LeMoigne, Guy, Shawki Barghonti, Gershon Feder, Lisa Garbus and Mei Xie, (1992), "Country Experiences with Water Resources Management: Economic, Institutional, Technological and Environmental Issues", *World Bank Technical Paper* No. 175, The World Bank, Washington DC.

Little, I., (1982), *Economic Development: Theory, Policy and International Relations,* Twentieth Century Fund, Basic Books, New York.

Mahajan, Gautam, (1989), *Evaluation and Development of Ground Water,* Ashish Publishing House, New Delhi.

Malik, R.P.S, (2007), "Water and Poverty", in Briscoe and Malik, (eds.), (2007), *Handbook of Water Resources in India: Development, Management and Strategies,* The World Bank, Oxford University Press, New Delhi, pp. 137-183.

Maloney, Clarence and K.V. Raju, (1994), *Managing Irrigation Together: Practice and Policy in India,* Sage Publications, New Delhi.

Marothia, Dinesh K., (2003), "Enhancing Sustainable Management of Water Resources in Agriculture Sector: The Role of Institutions", *Indian Journal of Agricultural Economics,* Vol. 58, No. 3, July-September, pp. 406 – 426.

Marothia, Dinesh K., (2005), "Institutional Reforms in Canal Irrigation System: Lessons from Chattisgarh", *EPW,* July 9, pp. 3074-3084.

Marothia, Dinesh K., (2005), "Water Property Rights Regimes: An Inquiry into Institutional and Legislative Economics", IDS, Jaipur.

Mate, M.S., (1998), *A History of Water Management and Hydraulic Technology in India (1500 B.C. to 1800 A.D.),* B.R. Publishing Corporation, Delhi.

Mathews, Olen Paul, (1987), *Water Resources: Geography and Law,* Scientific Publisher, Jodhpur.

Maxwell, W.H.C., (ed.), (1983), *Water for Human Consumption,* Results of the IV World Congress (5-9 September 1982), of the International Water Resources Association (IWRA), Tycooly International Publishing Ltd., Dublin.

Mayor, Federico and Jerome Binde, (2001), *The World Ahead: Our Future in the Making*, Zed Books, London.

McDonald, A. and D. Kay, (1988), *Water Resources: Issues and Strategies*, Longman Scientific and Technical Publishers Ltd., London.

Meharg, A.A., (2005), *Venomous Earth How Arsenic Caused the World's Worst Mass Poisoning*, Macmillan, New York.

Mehta, Lyla, (2005), *The Politics and Poetics of Water: Naturalization of Scarcity in Western India*, Orient Longman, New Delhi.

Meigh, J.R. and C.A. Sullivan, (2003), "The Impact of Climate Change on Water Resources: Problems and Prospects for a more Realistic Assessment", *Conference on Monsoon Environments: Agricultural and Hydrological Impacts of Seasonal Variability and Climate Change*, Trieste, Italy.

Menon, Ajit, et.al., (2007), *Community-based Natural Resource Management: Issues and Cases from South Asia*, Sage Publications India Pvt. Ltd., New Delhi.

Mirovitskaya, Natalia and William L. Ascher, (eds.), (2002), *Guide to Sustainable Development and Environmental Policy*, Duke University Press, Durban.

Mishra, P.N. and Vinay Bhardwaj, (2006), "Ground Water Recharge by Rain Water Harvesting in Jaipur Urban Area: A Remedy for Depleting Ground Water Resources", Briefing Paper in Joshi, Sharad, (2006), *Rajasthan Pani Utsav*, Cecoedecon, Jaipur.

Misra, A., (1995), *Rajasthan ki Rajat Bunden*, Gandhi Pratishthan, New Delhi.

Modi, Jayanti Lal, *Census of India, 2001, Rajasthan: Provisional Population Totals* (paper 1, 2, 3 of 2001), Controller of Publications, Delhi, 2001.

Moench, M., (1998), "Allocating the Common Heritage: Debates over Water Rights and Governance Structures in India", *EPW*, June 27, pp. 46-50.

Moench, M., (2002), "Water and the Potential for Social Instability: Livelihoods, Migration and the Building of Society", *Natural Resources Forum*, Vol. 26, pp. 195-204.

Moench, M., (ed.), (1995), *Groundwater Availability and Pollution: The Growing Debate over Resource Condition in India*, Vikram Sarabhai Centre for Development Interaction (VIKSAT), Natural Heritage Institute, Ahmedabad, Gujarat.

Mollinga, Peter P., (ed.), (2000), *Water for Food and Rural Development: Approaches and Initiatives in South Asia*, Sage Publications, New Delhi.

Morgan, Monroe T., (1991), *Environmental Health*, WCB Brown and Benchmark Publishers, Wisconsin, USA.

Mukundan T.M., (2006), *The Ery System of South India*, Akash Ganga Trust, Chennai.

Munasinghe, M., (1990), "Water Supply Policies and Issues in Developing Countries", *Natural Resources Forum*, Vol. 14, No. 1, February, pp. 33-48.

Muralidhar, S., (2006), "The Right to Water: An Overview of the Indian Legal Regime", *International Environmental Law Research Centre*, Geneva, pp. 1-10.

Murty, J.V.S., (1995), *Watershed Management in India*, Wiley Eastern Limited, New Age International Limited, London.

Narain, P. and M.A. Khan, (2000), "Water Resources Development and Utilisation for Drinking and Plant Management in Indian Arid Regions", in *Advances in Land Resources Management for Twenty First Century*, International Conference on land Resources Management for Food, Employment and Environmental Security, Proceedings, Soil Conservation Society of India, New Delhi, pp. 404-414.

Narain, P., M.A. Khan and G. Singh, (2005), "Potential for Water Conservation and Harvesting Against Drought in Rajasthan, India", Working Paper 104, Drought Series: Paper 7, *International Water Management Institute*, Sri Lanka.

Narayan, V.V. Dhruva, G. Sastry and U.S. Patnaik, (eds.), (1990), *Watershed Management*, Publications and Information Division, ICAR, New Delhi.

Narayanamoorthy A. and R.S. Deshpande, (2005), *Where Water Seeps! Towards a New Phase in India's Irrigation Reforms*, Academic Foundation, New Delhi.

Ohlsson, L., (1999), "Water Conflicts and Social Resource Scarcity", paper prepared for the European Geophysical Society, Den Haag.

Otto, Eckstein, (1958), *Water Resources Development: The Economics of Project Evaluation*, Harvard University Press, Harvard.

Overman, Michael, (1969), *Water: Solutions to a Problem of Supply and Demand,* Doubleday Science Series, Doubleday and Company Inc., Garden City, New York.

Pangare, G., V. Pangare and Binayak Das, (2006), *Springs of Life – India's Water Resources,* World Water Institute, Bharathi Integrated Rural Development Society (BIRDS) and Academic Foundation, New Delhi.

Pathak, B.D., (1978), "Exploration and Exploitation of Ground Water with special reference to Recharge", *The National Geographical Journal of India,* Vol. 34.

Postel, S., (1996), "Dividing the Waters: Food Security, Ecosystem Health, and the New Policies of Scarcity", *Worldwatch,* No. 132, p. 29. Worldwatch Institute, Washington DC.

Postel, S., (1997), "Water for Food Production: Will there be enough in 2025 ?", *International Water Resources Association IXth Congress,* Montreal, Canada.

Prakash, M. and C. Gopinath, (1962), "Tanka for Human and Livestock Consumption", *Indian Forester,* Vol. 88, pp. 861-864.

Ragade, Indukanth S., (2006), *Self Reliance in Water,* Chennai.

Rajora, Rajesh, (1998), *Integrated Watershed Management: A Field Manual for Equitable, Productive and Sustainable Development,* Rawat Publications, Jaipur.

Ramanathan, S., (1994), *Indigenous Water Harvesting Systems in Rajasthan,* IDS, Jaipur.

Ramanthan, Usha, (1992), "Legislating for Water: The Indian Context", Working Paper 1992-1, *International Environmental Law Research Centre,* Geneva, pp. 1-13.

Rao, A.V., D.C. Ojha and Anruag Saxena, (1998), *Fifty Years of Arid Zone Research in India 1947-1997,* (Monograph), Central Arid Zone Research Institute, Scientific Publishers, Jodhpur.

Rao, C.H. Hanumantha, (2000), "Watershed Development in India: Recent Experience and Emerging Issues", *EPW,* November 4, pp. 3943-3947.

Rao, K.L, (1975), *India's Water Wealth: Its Assessment, Uses and Projections,* Orient Longman, New Delhi.

Rao, V.V., K.K. Kumar and K.V.R. Murthy, (1980), "A New Approach of Water Management", *The National Geographical Journal of India,* Vol. 25, No. 1 and 2, pp. 70-74.

Rathore, M.S. and V. Ratna Reddy, (1996), *Urban Water Management*, Rawat Publications, Jaipur.

Rathore, M.S., (2001), "Ground Water Drought in Rajasthan: A Man Made Disaster", *IDS*, Jaipur.

Reddy, V. Ratna and S. Mahendra Dev, (eds.), (2006), *Managing Water Resources: Policies, Institutions and Technologies*, Oxford University Press, New Delhi.

Reddy, V. Ratna, (1996), *Urban Water Crisis: Rationale for Pricing*, IDS, Rawat Publication, Jaipur.

Reddy, V. Ratna, (2000), "Sustainable Watershed Management: Institutional Approach", *EPW*, September 16, pp. 3435 - 3444.

Reddy, V. Ratna, (2002), "Water Security and Management Lessons from South Africa", *EPW*, July 13.

Rosegrant, Mark W., Ximing Cai and Sarah A. Cline, (2002), *World Water and Food to 2025: Dealing with Scarcity*, International Food Policy Research Institute (IFPRI), Washington DC.

Rosegrant, Mark W., Ximing Cai, et.al., (2002), *Global Water Outlook to 2025: Averting on Impending Crisis*, United Nations-2002, Johannesburg World Summit on Sustainable Development, Washington DC.

Roy, Ashim Kumar, (1978), *History of the Jaipur City*, Manohar, New Delhi.

Roy, Joyashree, *et al.*, (2004), "An Economic Analysis of Demand for Water Quality", *EPW*, January 10, pp.186-192.

Sachs, J.D., (2001), "Macroeconomics and Health: Investing in Health for Economic Development", *Report of the Commission on Macroeconomics and Health*, WHO.

Sachs, J.D., (2005), *Investing in Development: A Practical Plan to Achieve the Millennium Development Goals*, Earthscan, London.

Saleth, Maria R., (ed.), (2002), *Water Resources and Economic Development*, Edward Elgar Publishing Ltd., Cheltenham, U. K.

Saleth, R. Maria, (1996), *Water Institutions in India: Economics, Law and Policy*, Commonwealth Publishers, New Delhi.

Saleth, R. Maria, (2004), "Strategic Analysis of Water Institutions in India: Application of a New Research Paradigm", Research Report 79, International Water Management Institute, Sri Lanka.

Sanctuary, Mark, and Hakan Tropp, (2005), "Making Water a Part of Economic Development: The Economic Benefits of Improved Water Management and Services." *Stockholm International Water Institute*, Stockholm.

Sandbergen, Loes Scheuk, (2004), "Some Gender Dimensions in Managing Water Scarcity", in Vaidyanathan A. and H.M. Oudshoom, (eds.), (2004), *Managing Water Scarcity – Experiences and Prospects*, Manohar Publishers, New Delhi.

Saravanan, V.S., (2006), "Integrated Water Resource Management", *EPW*, September 23, pp. 4086-4087.

Scoones, I., (1998), "Sustainable Rural Livelihoods: A Framework for Analysis", *IDS Working Paper No. 72*. IDS, Brighton.

Sen, A., (1981), "Poor, Relatively Speaking", *Oxford Economic Papers*, No.35.

Sen, A., (1985), *Commodities and Capabilities*, North Holland, Amsterdam

Sen, Amartya and Jean Dreze, (1995), *India: Economic Development and Social Opportunity*, Oxford University Press, New Delhi.

Shaban, Abdul and R.N. Sharma, (2007), "Water Consumption Patterns in Domestic Households in Major Cities", *EPW*, June 9, pp. 2190-2197.

Shah, Amita, (1998), "Watershed Development Programmes in India: Emerging Issues for Environmental-Development Perspective", *EPW*, June 27, pp. 66-79.

Shah, C.H., (2005), "Economic Analysis of a Drinking Water Project in Andhra Pradesh", *EPW*, January 29, pp. 474-481.

Shah, Tushaar and Barbara van Koppen, (2006), "Is India Ripe for Integrated Water Resources Management?", *EPW*, August 5, pp. 3413-3421.

Shah, Tushaar, (2004), "The Deepening Divide: Diverse Responses to the Challenge of Ground Water Depletion in Gujarat", in Vaidyanathan A. and H.M. Oudshoom, (eds.), (2004), *Managing Water Scarcity – Experiences and Prospects*, Manohar Publishers, New Delhi.

Shah, Tushaar, (2007), "Institutional and Policy Reforms", in Briscoe and Malik, (eds.), (2007), *Handbook of Water Resources in India: Development, Management and Strategies*, The World Bank, Oxford University Press, New Delhi, pp. 306-326.

Sharma, K.B. and P.R. Ojasvi, (1998), "Surface Water Management", in Faroda, A.S. and Manjit Singh, (eds.), (1998), *Fifty Years of Arid Zone Research in India,* Central Arid Zone Research Institute, Jodhpur, pp. 175-187.

Sharma, K.D. and D.C. Joshi, (1981), "'Nadis' the Vital Water Resources of the Indian Arid Zone", *Journal of Arid Environments,* Vol. 4, pp. 247-251.

Sharma, K.D. and D.N. Bohra, (1990), "Rainfall Analysis for Rainwater Management in a Drought-prone Area", *Annals of Arid Zone,* Vol. 29, pp. 165-169.

Sharma, Ram Avatar and Sushama Yadav, (2005), *Jal: Kal, Aaj aur Kal,* (in Hindi), Aakar Books, Delhi, 110091.

Shukla, S.R., (1988), *National Water Supply and Sanitation Programme,* NIHFW, New Delhi.

Shuval, Hillel I., (ed.), (1980), *Water Quality Management under Conditions of Scarcity,* Academic Press, London.

Signastam, Lisa, (2002), "Indicators of Environment and Sustainable Development: Theories and Practical Experience", *The World Bank Environment Department,* Environment Economic Series, Paper No. 89, The World Bank, Washington DC, USA.

Singh, Chhatrapati, (1991), *Water Rights and Principles of Water Resources Management,* N.M. Tripathi Pvt. Ltd., Bombay.

Singh, Katar, (2005), "Property Rights for Managing Ground Water: Lessons of Experience from Southern California and India", *IDS,* Jaipur.

Singh, M.P., A. Waris, K.N.K. Chauhan and B.B. Rathore, (2000), "Tanka – A Boon for Arid Zone Farmers", *Intensive Agriculture,* Vol. 38, No. 9-10, Oct.-Nov., pp. 28-31, CAZRI, Jodhpur.

Singh, R.P and M.A. Khan, (1999), "Rainwater Management: Water Harvesting and Its Efficient Utilisation", in Singh, H.P., Y.S. Ramkrishna, K.L. Sharma and B. Venkateshwarlu, (eds.), *Fifty Years of Dryland Research in India,* Central Research Institute of Dryland Agriculture, Hyderabad, pp. 301-313.

Sinha, Bakshi D. and P.S.K. Menon, (1996), *Environmental Sanitation, Health and Panchayati Raj,* Institute of Social Sciences, Concept Publishing Company, New Delhi.

Sivaraman K.R. and Govindrajan S. Thillai, (2003), *Manual on Rain Water Harvesting*, Sastha Foundation, Chennai.

Smith, Adam, [1776] (1976), *An Inquiry into the Nature and Causes of the Wealth of Nations*, Oxford University Press, Oxford.

Soni, Vikram, (2003), "Water and Carrying Capacity of a City: Delhi", EPW, November 8, pp. 4745-4748.

Stauffer, Julie, (1998), *The Water Crisis: Constructing Solutions to Freshwater Pollution*, Earthscan Publications, London.

Streeten, P., (1994), "Human Development: Means and Ends", *American Economic Review*, Vol. 84, No. 2, pp. 232-237.

Sullivan C.A. and J.R. Meigh, (2003), "The Water Poverty Index: Its Role in the Context of Poverty Alleviation, *Water Policy*, Vol. 5, No. 5.

Sullivan C.A., J.R. Meigh and P. Lawrence, (2005), "Application of the Water Poverty Index at Different Scales: A Cautionary Tale", *Agriculture, Ecosystems and the Envrionment*, Special issue.

Sullivan, C., (2002), "Calculating a Water Poverty Index", *World Development*, Vol. 30, No. 7, pp. 1195-1211.

Sullivan, C.A. and J.R. Meigh, (2005), "Targeting Attention on Local Vulnerabilities using an Integrated Indicator Approach: The Example of the Climate Vulnerability Index", *Water Science and Technology*, Special Issue on Climate Change, Vol. 51, No. 5, pp. 69-78.

Sullivan, C.A., (ed.), (2000), "Constructing a Water Poverty Index: A Feasibility Study", *Centre for Ecology and Hydrology and DFID* (Department for International Development), Wallingford, Oxfordshire, UK.

Sullivan, C.A., et.al., (2003), "The Water Poverty Index: Development and Application at the Community Scale", *Natural Resource Forum*, Vol. 27, pp. 189-199.

Sullivan, C.A., J.R. Meigh and T.S. Fediw, (2002), *Derivation and Testing of the Water Poverty Index*, Research Project, Centre for Ecology and Hydrology, Wallingford.

Szreter, Simon, (1997), "Economic Growth, Disruption, Deprivation, Disease, and Death: On the Importance of the Politics of Public

Health for Development.", *Population and Development Review*, Vol. 23, No. 4, pp. 693–728.

Taylor, J.A., (1974), *Climatic Resources and Economic Activity*, David and Charle Newton Abbot, London.

Taylor, James A., (1970), *The Role of Water in Agriculture*, Pergamon Press, Oxford.

Thanh, N.C. and Asit K. Biswas, (eds.), (1990), *Environmentally-Sound Water Management*, Oxford University Press, Delhi.

The World Bank Allied Publishers (1999), *Rural Water Supply and Sanitation*, New Delhi.

Tideman, E.M., (1996), *Watershed Management: Guidelines for Indian Conditions*, IGBP, (7th Reprint in 2000), Omega Scientific Publisher, New Delhi.

Todaro Michael P., Smith Stephen C., (2004), *Economic Development*, Pearson Education, Delhi.

Tolman, C.F., (1937), *Ground Water*, McGraw Hill Book Company, Inc., New York.

Upadhyay, V., (2001), *Legal Conflict over Land, Forests and Water in India: A Review of Cases and Concepts*, Aga Khan Foundation.

Urs, Kshithij, Richard Whittell, (2009), *Resisting Reform ? - Water Profits and Democracy*, Sage Publications, New Delhi.

Vaidyanathan, A. and H.M. Oudshoom, (eds.), (2004), *Managing Water Scarcity – Experiences and Prospects*, Manohar Publishers, New Delhi.

Vaidyanathan, A. and K. Subramaniyan, (2004), "Efficiency of Water Use in Agriculture", *EPW*, July 3, pp. 2989-2996.

Vaidyanathan, A., (1999), *Water Resource Management: Institutions and Irrigation Development in India*, Oxford University Press, New Delhi.

Vaidyanathan, A., (2001), "Policy Dimensions: Reviving Decaying Systems, A Case for Rainwater Harvesting", in Agrawal, Anil, Sunita Narain, Indira Khurana, (eds.), (2001), *Making Water Everybody's Business: Practice and Policy of Water Harvesting*, Centre for Science and Environment, New Delhi, pp. 295 – 302.

Vaidyanathan, A., (2006), *India's Water Resources: Contemprorary Issues on Irrigation*, Oxford University Press, New Delhi.

Vangani, N.S. and P.C. Chatterjee, (1979), "A Method of Evaluating Development Priority based on Inventory of Water Resources in Arid and Semi-arid Areas", *Annals of Arid Zone*, Vol.18, pp. 35-47.

Vangani, N.S., K.D. Sharma and P.C. Chatterji, (1988), *Tanka – A Reliable System of Rainwater Harvesting in Indian Desert*, (Monograph), ICAR, CAZRI Publication No.33, Jodhpur.

Veeman, Terrence S., (1978), "Water Policy and Water Institutions in Northern India: The Case of Ground Water Rights", *Natural Resources Journal*, Vol. 18, No. 3, pp. 569-87.

Veerashekharappa, (2000), "Reforms in Rural Drinking Water Supply", *EPW*, February 12-18.

Verma, C.V.J. and A.R.G. Rao, (eds.), (1983), *Research in Water Resources Development in India*, Central Board of Irrigation and Power, New Delhi.

Wasi-Ullah, A.K. Chakravarty, C.P. Mathur and N.S. Vangani, (1972), "Effects of Contour Furrows and Contour Bunds on Water Conservation in Grasslands of Western Rajastham", *Annals of Arid Zone*, Vol. 11, No. 3 and 4, pp. 179-182.

Wiener, A., (1972), *The Role of Water in Development*, McGraw Hill Book Company, New York.

Winpenny, James, (1994), *Managing Water as an Economic Resource*, Routledge, London.

Wolters, Henk, (2005), "Water Distribution under Stress Conditions: Policy Development and Operational Aspects", *International Workshop on Value of Water – Different Approaches in Transboundary Water Management*, Koblenz, Germany.

Wright, Forest B., (1950), *Rural Water Supply and Sanitation*, John Wiley and Sons, Bombay.

Zerah, Marie – Helene, (2000), *Water: Unreliable Supply in Delhi*, Manohar Publishers and Distributors, Delhi.

Zwarteveen, Margaret Z., (1997), "Water: From Basic Need to Commodity: A discussion on Gender and Water Rights in the Context of Irrigation", *World Development*, Vol. 25, August, pp. 1335-49.

II. Reports

All India Soil and Land Use Survey, (1990), Watershed Atlas of India, Department of Agriculture and Cooperation, IARI Campus, New Delhi.

American Water Works Association, (1971), Water Quality and Treatment: A Handbook of Public Water Supplies, Third Edition, McGraw Hill Book Company, New York, pp. 654.

Annual Report 2005-06, Association of Rural Advancement through Voluntary Action and Local Involvement (ARAVALI), Jaipur.

Asian Development Bank, (1990), *Water Supply and Sanitation: Beyond the Decade,* Proceedings of the Asian and Pacific Regional Consultation, Manila.

Asian Development Bank, (1993), *Water Utilities Data Book,* Asian and Pacific Region, Philippines.

Asian Productivity Organization, (1991), *Farm Level Irrigation Water Management,* Report of a Study Meeting in Lahore, Pakistan, 7-18 February 1989, (APO Project Code STM/IV/88), Tokyo.

CAZRI Annual Report, (2000), Indian Council of Agricultural Research, Jodhpur.

CECOEDECON, (1997), *Social Assessment of Baran District for District Poverty Initiatives Project,* Institute of Development Studies, Jaipur.

Census of India, (1981), *General Economic Tables 1981* Part III, A & B, Vol. I (ii), Registrar General of India, New Delhi.

Census of India, (1991), *Provisional Population Totals 1991,* Registrar General of India, New Delhi.

Census of India, (1991), *Rajasthan State District Profile 1991,* Registrar General of India, New Delhi.

Census of India, (1991), State Profile 1991 – India, Registrar General of India, New Delhi.

Central Public Health and Environmental Engineering Organization, (1999), *Manual on Water Supply and Treatment,* Ministry of Urban Development, Government of India, Third edition, Revised and updated in May 1999, New Delhi.

Central Research Institute for Dryland Agriculture (CRIDA), (1990), *Field Manual on Watershed Management,* CRIDA, Hyderabad.

Central Water Commission, (1998), *Water and Related Statistics,* New Delhi.

Centre for Science and Environment, (1982), *The State of India's Environment: A Citizen's Report*, New Delhi.

Centre for Science and Environment, (1986), *The State of India's Environment 1984-85*: The Second Citizen's Report, New Delhi.

FAO, (1995), *Methodology for Water Policy Review and Reform*, Water Report, United Nations, Rome, Italy.

FAO, (1996), "Food Production: The Critical Role of Water", *Technical Background Document for the World Food Summit*, Rome.

FAO, (2005), *Freshwater Resources 2005*, Population Division of the Department of Economic and Social Affairs, United Nations Secretariat, The World Bank.

Global Committee for the Water Contract, (1998), *The Water Manifesto: The Right to Life*, Lisbon, Valencia, Brussels.

Government of Andhra Pradesh, (1997), "Corporation Act 1997", *Water Resources Department*, Hyderabad.

Government of Arunachal Pradesh, (2006), "The Arunachal Pradesh Water Resources Management Authority Bill, 2006", *The Arunachal Pradesh Gazetteer*, Naharlagun.

Government of Himachal Pradesh, (2005), "The Himachal Pradesh Ground Water (Regulation and Control of Development and Management) Act, 2005", Shimla.

Government of India, (1977), *Manual of Water Supply and Treatment*, Second edition, Ministry of Works and Housing, New Delhi.

Government of India, (1979 and 1980), *Accessibility of the Poor to the Rural Water Supply*: A Quick Evaluation Study, Planning Commission, New Delhi.

Government of India, (1982), *Accessibility of the Poor to the Rural Water Supply*: A Planning and Design Manual, Planning Commission, New Delhi.

Government of India, (1983), *National Master Plan – India: International Drinking Water and Sanitation Decade 1981-1990*, Vol. I, Ministry of Works and Housing, New Delhi.

Government of India, (1986), *Guidelines for Implementation of Accelerated Rural Water Supply Programme* (ARWSP), Department of Rural Development, Ministry of Agriculture, New Delhi.

Government of India, (1986), *Technology Mission Drinking Water and*

Related Water Management (Project Development), Department of Rural Development, Ministry of Agriculture, New Delhi

Government of India, (1987), *Current Evaluation of Rural Water Supply*, Status Report, New Delhi.

Government of India, (1987), *Submission on Desalination of Water*, Technology Mission on Drinking Water in Village and Related Management, New Delhi.

Government of India, (1987), *Voluntary Agencies and NGOs*, Technology Mission on Drinking Water in Village and Related Management, New Delhi.

Government of India, (1993), *Water Quality and De-fluoridation Techniques*, Rajiv Gandhi National Drinking Water Mission, New Delhi.

Government of India, (1994), *Guidelines for Watershed Development*, Ministry of Rural Development, New Delhi.

Government of India, (1994), *Report of the Expert Committee on Rural Water Supply*, Rajiv Gandhi National Drinking Water Mission, New Delhi.

Government of India, (1996), *National Workshop on Operation and Maintenance of Rural Water Supply and Sanitation Systems*, New Delhi.

Government of India, (1998), *Water Quality: An Overview*, Department of Drinking Water Supply, Ministry of Rural Development, New Delhi.

Government of India, (1998, 1999), *Economic Survey*, Ministry of Finance, New Delhi.

Government of India, (1999), *Guidelines for Implementation of Rural Water Supply Programme*, Department of Rural Development; Ministry of Rural Areas and Employment, New Delhi.

Government of India, (1999), *Report of the National ·Commission for Integrated Water Resources Development Plan*, Ministry of Water Resources, New Delhi.

Government of India, (1999), *Sector Reform Project Guidelines*, Department of Drinking Water Supply, Ministry of Rural Development, New Delhi.

Government of India, (2000), *Central Ground Water Board*, Chapter 11, Ministry of Water Resources, New Delhi.

Government of India, (2000), *Rajiv Gandhi National Drinking Water Mission,* Department of Drinking Water Supply, Ministry of Rural Development, New Delhi.

Government of India, (2001), *Report on Drinking Water, Sanitation and Hygiene in Rajasthan,* 54th Round of NSS (Jan-June 1998), State Sample, Directorate of Economics and Statistics, Jaipur.

Government of India, (2002), "Drinking Water Supply and Sanitation (Rural and Urban)", *Report of the Steering Committee,* Tenth Five Year Plan, Planning Commission, New Delhi.

Government of India, (2002), *National Human Development Report 2001,* Planning Commission, Oxford University Press, New Delhi.

Government of India, (2003), *4th Editor's Conference on Social Sector Issues* – 28th August 2003, Ministry of Water Resources, New Delhi.

Government of India, (2004), *Induction Material,* Ministry of Water Resources, New Delhi.

Government of India, (2004), *Swajaldhara,* Department of Drinking Water Supply, Ministry of Rural Development, New Delhi.

Government of India, (2004), *Terms of Reference for the Evaluation Study of Sector Reform Pilot Projects* (SRP), Department of Drinking Water Supply, Ministry of Rural Development, New Delhi.

Government of India, (2004), *Total Sanitation Campaign, Department of Drinking Water Supply,* Ministry of Rural Development, New Delhi.

Government of India, (2005), "Scheme for Support to Public Private Partnership in Infrastructure", *Department of Economic Affairs,* New Delhi.

Government of India, (2006), *Rajasthan Development Report,* Planning Commission, Academic Foundation, New Delhi.

Government of India, Department of Drinking Water Supply, (2002), "Guidelines on Swajaldhara, 2002", *International Environmental Law Research Centre,* Geneva, pp. 1-15.

Government of India, *Jaipur Declaration on Water Quality Management: Vision 2025,* Department of Drinking Water Supply, New Delhi.

Government of India, Ministry of Water Resources, (2003), "Statewise Water Resources Situation in India", *EPW,* October 4, p. 4199.

Government of Karnataka, (2000), "The Karnataka Irrigation and Certain Other Law (Amendment) Act 2000", *Water Resources Department*, Bangalore.

Government of Karnataka, (2002), "State Water Policy", *Water Resources Department*, Bangalore.

Government of Kerala, (2004), "Rainwater Harvesting", *Local Self Government Department*, Thiruvananthpuram.

Government of Madhya Pradesh, (2003), "State Water Policy 2003", *Water Resources Department*, Bhopal.

Government of Maharashtra, (2003), "Maharashtra State Water Policy", Mumbai.

Government of Rajasthan, (1981, 2003), *Statistical Abstract Rajasthan*, Directorate of Economics and Statistics, Jaipur.

Government of Rajasthan, (1990 and 1991, 1994, 1995, 1995-2001, 1996, 2001, 2003), *Some facts about Rajasthan*, Directorate of Economics and Statistics, Jaipur.

Government of Rajasthan, (1999), *Ground Water Atlas of Rajasthan*, Ground Water Department, Jodhpur.

Government of Rajasthan, (1999), *State Water Policy 1999*, Jaipur.

Government of Rajasthan, (1999), *The White Paper on the State of Economy in Rajasthan*, Jaipur.

Government of Rajasthan, (2000), *Water Resource Vision 2045*, Department of Water Resources, Jaipur.

Government of Rajasthan, (2001), *Rajasthan Mein Jalgrahana Vikas: Gatividhiyan Evam Upalabdhiyan*, Department of Watershed Development and Land Conservation, Jaipur.

Government of Rajasthan, (2003), *Report of the Review Mission to Rajasthan*, 20-24 May, 2003, Jaipur.

Government of Rajasthan, (2004), *Ground Water Scenario in Jaipur District*, Ground Water Department, Jaipur.

Government of Rajasthan, (2004), *Reappraisal of Ground Water Resources of Jaipur District* (as on 31.3.2004), Ground Water Department, Jaipur.

Government of Rajasthan, (2004), *Vision-2025 for Rajasthan*, Central Ground Water Board, Western Region, Jaipur.

Government of Rajasthan, (2004), *Vision-2045: Water Resources*, Irrigation Department, Jaipur.

Government of Rajasthan, (2005), *Economic Review 2004-05*, Directorate of Economics and Statistics, Jaipur.

Government of Rajasthan, (2005), *Rajasthan Water Sector Restructuring Project*, RUIDP, Jaipur.

Government of Rajasthan, (2005), *State Water Policy (Draft)*, Jaipur.

Government of Rajasthan, (2006), "Kisan Mahotsav - Jal Chetna Yatra: A Mega Campaign in Rajasthan (16 May - 16 June, 2006)", Jaipur.

Government of Rajasthan, (2006), *Ground Water in Jaipur District: Problems and Solutions*, Ground Water Department, Jaipur.

Government of Rajasthan, (2006), *Rainwater Conservation and Recharge*, PHED, Jaipur Action Group, Ground Water Department, Jaipur.

Government of Rajasthan, (2006), *Rainwater Harvesting, Conservation and Groundwater Recharge Report*, Secretary, Public Health Engineering and Ground Water Department and Nodal Officer (Water), Jaipur Action Agenda Group (JAAG), Jaipur.

Government of Rajasthan, (2006), *Report on Wasteland Watershed Development and Land Conservation* Department, Rajasthan State Cooperative Press, Jaipur.

Government of Rajasthan, Watershed Development and Land Conservation, *Annual Reports 2002-03, 2004-05*, Directorate of Watershed Development and Land Conservation, Pant Krishi Bhavan, Jaipur.

Government of Uganda, (2005), "Uganda: Poverty Reduction Strategy Paper." Kampala, quoted from HDR, 2006.

Government of Uganda, (2004), "Poverty Eradication Action Plan (2004/5–2007/8)." Ministry of Finance, Planning and Economic Development, Kampala, quoted from HDR 2006.

Gupta, Savitri, (1987), *Rajasthan District Gazetteers: Jaipur*, Directorate, District Gazetteers, Government of Rajasthan, Jaipur.

India Infrastructure Report 2006: *Urban Infrastructure*, Oxford University Press, New Delhi

McIntosh, Arthur C. and Cesar Yniguez, (eds.), (1997), *Second Water Utilities Data Book*, Asian and Pacific Region, Asian Development Bank, Philippines.

Modi, Jayanti Lal, (2001), *Rajasthan: Provisional Population Totals* (Paper 1, 2, 3), Census of India, Controller of Publications, Delhi.

National Council of Applied Economic Research, (2002), *West and Central India: Human Development Report*, Oxford University Press, New Delhi.

Parikh, Kirit S. and R. Radhakrishna, (2002), *India Development Report 2002*, IGIDR, Oxford University Press, New Delhi.

Parikh, Kirit S., (ed.), (1997), *India Development Report 1997*, IGIDR, Oxford University Press, New Delhi.

Reducing Poverty, Accelerating Development, (2000), The World Bank, Oxford University Press, New Delhi.

Report on the Administration of Jaipur State for 1931-32, Government of India Press.

Sanctuary, Mark, Hakan Tropp and Laurence Haller, (2006), *Making Water a Part of Economic Development*, Report by the Government of Norway and Sweden, Stockholm International Water Institute.

Srivastava, I.C., (1981), *Census of India, District Census Handbook*, Village and Town Directory, Rajasthan Series 18, Part XIII, A&B.

Srivastava, I.C., Bhagirath Sharma and S.K. Kulshrestha, (2005), *Sector Policy for Rural Drinking Water and Sanitation* (Draft), State Policy for Rural Drinking Water and Sanitation, UNICEF and Government of Rajasthan.

State Development Report on Urban Development and Housing, Rajasthan, (2007), Submitted by Centre for Management Studies, HCM RIPA, Jaipur.

The World Bank, (1991, 1992), *World Development Report 1991*, Oxford University Press, New York.

The World Bank, (1993), "Privatization and User Participation in Water Resources Management", in World Bank, *Water Resources Management*: A World Bank Policy Paper, Appendix-C, Washington, D. C., pp. 100-115.

The World Bank, (1993), "The Demand for Water in Rural Areas: Determinants and Policy Implications", *World Bank Research Observers*, Vol. 8, January, pp. 47-70.

The World Bank, (1998), *Inter Sectoral Water Allocation, Planning and Management Report*, under the Indian Water Resources Management Sector Review Programme, South Asia Rural Development Unit, Washington DC.

The World Bank, (1999), *India: Water Resource Management – The Irrigation Sector*, Allied Publishers, New Delhi.

The World Bank, (2003), *World Development Report 2003, Sustainable Development in a Dynamic World: Transforming Institutions, Growth, and Quality of Life*, Washington DC.

The World Bank, (2005), *World Development Indicators 2005*, Washington DC.

Tomar, R.P., *Rajasthan, Part XII* – A & B, District Jaipur, Census of India, 1991: Series 21, General Administration Department, Government of Rajasthan, Jaipur.

UN Water Conference Report 1977, (1978), "Resources and Needs: Assessment of the World Water Situation", in Asit K. Biswas, (ed.), (1978), *Water Development and Management*, Pergamon Press, Oxford, pp. 1-44.

UNDP, (1990), *Secretariat for the Global Consultation on Safe Water and Sanitation for the 1990s*, New Delhi, September 10-14, 1990, Background Paper, New York.

UNEP, (1989), "Sustainable Water Development and Management", *International Journal of Water Resources Development*, Vol. 5, No. 4, December, pp. 225-51.

UNESCO - WWAP, 2003, Water for People, Water for Life, Executive summary. http://unesdoc.unesco.org/images/0012/001295/129556e.pdf.

UNESCO, (1977), "Socio-eonomic Aspects of Urban Water Resources Planning and Management", in Biswas, Asit K., (ed.), (1977), *Water Development, Supply and Management*, Proceedings of the United Nations Water Conference, Vol. 1, Pt. 4, United Nations and Pergamon Press, Oxford, pp. 685-697.

UNICEF, (2005), *Proposed Water Policy of State Government of Rajasthan*, Jaipur.

United Nations Development Programme, Human Development Report (1993, 1995, 1997, 1998, 1999, 2000, 2001, 2002, 2004, 2006, 2007, 2008), (Beyond Scarcity: Power, Poverty and the Global Water Crisis), New York.

United Nations Environment Programme, (2003), "Water for the Future", *Environment for Development*, United Nations, New York, pp. 6-13.

United Nations Report, (2006), *Water Woes traced to Farm Ethics*, Fourth World Water Forum, United Nations.

Vyas, V.S., (2005), *Water in Rajasthan: Report of the Expert Committee on Integrated Development and Management of Water Resources*, Government of Rajasthan, Jaipur.

WHO, (1987), *Achieving Success in Community, Water Supply Scheme and Sanitation Projects*, New Delhi.

WHO, (1987), *Technology for Water Supply Scheme and Sanitation in Developing Countries*, Geneva.

WHO, (2001), *Macroeconomics and Health: Investing in Health for Economic Development*, Report of the Commission on Macroeconomics and Health, Geneva.

WHO and Division of Environmental Health, (1984), *Human Resource Development Handbook*, Guidelines for Ministries and Agencies Responsible for Water Supply and Sanitation by Carefoot, Weil and Gibson, Howard, Geneva.

WHO, (1993), *Guidelines for Drinking Water Quality*, Second Edition, Vol. I, Recommendations, Geneva.

WHO, (1994), *Operation and Maintenance of Urban Water Supply and Sanitation Systems*: A Guide for Managers, Geneva.

World Bank, (2004), "Water Resource Sector Strategy, Strategic Directions for World Bank Engagement", Washington DC.

World Bank, (2001, 2004 and 2005), *World Development Indicators*, The World Bank, Washington DC.

World Economic Forum, Yale Center for Environmental Law and Policy, and Center for International Earth Science Information Network, Columbia University, *2001 Environmental Sustainability Index* (http://www.ciesin.columbia.edu/indicators/ESI), January 2001

World Resources: *A Guide to the Global Environment – The Urban Environment, 1996-97*, The World Resources Institute, UNEP, UNDP, The World Bank, Oxford University Press, New York, 1996.

World Water Commission, (2000), *World Water Vision: A Water Secure World*, London.

❑❑❑

Index

❑❑❑